Digital Platforms, Imperialism and Political Culture

> "This book is a timely and important contribution to our understanding of imperialism in an age of digital media. Advancing his theory of platform imperialism, Jin manages to eloquently illustrate the contingency of new technologies on the global inequalities of the contemporary world order. This is a very welcome and sophisticated intervention in the field."
>
> —*Lina Dencik, Cardiff University, UK*

In the networked twenty-first century, digital platforms have significantly influenced capital accumulation and digital culture. Platforms, such as social network sites (e.g., Facebook), search engines (e.g., Google), and smartphones (e.g., iPhone), are increasingly crucial because they function as major digital media intermediaries. Emerging companies in non-Western countries have created unique platforms, controlling their own national markets and competing with Western-based platform empires in the global markets. The reality though is that only a handful of Western countries, primarily the U.S., have dominated the global platform markets, resulting in capital accumulation in the hands of a few mega platform owners. This book contributes to the platform imperialism discourse by mapping out several core areas of platform imperialism, such as intellectual property, the global digital divide, and free labor, focusing on the role of the nation-state alongside transnational capital.

Dal Yong Jin is Associate Professor in the School of Communication at Simon Fraser University, Canada. He is also Visiting Associate Professor at Yonsei University, Korea.

Routledge New Developments in Communication and Society Research

Series Editor: James Curran, *Goldsmiths, University of London*

1 **How Media Inform Democracy**
   A Comparative Approach
   Toril Aalberg and James Curran

2 **Communicating Climate Change and Energy Security**
   New Methods in Understanding Audiences
   Greg Philo and Catherine Happer

3 **Digital Platforms, Imperialism and Political Culture**
   Dal Yong Jin

Digital Platforms, Imperialism and Political Culture

Dal Yong Jin

New York London

First published 2015
by Routledge
711 Third Avenue, New York, NY 10017

and by Routledge
2 Park Square, Milton Park, Abingdon, Oxon OX14 4RN

First issued in paperback 2017

Routledge is an imprint of the Taylor & Francis Group, an informa business

Library of Congress Cataloging in Publication Data

Jin, Dal Yong, 1964–
Digital platforms, imperialism and political culture / by Dal Yong Jin.
pages cm. — (Routledge New Developments in Communication and Society ; 3)
Includes index.
1. Digital electronics—Social aspects. 2. Technological innovations—Social aspects.
3. Political culture. 4. Mass media and globalization. 5. Imperialism. I. Title.
HM851.J56 2015
303.48'33—dc23 2014040954

ISBN 13: 978-1-138-09753-7 (pbk)
ISBN 13: 978-1-138-85956-2 (hbk)

Typeset in Sabon
by codeMantra

For my family, Kyung Won, Yu Sun, and Yu Young

Contents

Acknowledgments

The ideas and arguments in this book were conceived in 2011 when digital platforms, such as social networking sites, search engines, and smartphones, started to fundamentally change our daily activities. During my days in both Korea and Canada between 2009 and 2011, I experienced undeniable influences formed by these digital platforms, and I started to perceive their role in our modern society. My interactions with people over the next several years, including students at both Simon Fraser University in Canada and KAIST in Korea, presenters and discussants at several conferences, and colleagues in my academic discipline, all provided valuable opinions that shaped and advanced my ideas and discussion topics.

It is impossible to thank everyone who helped me to produce this book. I would like to single out a few graduate students at the University of Illinois at Urbana–Champaign who invited me to talk about my preliminary ideas on digital imperialism in the era of globalization. As the co-organizers of the Focal-Point Speaker Series, Robert Mejia, Erin Crocodile, and Jungmin Kwon gave me a wonderful opportunity to test my arguments. They are now emerging scholars and good colleagues of mine. Several faculty members, including Dan Schiller who was my dissertation advisor, John Nerone, Kent Ono, and James Hay provided their insightful views and conveyed some feedbacks to develop my ideas. When I visited Champaign, Illinois, Clifford Christians personally picked me up at the airport to have dinner with him and his wife and encouraged me to think deeply and thoroughly. This book certainly benefited from their thoughtful and warm comments and provocative questions.

Selections of this book were presented in preliminary form at several conferences and symposia organized by several institutions, such as Simon Fraser University and Seoul National University of Science and Technology, as well as a couple of international conferences. Several scholars that I met in these venues, including Kaarle Nordenstreng, Jack Qiu, and Kwang Suk Lee provided important comments. I also would like to thank Christian Fuchs and Dwayne Winseck who offered very kind critiques and observations on my first piece of work that was later published in *triple-c: Communication, Capitalism & Critique. Open Access Journal for a Global Sustainable Information Society.* Their suggestions were highly instructive and valuable to my later analysis of digital platforms.

Simon Fraser University also provided a very important intellectual environment. Michael Borowy, as my research assistant, read the manuscript and gave me several suggestions that helped me to further enhance the structure of this work. Seongbin Hwang, during his stay as a visiting professor in Vancouver, generously listened to my project and showed his interests and comments, which gave me opportunities to double check the soundness of the book. Andrew Feenberg also challenged me to carefully think about several important issues, including digital labor and the role of social media, which helped me to advance key debates.

I am also grateful for the support of two agencies, partially because this work was made possible by their funds. These agencies are the Social Sciences and Humanities Research Council (SSHRC) of Canada and the National Research Foundation of Korea Grant funded by the Korean Government (NRF-2013S1A3A2054849).

Most of all, I dedicate this book to my daughters, Yu Sun Jin and Yu Young Jin, and to my wife, Kyung Won Na. I completed most of the book during my daughters' most important years at high school. My family's generous understanding for my research and writing helped me keep my academic journey in prosper. This book is my small present to their love.

Part I

Imperialism Is Back

1 Platform Technologies and Political Culture

INTRODUCTION: POWER SHIFT FROM THE WORLD WIDE WEB TO PLATFORMS

> "You wake up and check your email on your bedside iPad—that's one app. During breakfast you browse Facebook, Twitter, and *The New York Times*—three more apps. On the way to the office, you listen to a podcast on your smartphone. Another app. At work, you have Skype and IM conversations. More apps. At the end of the day, you come home, make dinner while listening to Pandora, play some games on Xbox Live, and watch a movie on Netflix's streaming service. You've spent the day on the Internet—but not on the Web. And you are not alone. Over the past few years, one of the most important shifts in the digital world has been the move from the wide-open Web to semiclosed platforms that use the Internet for transport but not the browser for display."
>
> (Anderson, 2010)

In August 2010, *Wired* magazine announced the 'Death of the Web,' based on the premise that platforms are becoming the primary mode of access to the Internet. It was only a few years ago when the same *Wired* chanted the powerful role of the World Wide Web in our networked society (Long, 2008). In July 2008, it clearly stated:

> "the Web became publicly available on the Internet for the first time in 1991. The web has changed a lot since Tim Berners-Lee posted the first web pages summarizing his World Wide Web project, a method of storing knowledge using hypertext documents.[1] Today's web is far more powerful and sophisticated than the research tool developed by Berners-Lee and Cailliau but continues operating on basically the same principles they established a quarter of a century ago."

This rather shocking contrast between the end of the Web and the emergence of platforms within only a handful of years undoubtedly exemplifies the swift change in the field of information and communication technology

(ICT). Since the first use of the World Wide Web (hereafter Web) in 1991, the Web has indeed been the primary engine for the growth of the Internet. The dominant position of the Web in the networked society has not been challenged until now as platforms are suddenly replacing it. Of course, this does not mean that we are actually witnessing and/or expecting the death of the Web, given its continuous role in our network society. We also cannot separate platforms from the Internet age in which the Web plays a primary role because people certainly use both the Web and applications in order to maximize the benefits from these digital technologies.[2]

What we are able to admit is that the era of platforms is not the same as the Web-based Internet because applications (apps), which are software, play a key role as one of the primary digital intermediaries. For example, Facebook won the Web, partially because of its innovative features that set it apart from other social network sites. First and foremost, the 2007 launch of the Facebook Platform was key to Facebook's success. This open application programming interface made it possible for third-party developers to create applications that work within Facebook itself. Almost immediately after being released, the platform gained a massive amount of attention, and now there are hundreds of thousands of apps built on the platform—so many that Facebook has recently launched the Facebook App Store to organize and display them all (Goble, 2012). As the smartphone is rapidly replacing traditional mobile phones, many users also select their own smartphones because they primarily want to use multiple applications. As a few smartphone makers, such as Apple and Samsung, have rapidly advanced their new gadgets, applications also become some of the most significant factors for the users in selecting their own smartphones.

Platform is a useful term because it is a broad enough category to capture several distinct phenomena, such as social networking, shift from desktop to tablet computing, and smart phone and app-based interfaces, as well as the increasing dominance of centralized cloud-based computing (Hands, 2013a). The platform is also specific enough to "indicate the capturing of digital life in an enclosed, commercialized and managed realm. While the presence of the Internet must not be forgotten, theories of network culture need to be supplemented with new frameworks and paradigms" (Hands, 2013a, 1).[3] Although it was not long ago when people began to witness the emergence of platforms, platform technologies and politics are suddenly ubiquitous in everyday life. They are deeply woven into contemporary life, politically, economically, culturally, and technologically.

PLATFORMS IN THE DIGITAL ECONOMY AND CULTURE

Platforms, such as social network sites (SNSs) (e.g., Facebook and Twitter), search engines (e.g., Google), and smartphones (e.g., iPhone and Galaxy)[4] and their operating systems (e.g., Android and iOS), are known as digital intermediaries. They have greatly changed and influenced people's daily lives. Social network sites and smartphones have become necessary tools for high school students to connect with friends. The popularity of social networks for democracy as in the case of Arab Spring (2010) continues to grow exponentially. As James Curran (2012, 3) argues, the Internet which can be accessed through the Web would rejuvenate democracy by enabling direct e-government through popular referenda, and it would democratize our society. In the early 21st century, platform technologies, including Facebook and Twitter, as well as smartphones have further enabled the fundamental shift from the mass-mediated public sphere to platform-driven public sphere (Benkler, 2006) because platforms provide opportunities for people to mobilize themselves effectively for social change. Global youth also rapidly access Facebook and Twitter on spots as their new communication method. With the rise of new platforms, communication and cooperation have become more important features of the digital society (Fuchs, 2008). The phenomenal growth and use of smartphones and relevant apps have had a huge impact on our society in a shorter period of time than have any other technologies.

In the era of globalization, platforms have also gained significance for the digital economy, because people heavily access and use these platforms. As Facebook and Google are for-profit, U.S.-based platforms, user activities, not only as customers but also as producers of content for these platforms, become a new revenue source for platform owners. Platform owners who are mega media and technology giants have developed their strategies to appropriate user activities in order to transform users' daily performances into monetary revenue resources. While it is not new to witness the commodification of customers in previous media, including television and the Internet, the massive commercialization of platform users has further raised concerns because only a handful of platforms dominate the global markets. Therefore, the digital platform has emerged "as an increasingly familiar term in the description of the online services of content intermediaries, both in their self-characterizations and in the broader public discourse of users, the press and commentaries" (Gillespie, 2010, 349).

Due to the significance of platforms in both the digital economy and culture, several countries have developed their own SNSs and smartphones—not only as hardware architecture but also as software frameworks that allow software to run—for the digital economy and culture, including intellectual property and participatory culture. Unlike the era of the Web, platforms are themselves centered on intellectual property rights as one of the most significant tools to accumulate capital in the hands of a few platform owners and the countries, as in the case of the tug-of-war between Apple and Samsung.

Many corporations in several countries, from start-ups to mega information technology firms, have invented their own platforms. Several social network sites preceded Facebook. Asian Avenue—targeting an Asian-American community—launched in July 1997, and Cyworld in Korea originally started in 1999. Skyrock (formerly Skyblog), which was a French blogging service before adding SNS features, was born in 2002. These few players have advanced their unique platforms, controlled their own national markets and/or communities, and competed with U.S.-based platforms in the global markets. Later, several non-Western countries also developed their own smartphones, including Samsung Galaxy III in Korea, HTC in Taiwan, and Huawei in China.

At a glance, therefore, the massive switch to the digital economy has provided a surplus of capital for several emerging powers, including China, India, and Korea, with which to challenge the longer-term U.S. dominance (Boyd-Barrett, 2006, 24). These countries have presumably competed with Western countries, in particular the U.S., and they are supposed to build a new global order with their advanced digital technologies. Some theoreticians indeed focus on the emergence of a few non-Western countries as major players in the platform market.

The reality is that only a handful of Western countries, primarily the U.S., have developed social network sites, such as Twitter and Facebook, encompassing several new features and functions (boyd and Ellison, 2008) and smartphones, and have dominated the global platform market. Although the U.S. is not the sole player in the platform business, the extensive role of the U.S. is not deniable in the early 21st century. There are doubts as to whether non-Western ICT corporations have reorganized the global flow and constructed a balance between the West and the East. The panacea of technology may reduce imperialism and domination to vestiges of the past; however, technology will always be the reality of human hierarchy and domination (Maurais, 2003; Demont-Heinrich, 2008), and digital technologies have buttressed U.S. hegemony.

In fact, non-Western countries have not, and likely cannot, construct a balanced global order because Google (including its Android operating system), Facebook, Twitter, and Apple's iPhones (and iOS), as well as YouTube, are indices of the dominance of the U.S. in the digital economy and political culture. Again, several developing countries, such as China and Korea, have invented and advanced their platforms, but their use is mainly limited to their own territory or their own diaspora with a few exceptions. Therefore, it is not controversial to say that American dominance has been continued with platforms. Platforms have functioned as a new form of distributor and producer that the U.S. dominates. Arguably, we are still living in the imperialist era.

The hegemonic power of American-based platforms is especially crucial because Google, Facebook, iPhone, and Android have functioned as major digital media intermediaries thanks to their advanced roles in aggregating several services. Of course, platforms are not only gathering information from users, but also commercializing user information as commodity, resulting in massive capital accumulation for the owners of these platforms as well as their countries. Although user activities are mainly voluntary when it comes to platforms, activities are commodified by platform owners. The U.S., which had traditionally controlled non-Western countries with its military power, capital, and, later, cultural products, now seems to dominate the world with platforms, benefitting from these platforms in terms of both capital accumulation and spreading symbolic ideologies and cultures.

This new trend raises the question of whether the U.S., which has always utilized its imperial power, not only with military force, capital, and cultural products, but also with technologies, continues to control the majority of the world in order to actualize the same dominance, this time, with platform technologies. Since several countries have also developed their own platforms and competed with U.S.-based platforms, it is critical to determine whether these countries are able to overcome Western influences and become major players both nationally and globally. Since platforms have become crucial as the primary component of the digital economy and culture, it is significant to understand the close relations between platform owners, mostly located in the U.S., and platform users in the majority of countries globally. The goal is ultimately to comprehend whether platform technologies and relative ideologies have intensified asymmetrical power relations between a few Western countries, in particular the U.S., and the remaining countries, as can be seen in several areas, including in the realm of culture over the last several decades.

HOW TO UNDERSTAND PLATFORM POLITICS

What Is a Platform?

The term platform has recently arisen in describing the current use of technology and culture. Many scholars, policy makers, and corporations have rapidly adopted and used the notion of platforms as one of the most significant areas, yet they make no reliable definitions. While the conceptualizations of platforms were abundant, the meaning of platforms was barely addressed.[5] As some media and analysts state, in our contemporary society, a platform is any base of technologies upon which other technologies, applications, data blocks, or even dedicated computing processes are built (Bridgwater, 2013). When Joss Hands and Greg Elmer organized the first ever conference on platform politics in 2011, they defined platforms as "portals or applications that offer specific Internet services, frameworks for social interaction, or interfaces to access other networked communications and information distribution systems." In the call for papers, they also stated, "additionally the prevalence of mobile computing and its operating systems, that prioritize Internet access via 'apps' not web browsers, is intensifying this transformation, and this model is now being applied to tablet computing—and may well soon spread into general computing and computer mediated communication" (Exploring New Configurations of Network Politics, 2011).

Later, as Joss Hands (2013b, 3) himself points out, "a platform is, in its most general sense, a software framework running on the world wide web or Internet, in the forms of social media interfaces, apps, or most commonly 'Web 2.0' portals that gather users in interfaces with each other and with the Web and Internet itself; key is the provision for user generated content and intensive interaction."[6] In other words, the platform has been a concept to explain "the online services of content intermediaries, both in their self-characterizations and in the broader public discourse of users, the press and commentaries" (Gillespie, 2010, 349).

> "Intermediaries like YouTube and Google, those companies that provide storage, navigation and delivery of the digital content of others, are working to establish a long-term position in a fluctuating economic and cultural terrain. Like publishers, television networks and film studios before them, established companies are protecting their position in the market, while in their shadows, smaller ones are working to shore up their niche positions and anticipate trends in the business of information delivery."
>
> (Gillespie, 2010, 348)

However, van Dijck (2013, 29) points out, "a platform is a mediator rather than an intermediary," because it shapes the performance of social acts instead of merely facilitating them:

> "Technically speaking, platforms are the providers of software, (sometimes) hardware, and services that help code social activities into a computational architecture; they process (meta) data through algorithms and formatted protocols before presenting their interpreted logic in the form of user-friendly interfaces with default settings that reflect the platform owner's strategic choices."
>
> (van Dijck, 2013, 29)

Given the short history of platform technologies and political ideologies, it is not surprising to find that there has been no confirmed definition, and, as explained above, some scholars have just started to think about the notion, and therefore the evolution, of platforms. Therefore, we believe that the concept of platforms can be explained in three different, but interconnected ways.

First, we should think of a platform not only as hardware architecture but also as a software framework that allows other programs to run (Tech Coders.com, 2012). While people associate platforms with their computational meaning (Bodle, 2010), which is an infrastructure that supports the design and use of particular applications or operating systems, the platform is beyond the computations domain. Technically, "a platform may refer to a hardware configuration, an operating system, a software framework or any other common entity on which a number of associated components or services run" (Ballon and Heesvelde, 2011, 703). This means that platforms allow code to be written or run, and a key aspect is that they also enhance the ability of people to use a range of Web 2.0 technologies to express themselves online and participate in the commons of cyberspace (Gillespie, 2010). Lev Manovich (2013, 7) also points out, "platforms allow people to write new software," and "these platforms, such as Google, Facebook, iOS, Android, are in the center of the global economy, culture, social life, and, increasingly, politics."

Second, platforms "afford an opportunity to communicate, interact, or sell" (Gillespie, 2010, 351). Platforms can be analyzed from the corporate sphere because "their operation is substantially defined by market forces and the process of commodity exchange" (van Dijck 2012, 162). Economically, platforms and their providers mediate and coordinate between various stakeholder constituencies (Ballon and Heesvelde, 2011). Platforms themselves are economic entities with both a direct economic role as creators of surplus value through commodity production and exchange and an indirect economic role, through advertising, in the creation of surplus value within other sectors of commodity production (Garnham, 1997). As Baldwin and Clark (2006) point out, successful firms are those that possess architectural knowledge about bottlenecks and use this knowledge in order to shrink their footprint and selectively outsource activities. In this way, they gain an advantage in terms of invested capital, while keeping control over the most critical bottlenecks (see Figure 1.1).

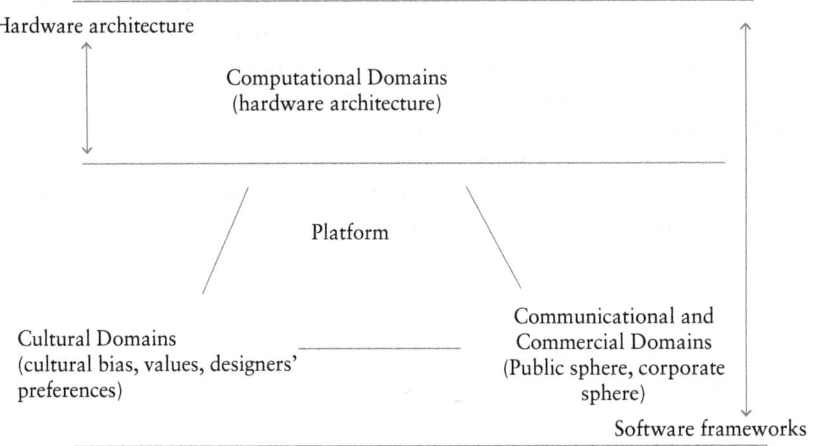

Figure 1.1 How to Understand Platforms.

Finally, it is also crucial to understand the nature of platforms, whether applications or software, because a platform's value is embedded in design. As several theoreticians argue (Feenberg, 1991; Salter, 2005; Ess, 2009), technologies are not value neutral but reflect the cultural bias, values, and communicative preferences of their designers. Likewise, platforms often "reinforce the values and preferences of designers," either explicitly or implicitly, while sometimes "clashing with the values and preferences" of their intended uses (Ess, 2009, 116). Bodle (2010, 15) specifically points out, "the technological design of online spaces, tools, and operating systems constitutes a contested terrain where the imposition of designers' values and preferences are at odds with the values and preferences of the intended user base." More specifically, they are commercial values because these platforms are designed primarily to facilitate consumption, not creation (Wum, 2011).

What we also have to understand is that platforms are deeply involved in political culture, not only as corporate strategies in developing close relations with the nation-state in the pursuit of favorable government policies for their businesses but also as delicate corporate policies in avoiding any particular responsibilities. Political culture refers to the symbolic environment of political practice, and it has been shaped by historical experiences and philosophical and religious traditions (Kluver, 2005). This also includes the assumptions, expectations, mythologies, and mechanisms of political practice within a nation, as Kluver and Banerjee (2005) aptly put it. Therefore, political culture here includes the role of nation-states and symbolic hegemony in tandem with platform technologies.

Several platforms, such as Google, YouTube, and Facebook, sometimes downplay their role to merely an intermediary to limit their liability for the users' activity (Gillespie, 2010). For example, Facebook's design of privacy controls, dissemination of user content to advertisers, and public release of profile information disregards the values of privacy. The company's preference for compulsory sharing directly clashes with social network members' need for privacy and control over their own information. Apple's refusal to run Flash-enabled applications or videos on iPhones in order to control the environment for maximum monetization from the sale of applications and control of future video codecs is another example of clashing values (Bodle, 2010, 15). Salter (2005, 292) also argues that "technologies are the result of innovations with users in mind." Platforms sometimes limit their major functions as a mere intermediary, while at other times they define them as an active intermediary to appropriate user activities.

In particular, Bodle (2010, 15) further points out that "identifying market-oriented values in technical design" (in this case platforms) that seek to undermine users' need for "privacy, control, autonomy, online encounters and access illustrated" how platform can serve as agents of platform imperialism (see also Ess, 2009). Bodle (2010, 15) also claims, "the technological design of online spaces, tools, applications and devices constitutes a contested terrain where the imposition of designers' values and preferences are at odds with the values and preferences of the intended user base." Indeed, technical standards become imperative. "Once they are set, the firm that holds the patent is off to the races. It is in the public interest that these standards not privilege a single firm, but that is not always possible. Smart firms do what they can to make their technical system the industry standard, hence giving them the pole position and a two-lap lead in a three-lap race" (McChesney, 2013, 133).

Patent laws have indeed been a cornerstone of the industrial economy. William Melody (2009, 65) also argues that "copyrights laws may be even more important than in the knowledge economy,"[7] although Melody (2009, 66) emphasizes that "the knowledge economy revolution is being driven primarily by skilled labor." It may be true to say that, for the first time in the history of capitalism, the primary driving economic force may not be physical capital, but human capital—the investment in skilled labor. However, in the era of the platform, it is significant to acknowledge that the major players are not only skilled labor as designers and developers, but general users who create content as unpaid workers.

As such, all three of these areas are relevant to why platforms have emerged in reference to online and mobile content-hosting intermediaries. Drawing these meanings together allows us to see that platforms emerge not simply as indicating a functional computational shape but with cultural values and communicational aspects, including both public and corporate spheres, embedded in them. As the growth of new media cannot be separated from society, we must interpret the triple helix as a complicated but interconnected whole in order to understand platform. A closer interpretation of the technological functions, traits of platforms as either public sphere or corporate sphere, and cultural values will help determine unique challenges and opportunities in understanding global platforms as a new tool for imperialism.

Platform Imperialism

This book will analyze the evolutionary development of various theories of imperialism and examine whether we might be moving towards the construction of platform imperialism. Since the new concept of imperialism functions through digital technologies, first information and second platform technologies in the 21st century, it is significant to interpret whether such technologies play a primary role in changing the notions of imperialism.

As briefly discussed, platforms are crucial for people's everyday information flows and capitalism, not only on a national level, but also on a global level. Platforms suggest a progressive and egalitarian arrangement, promising to support those who stand upon them in the contemporary global society (Gillespie, 2010). However, arguably, global flows of culture and technology have been asymmetrical, as theories of cultural imperialism (e.g., H. Schiller, 1976) and media imperialism (e.g., Boyd-Barrett, 1977) have long asserted. Thus the focal point here is whether asymmetrical relationships between a few developed and many developing countries exist in the case of platforms. Accepting platforms as digital media intermediaries, the idea of platform imperialism in this book refers to an asymmetrical relationship of interdependence in platform technologies and political culture between the West, primarily the U.S., and many developing countries, including two great powers—both nation-states and transnational corporations—as Lenin (1917) analyzed. As detailed in Chapter 2, Lenin (1917) emphasized the interplay of the nation-state and transnational corporations (TNCs) within the notion of great powers; therefore, it is vital to understand platform imperialism as the result of the state-industry complex phenomenon. This means that platform imperialism is not only about the forms of technological disparities but also the forms of intellectual property, symbolic hegemony, and user commodity because these issues concentrate capital into the hands of a few U.S.-based platform owners, resulting in the expansion of the global divide.

Characterized in part by unequal technological exchanges and therefore capital flows, the current state of platform development implies a technological domination of U.S.-based companies that have greatly influenced the majority of people and countries. Unlike other fields, including culture and hardware, in which the method for maintaining unequal power relations among countries is primarily the exportation of these goods and related services, in the case of platform imperialism, the means of dominating foreign countries are different because intellectual property and commercial values are embedded in platforms and in ways that are more significant for capital accumulation and the expansion of power.

PURPOSES OF THE BOOK

This book, as the first attempt to comprehensively analyze platform technologies and political culture, explores the evolution of platforms. It critically and historically contextualizes the recent development of platform technologies and political culture within the debates of imperialism. The critical analysis of platform politics should not be taken as totally rejecting positive changes happening with the rapid growth of social network sites, smartphones, and search engines as new forms of participatory culture and the digital economy. However, we also understand that platform technologies have become some of the most significant means for the capital accumulation and dominance of a handful of Western countries. Unlike the realm of popular culture, in which several emerging forces, such as Brazil, Mexico, and Korea, are gradually competing with Western forces, although the degree is not able to compare with American popular culture, platform technologies are mostly invented by Western-based transnational corporations and/or start-ups. Furthermore, the nature of dominance in terms of the market share of these U.S.-based platforms in the majority of national markets has soared, which has resulted in the intensification of American dominance.

To begin with, the major goal of this book is to determine the primary role of platforms in our networked global society and to discuss whether platform politics is useful for explaining the contemporary power relations and inequality between the U.S. and non-Western countries. More specifically, the book investigates whether the recent growth of American-based platforms has resulted in a change to the norm of the imperialism thesis because the panacea of technology, in this case platforms, may not reduce American domination; instead, technology is always the reality of human hierarchy and domination (Demont-Heinrich, 2008). Given that the U.S. has intensified its dominant power in the area of platforms, the book contributes to the platform imperialism discourse as a form of new imperialism by mapping out several core areas of platform imperialism, including the swift growth and global dominance of SNSs and smartphones. We eventually intend to develop platform imperialism theory, focusing on the role of the nation-state alongside transnational capitals. In other words, we investigate the primary role of the nation-state in the platform industries. The book especially articulates how the U.S. government has cultivated the free flow of information norm in global affairs in the era of social media.

Secondly, platforms are closely related to several important issues surrounding the growth of platform technologies and political culture, such as intellectual property rights, which are some of the most significant components of platform imperialism, global digital divide, and the spiritual hegemony of American-based entrepreneurship. This book critically analyzes political culture, including both intellectual property rights and the current debates on the global digital divide, which becomes enlarged due in large part to the asymmetrical growth and use of platform technologies. Since platform imperialism is also about the ideological dominance of Western countries and developers, this book addresses the ways in which symbolic hegemony influences the intensification of the global digital divide, which has resulted in the formation of platform imperialism. In other words, platforms promote imperialism which promotes asymmetrical information flows and discrimination in their design and use.Platforms establish norms and attitudes about their uses, standards, and practices of systemic colonization (Salter, 2005, cited in Bodle, 2010). These norms and practices include a disregard for privacy and a lack of transparency in intellectual property right.

As Gross (2006, 115) points out, "a method for maintain unequal power relations among nations is the exportation and forced importation of intellectual property rights, resulting in a massive transfer of wealth from countries of the South to those of the North, and a one way flow of ideas from the North to the South—a form of information of age colonialism." Platforms also have the potential to inflame the social divide. Given the global growth and influence of platforms, a critical interpretation of these issues is urgently needed.

Finally, we analyze the commodification of platforms and the appropriation of users as free labor, because platforms are engaged in the commodification of what can be understood as free labor. In the era of platforms, users are the core driving force behind the digital economy. Thus, we contextualize an attempt to understand the role of users in the reproduction of capital relations towards the user commodity, which is now a primary means of capital accumulation in platforms because access is key. The book then examines the capitalization of platforms and their global expansion. We eventually endeavor to make a contribution to the discourse of platform imperialism as a new form of imperialism, focusing on the nexus of great powers encompassing nation-states and TNCs, such as Google and Apple.

In the 21st century, there is a distinct connection between platforms, globalization, and capitalist imperialism. Platforms can be situated within more general capitalist processes that follow familiar patterns of asymmetrical power relations between the West and the East, as well as between workers and owners, commodification, and the harnessing of user power. Of course, this does not mean that the current form of platform imperialism resembles them. Instead, we need to challenge and extend the previous forms of imperialism in the realm of platforms—as an active intermediary—in the era of globalization, because platform imperialism is distinctive and differs from its predecessors.

POLITICAL ECONOMY AS AN APPROACH

The development and penetration of information and communication technologies (ICTs) are no longer discrete and distinct sectors from society. All its circuits, technology, texts, and promotion have become intertwined with the wider orbits of digital networks as critical zones for growth and profits (Jin, 2010). Platform technologies should be defined based on specific combinations of technical, political, cultural, and economic characteristics and not exclusively on any one of these alone. Through the examination of platforms in light of their sociocultural elements and critical studies contingencies, we illuminate some of the underexamined complexities inherent in the conception, development, implementation, and reception of platforms in a global arena.

As such, we primarily employ political economy approaches, emphasizing the historical documentation of the growth of imperialism and platform technologies. We employ a historical approach and the critical research of communication because political economy grounds its historical analysis in the organization and dynamics of both production and consumption. The historical approach is very useful to determine the causes behind the changing process of the imperialism theory. The political economy of new media and technology is suitable for analyzing contemporary society, in which platforms are major forces influencing the digital economy and culture because it addresses the nature of the relationship of platforms to the broader structure of society.

As several political economists, such as Vincent Mosco (2009), Dan Schiller (1999, 2007), and Robert McChesney (1999, 2013), emphasize, political economy looks at how ownership and supporting mechanisms, including advertising, and government policies influence media and technology systems. This approach leads us to understand the close relationship between platforms and surrounding environments, such as the role of the nation-state, intellectual property rights, the global digital divide, and users as commodities, as well as the concentration of ownership of platforms. As McChesney (2013, 13) points out, "political economy should be the organizing principle for evaluating the digital revolution" because the ways capitalism works and does not work determine the role platforms might play in society. As he admits (2013, 19), political economy does not provide all the necessary answers to all the questions, but "it provides valuable and indispensable context and insight for the most important questions."

However, it is also significant to understand that political economy is no longer about production. With the rapid growth of digital technologies, the role of audiences as content providers and consumers has become significant, and without understanding consumption correctly, it is not possible to utilize a fair political economy approach. As Dan Schiller (1999, 128) aptly puts it, "the extent to which cyberspace becomes a commercial consumer medium will be very largely determined by profit-seeking companies themselves." Since platform technologies and political culture are not only about production, but also consumption, we attempt to determine whether the role of users as prosumers has changed the traditional notion of imperialism emphasizing the tensions between classes as well as between countries in the form of asymmetrical power relations.

Manuel Castells (2009, cited in van Dijck, 2013) also points out that Web 2.0 is shaped by a clash between users asserting communicative and creative freedom and owners curbing users' newly acquired technological power. His analysis engages more with institutional actors, such as governments or corporations, than with user activity when he recommends that "theory identify the concrete social actors who are power holders and examine their global networking and their local workings" (Castells, 2009, 430). However, he also emphasizes "the users, including political grassroots groups using social media as a means to counter power" (van Dijck, 2013, 27). While we do emphasize the macro-level political economy approach in analyzing the emergence of platforms, what we also need to understand is the importance of the examination of the culture of connectivity. The contemporary political economy approach in the Web 2.0 era must consider the users as the major part of the analysis because they are not only consumers but also producers, unlike the pre-Web 2.0 era. Users and owners of platforms share the significance of having good content flow sinuously (van Dijck, 2013), but their interests diverge, resulting in power struggles between them.

ORGANIZATION OF THE BOOK

The book is organized as follows. In Chapter 2, we historicize the notion of imperialism in the globalized 21st century. The chapter investigates whether the recent growth of American-based platforms has resulted in a change to the norm of the imperialism thesis by analyzing the evolutionary nature of imperialism, such as (1) Lenin's imperialism, (2) cultural imperialism, (3) information imperialism, and (4) platform imperialism. Given that the U.S. has continued its power with platforms, we especially endeavor to make a contribution to the platform imperialism discourse as a form of new imperialism, focusing on the role of transnational corporations, including spiritual hegemony of America-based entrepreneurships. In other words, we primarily investigate whether platforms and their owners, such as Facebook, Google, and Apple, alongside the nation-state, play a key role in the construction of platform imperialism. Eventually, the chapter analyzes the power relations between the West and the East because the historical development of imperialism theory has been influenced by the tension between great powers, including TNCs in these two areas, as Lenin emphasized (1917).

Chapter 3 empirically analyzes the construction of platform imperialism with the growth of platforms around the world. By examining the recent growth of platforms, including Facebook, Google, and Twitter, in the global markets, it discusses the capitalization of platforms and their global expansion in the digital age. The chapter finally argues whether platform imperialism is useful for explaining the current power relations between the U.S. and non-Western countries. It articulates the ways in which only a few Western countries, in particular the U.S., have dominated the development of platform technologies and the global penetration of these new technologies. It eventually endeavors to make a contribution to the platform imperialism discourse as a form of new imperialism, focusing on the nexus of great powers encompassing nation-states and TNCs, such as Google and Apple. The chapter finally argues whether platform imperialism is useful for explaining the current power relations between the U.S. and non-Western countries.

Chapter 4 investigates the changing role of nation-states in conjunction with platforms. Platforms are not separate from the government because they are primary engines for the digital economy. While TNCs have advanced new technologies, the U.S. government and other governments have also been major players in the globalized world because they need to support the growth of their own platforms. Several theoreticians argue that imperialism, which relied on sovereign nation-states, no longer exists in the midst of the globalization process. However, the nation-state has always been significant in international negotiations alongside TNCs. For example, in the middle of the conflicts between the Chinese government and Google, the U.S. as a nation-state has strongly supported Google, primarily because the principle of the free flow of information has become a universal virtue to both the information industries and the U.S. government. Through the discourse of the tug-of-war between the Chinese government and Google (and its supporter, the U.S. government), this chapter examines the continuing, even intensifying, role of nation-states in the globalization era.

In Chapter 5, we investigate the significance of intellectual property rights as a major means of capital accumulation in the platform era. The diffusion of American SNSs and smartphones globally and their impacts on local customers and cultures has had far-reaching implications in the 21st century. The U.S. has benefited from innovation and intellectual property. SNSs, search engines, and smartphones alongside cultural products are crucial parts of the American empire, which is what the chapter tries to analyze. While platforms have been a new medium to accumulate capital through advertising and royalties from intellectual property rights, U.S.-based SNSs and smartphone producers have enjoyed dominant power in the global markets. These platform providers have reaped massive profits from hardware, software, and services protected by intellectual property laws, including copyright, patent, and trademark. This chapter examines the ways in which the U.S. has intensified its efforts to build global intellectual property (IP) standards, and it discusses the tension between a few countries as IP holders and the majority of countries as IP users.

Chapter 6 examines how users engage with SNSs. It focuses on providing a political economy analysis of SNS primarily in two ways, both through the commodification of SNSs as an emergent platform technology and the appropriation of users as free labor, because SNSs are engaged in the commodification of what can be understood as free labor. It contextualizes an attempt to understand the role of users in the reproduction of capital relations towards user commodities via the modification of Dallas Smythe's audience commodity thesis to a user commodity focus. It discusses the commodification of SNSs and their users in broader perspectives, including the 'user as free labor' in order to map out the comprehensive commodification process of SNS users. In other words, the chapter focuses on the nature of free labor because the voluntary involvement of immaterial labor has eventually turned itself into the commodification process, since corporations and advertising agencies systematically exploit their users' affective labor.

In Chapter 7, we attempt to develop new perspectives in the existing body of knowledge on the issue of the global digital divide by discussing its significant pertinence to platforms. We suggest that the digital divide be revisited in order to better contextualize it and that less linear explanations of the divide phenomenon should be developed. It thus discusses the theoretical examination of a few significant standards, such as smartphones in conjunction with software, intellectual property, and symbolic hegemony, as some of the most significant socio-cultural and ICT issues in determining the degree of the global digital divide. The chapter explores the chief reasons why these new measures as the nature of the problem itself and the manner in which it should be resolved are significant in the current debates on the global digital divide, and it explores what the implications are in our networked society.

Finally, Chapter 8 summarizes the major characteristics of platform politics, and it discusses whether we need to develop non-Western media theories explaining the rapid growth of local platform technologies and culture in the global markets or whether we have to apply and utilize current forms of these theories. This final chapter also discusses what we have to keep in mind for the future of platform discourse in the midst of neoliberal globalization.

NOTES

1. Tim Berners-Lee, a scientist at CERN, the European Organization for Nuclear Research, developed HyperText Markup Language (HTML). This technology continues to have a large impact on how we navigate and view the Internet today, after CERN introduced the World Wide Web to the public in 1991 (Zimmermann, 2012). The Web is a system of interlinked hypertext documents accessed via the Internet. With a web browser, such as Internet Explorer, Safari, Google Chrome, and Firefox, people can view web pages that may contain images, text, videos, and other multimedia, and they are able to navigate between them via hyperlinks.
2. The contrast between Web-based and app-based technologies is also evidenced in the definitions of social network sites. As one of the earliest concepts, boyd and Ellison (2008, 211) define "social network sites as web-based services that allow individuals to construct a public or semi-public profile within a bounded system." On the one hand, later, Alan Albarran (2013, 2) defines that "social media represents the technologies or applications that people use in developing and maintaining their social network sites." As these definitions also exemplify, it is difficult to separate the Web-based technologies from application-based technologies. However, it is also certain that only six years ago, boyd and Ellison emphasized the role of the Web in the development of new technologies because they did not witness the invention and advancement of several new technologies based on platforms, including the iPhone and Facebook Platform when they wrote the paper, while others later focus on the role of applications in the era of platforms.
3. Several theoreticians use different focuses in analyzing the contemporary form of monopoly capitalism. First, Lev Manovich (2013, 2) emphasizes the notion of software—programs such as Word, PowerPoint, Photoshop, Firefox, Blogger, and Google Earth, which enables users to create, publish, share, and remix images. However, platforms have both hardware and software functions. Therefore, the software side alone cannot properly explain platform technologies. Robert McChesney (2013) considers the Internet to be the most powerful driver of monopoly capitalism we have ever seen. Meanwhile, Vincent Mosco (2014) analyzes it with the term cloud systems, which is a powerful system for producing, storing, analyzing, and distributing data, information, applications, and services to organizations and individuals. Cloud systems are essential means of control, providing companies with opportunities to manage global supply

chains and to manage the workplace and through opportunities to rationalize business operations for profit. However, in this book, I employ the notion of platforms in order to specify three most significant and relevant areas, such as social network sites, search engines, and smartphones that are the primary drivers of modern capitalism, which have resulted in the construction of platform imperialism.

4. For example, the iPhone is more than just a gadget, it is a computer platform people can build on by developing and installing software for it (Grossman, 2007).
5. There have been several occasions where media scholars develop the notion of platforms and platform politics. For example, media scholars convened May 11–13, 2011, in Cambridge, United Kingdom, for the final event of the Network Politics conference, which talked about platform politics. Partially based on the conference, *Culture Machine*, an international open-access journal of culture and theory, published the journal special issue about platform politics, including twelve research papers, in 2013.
6. While there are several different definitions on Web 2.0., as discussed in Chapter 6, Web 2.0 is defined by the ability of users to produce content collaboratively. It is based on user-generated content that creates value from the sharing of information between participants and the business model in which users provide content, which is then leveraged into the user as free labor to be exploited (Ritzer and Jurgenson, 2010, 19; Cohen, 2008).
7. As William Melody (2009, 59) points out, "the knowledge economy shifts a primary focus on the transformation of material sources, that is, the physical production of goods, to a focus on improving and facilitating transactions capabilities, that is, generating and communicating information to facilitate exchange transactions. The ICT sector is driving productivity reforms primarily by improving the information and communication activities related to transactions."

REFERENCES

Albarran, A. (2013). (ed.). *The Social Media Industries*. London: Routledge.

Anderson, C. (2010). The Web is dead. Long live the Internet. *Wired*. 17 August. http://www.wired.com/magazine/2010/08/ff_webrip/.

Baldwin, C. & Clark, K. (2006). Architectural innovation and dynamic competition: The smaller footprint strategy. Harvard Business School Working Paper 07–14. http://www.hbs.edu/research/pdf/07-014.pdf.

Ballon, P. & Heesvelde, E.V. (2011). ICT platforms and regulatory concerns in Europe. *Telecommunications Policy* 35: 702–714.

Benkler, Y. (2006). *The wealth of networks: How social production transforms markets and freedom*. New Haven, CT: Yale University Press.

Bodle, R. (2010). Assessing social network sites as international platforms. *The Journal of International Communication* 16(2): 9–24.

boyd, d. & Ellison, N. (2008). Social network sites: Definition, history and scholarship. *Journal of Computer–Mediated Communication* 13(1): 210–230.

Boyd-Barrett, O. (2006). Cyberspace, globalization and empire. *Global Media and Communication* 2(1): 21–41.

Bridgwater, A. (2013). What is a platform anyway. *Computer Weekly*. 6 July. http://www.computerweekly.com/blogs/cwdn/2013/07/what-is-a-platform-anyway.html.

Castells, M. (2009). *Communication Power*. New York: Oxford University Press.

Cohen, N. (2008). The valorization of surveillance: Towards a political economy of Facebook, *Democratic Comunique* 22(1): 5–22.

Curran, J. (2012). Reinterpreting the Internet. In J. Curran, N. Fenton, and D. Freedman (eds.), *Misunderstanding the Internet*. London: Routledge.

Demont-Heinrich, C. (2008). The death of cultural imperialism—and power too? *International Communication Gazette* 70(5): 378–394.

Ess, C. (2009). *Digital Media Ethics*. Cambridge: Polity Press.

Exploring New Configurations of Network Politics (2011). Platform Politics, Call for Papers. http://www.networkpolitics.org/content/platform-politics-call-papers.

Feenberg, A. (1991). *The Critical Theory of Technology*. London: Oxford University Press.

Fuchs, C. (2008). *Internet and Society: Social Theory in the Information Age*. New York: Routledge.

Fuchs, C. (2010a). New imperialism: Information and media imperialism. *Global Media and Communication* 6(1): 33–60.

Fuchs, C. (2010b). Critical globalization studies and the new imperialism. *Critical Sociology* 36(6): 839–867.

Garnham, N. (1997). *Capitalism and Communication*. London: Sage.

Gillespie, T. (2010). The politics of platforms. *New Media and Society* 12(3): 347–364.

Goble, G. (2012). The history of social networking. 6 September. .http://www.digitaltrends.com/features/the-history-of-social-networking/#ixzz2kjqxOJtr.

Gross, R. (2006). Intellectual property rights and the information commons. In R.F. Jørgensen (ed.), *Human Rights in the Global Information Society*, pp. 107–120. Cambridge, MA: The MIT Press.

Grossman, L. (2007). Invention of the year: the iPhone. *Time*. November 1.

Hands, J. (2013a). Introduction: politics, power and platformativity. *Culture Machine* 14: 1–9.

Hands, J. (2013b). Platform communism. *Culture Machine* 14: 1–24.

Hardt, M. & Negri, A. (2000). *Empire*. Cambridge, MA: Harvard University Press.

Jin, D.Y. (2014). Critical analysis of user commodities as free labor in social networking sites: A case study of Cyworld. *Continuum: Journal of Media and Cultural Studies*.

Jin, D.Y. (2007). Reinterpretation of cultural imperialism: Emerging domestic market vs. continuing U.S. dominance. *Media, Culture and Society* 29(5): 753–771.

Kluver, R. & Banerjee, I. (2005). Political culture, regulation, and democratization: The Internet in nine Asian nations. *Information, Communication and Society* 8(1): 30–46.

Kluver, R. (2005). Political culture in Internet politics. In *Internet Research Annual*, vol. 2, 75–84. M. Consalvo and M. Allen (eds.). Peter Lang: New York.

Lenin, V. (1917). Imperialism, the highest stage of capitalism. In H. Christman (ed.), *Essential Works of Lenin*, pp. 177–270. New York: Dover.

Long, T. (2008). Ladies and Gentlemen, the World Wide Web. 7 July. http://www.wired.com/science/discoveries/news/2007/08/dayintech_0807.

Maurais, Jacques (2003). Towards a new linguistic order. In J. Maurais and M. Morris (eds.). *Languages in a Globalizing World*, 13–36. Cambridge: Cambridge University Press.

Manvich, Lev (2013). *Software Takes Command.* London: Bloomsbury.

McChesney, R. (1999). *Rich Media, Poor Democracy.* Urbana, IL: Champaign.

McChesney, R. (2013). *Digital Disconnect: How Capitalism Is Turning the Internet against Democracy.* New York: The New Press.

Melody, W. (2009). Markets and polices in new knowledge economies. In R. Mansell, C. Avgerou, D. Quah, and R. Silverstone (eds.), *The Oxford Handbook of Information and Communication Technologies*, 55–74. New York: Oxford University Press.

Mosco, V. (2009, 2nd ed.), *The Political Economy of Communication*. London: Sage.

Negri, A. (2008). *Reflections on Empire*. Cambridge: Polity.

Renzi, A. (2011). What is the politics of platform politics? *Television and New Media* 12(5): 483–485.

Salter, L. (2005). Colonization tendencies in the development of the World Wide Web. *New Media and Society* 7(3): 291–309.

Schiller, D. (1999). *Digital Capitalism: Networking the Global Market System*. Cambridge, MA: MIT Press.

Schiller, D. (2007). *How to Understand Information*. Urbana, IL: The University of Illinois Press.

Schiller, H. (1969). *Mass Communications and American Empire*. Oxford: Westview Press.

Schiller, H. (1976). *Communication and Cultural Domination*. White Plains, NY: International Arts and Sciences Press.

TechCoders.com (2012). Platforms for software development. Retrieved March 2, 2012, from http://www.techcoders.com/platforms-for-software-development.html/.

van Dijck, J. (2013). *The Culture of Connectivity: A Critical History of Social Media*. New York: Oxford University Press.

van Dijck, J (2012). Facebook as a tool for producing sociality and connectivity. *Television and New Media* 13(2): 160–176.

Zimmermann, K.A. (2012). Internet history timeline: ARPANET to the World Wide Web. 7 May. http://www.livescience.com/20727-internet-history.html.

2 The Evolution of Imperialism in the 21st Century

INTRODUCTION

> "A number of writers, some Marxists among them, are provocatively propounding the idea that imperialism is over and that we have arrived somewhere else. Hardt and Negri's *Empire*, the best-selling Marxist book of modern times, argues this...Partly in reaction to this, many have re-asserted that the monster is not only alive but is threatening the world with new dangers. And, among the latter category, a number are trying to see what is new about the current state of the world and to explore how historical-materialist and related theories can help to analyze it and ultimately to combat it."
>
> (Sutcliffe, 2006, 60)

Notions of imperialism have increased significantly with the rapid growth of asymmetrical power relationships between the U.S. and non-Western countries in the 21st century. As Marxism has regained its momentum with increasing inequality in many parts of the world, including in the areas of economy, culture, and politics, imperialism becomes one of the most revisited concepts in our contemporary capitalism in which the digital economy takes a major role (Sutcliffe, 2006; Hesmondhalgh, 2010; Fuchs and Mosco, 2012; Fuchs, 2012).[1]

It is controversial whether the U.S. continues its dominant position in the world due to the emergence of a few countries as major forces competing with a few Western countries. In the midst of globalization, the hegemonic power of a few Western countries has somewhat decreased in terms of their political and military power. However, it is also true that the U.S. continues to play a primary role in several areas, including culture and technology. In particular, in the early 21st century, only a handful of U.S.-created platforms, such as Facebook, iPhone (and its operating system iOS), and Google, have functioned as major digital media intermediaries, which results in capital accumulation for a few Western corporations thanks to their advanced roles in aggregating several services.

The primary goal of this chapter is to historicize the notion of imperialism in the globalized 21st century. It investigates whether the recent growth of American-based platforms has resulted in a change to the norm of the imperialism thesis by analyzing the evolutionary nature of imperialism, such as (1) Lenin's imperialism (mostly developed in the early 20th century), (2) cultural imperialism (mostly developed in the 1970s and 1980s), (3) information imperialism (in the 1990s), and (4) platform imperialism (in the early 21st century). This chapter attempts to document the evolution of imperialism theories so that we can make a contribution to the platform imperialism discourses as a form of new imperialism in following chapters. Our discussions in this chapter will shed light on the continuing debates on imperialism, in particular the power relations between the West and the East because the historical development of imperialism theory has been influenced by the tension between great powers, including both nation-states and transnational corporations in these two areas, as Lenin emphasized (1917).

THE EVOLUTION OF IMPERIALISM IN THE 20TH AND THE 21ST CENTURIES

Where the perception of imperialism has roots in early history, modern notions of imperialism go back a century and have become influential theoretical frameworks, although they have remained controversial in academia. The contemporary concept of imperialism is very different from the discourse developed in the early 20th century when it was primarily advanced by classical, Marxist-inspired theories of imperialism (e.g., Kautsky, Lenin, and Luxemburg). From a Marxist perspective, "imperialism is what happens when two forms of competition—the economic struggle among capitals and geopolitical rivalries between states—fuse" (Callinicos, 2007, 70). One of the central arguments of the Marxist tradition of imperialism is that there is an intrinsic relation between capitalism and expansion and that capitalist expansion inevitably takes the political form of imperialism (Marx, 1867). As Sutcliffe (2006, 60) points out, "the distinctive feature of the Marxist or historical-materialist method of analyzing imperialism consists of a special kind of dual vision. This consists of the hierarchies, conflicts and alliances—political, military and economic—between countries, and it is about dominance and exploitation of some countries by others."

Building on and modifying the theories of Karl Marx, there are several renditions of imperialism in the critical theory tradition. Lenin's pamphlet *Imperialism, the Highest State of Capitalism* (1917) provides an excellent place to start discussing imperialism because the Leninist theory of imperialism has exerted a considerable impact on the current era. What Lenin emphasized almost 100 years ago cannot be applied directly to the contemporary era due to vastly different social and economic conditions, as well as a different technological milieu. However, it is certainly worth trying to see whether Lenin's concepts can be applied to the 21st century.

Therefore, it is critical to historicize imperialism in the 21st century by analyzing the evolutionary nature of imperialism, from Lenin's imperialism, through cultural imperialism, to information imperialism, and finally to platform imperialism. The documentation of the evolution of different forms of imperialism guides us to address the issues of whether or not we are experiencing a new notion of imperialism by mapping out several core characteristics that define platform imperialism, including the swift growth and global dominance of U.S.-based SNSs and search engines.

Revisiting Lenin's Imperialism Thesis

Lenin argued that modern imperialism (or capitalist imperialism) constitutes a different stage in the history of capitalism. "The first stage was the competitive form of capitalism characterized by relatively small-scale enterprises, few of which dominated their market. That is the form of capitalism that mostly existed in Marx's day" (Harrison, 2007). The newer stage of capitalism, however, is characterized by huge monopolistic or oligopolistic corporations (Lenin, 1917). Lenin sharpened the temporal division between imperialism and the previous state of capitalism. He argued that "it was the transition to monopoly capital that drove the other changes in capitalist society" (McDonough, 1995, 356).

In his *Imperialism* pamphlet, Lenin remarked, "if it were necessary to give the briefest possible definition of imperialism, we should have to say that imperialism is the monopoly state of capitalism" (Lenin, 1917, 265). The key is that it was an economic analysis of the transition from free competition to monopoly. For Lenin, imperialism is the monopoly stage of capitalism, and imperialism is a new development that had been predicted but not yet seen by Marx. Lenin's term, monopoly capitalism, can be somewhat misleading because the way it is used by Lenin, and virtually all Marxists since his day, does not require that there be only one giant company, e.g., only one automobile manufacturer that has a 100 percent monopoly in its markets, or only one single steel producer, and so forth (Harrison, 2007). Instead, what Lenin referred to as monopoly capitalism is perhaps better known as an oligopoly today. What Lenin wanted to emphasize was that, at the fundamental economic level, what had most changed was that there were major aspects of monopoly in this new stage of capitalism and whether or not the consolidation of companies had reached the point where there was a single survivor in each industry. That is, even if there still are several huge companies in each industry, they tend to collude and jointly control the market to their mutual benefit (Harrison, 2007, 1, 10).

Later, Lenin gave a more elaborate, five-point definition of capitalist imperialism which emphasizes finance-capital—the dominant form of capital. The criteria are:

- the concentration of production and capital developed to such a stage that it creates monopolies which play a decisive role in economic life

- the merging of bank capital with industrial capital and the creation, on the basis of finance capital, of a financial oligarchy
- the export of capital, which has become extremely important, as distinguished from the export of commodities
- the formation of international capitalist monopolies which share the world among themselves
- the territorial division of the whole world among the greatest capitalist powers (Lenin, 1917)

Based on these five characteristics, Lenin defined imperialism as:

> "capitalism at that stage of development at which the domination of monopolies and finance capital is established; in which the export of capital has acquired pronounced importance; in which the division of the world among the international trusts has begun; in which the division of all the territories of the globe among the biggest capitalist powers has been completed.
>
> (Lenin, 1917, 237)

As Lenin's five-point definition of imperialism explains, finance capital uses the state machinery to colonize the periphery. In the periphery, capitalists would use oppressed peripheral labor to produce primary commodities and raw materials cheaply and create an affluent stratum (peripheral elite) to consume expensive commodities imported from the core, and undermine indigenous industry (Galtung, 1971). Johan Galtung (1971, 81) pointed out, "the world consists of center and periphery nations. Hence our concern is with the mechanism underlying this discrepancy between the center and the periphery. Thus, imperialism is a species in a genus of dominance and power relationships." For Lenin, imperialism is the power struggle for the economic and political division of the world, which gives rise to a transitional dependence between rentier states and debtor states:

> "the epoch of the latest stage of capitalism shows us that certain relations between capitalist associations grow up, based on the economic division of the world; while parallel to and in connection with it, certain relations grow up between political alliances, between states, on the basis of the territorial division of the world, of the struggle for colonies, of the struggle for spheres of influence."
>
> (Lenin, 1917, 239)

Indeed, Lenin himself implicitly discussed the role of the nation-state and his notion of state was great power, which also included transnational capitals. His argument for a strong state was a Commune worker state. The Commune was an armed and organized revolutionary section of the Parisian working class, but it was not a state (Lenin, 1964; Rothenberg, 1995). What

Lenin described was that both economic rivalry and military conflicts are indicative as conflicts for hegemony between great powers that constitute essential features for imperialism. As Fuchs (2011a, 198) aptly put it, in Lenin's statement, "great powers are not necessarily nation-states, because great powers are powerful actors, meaning that they can also be corporations as well as nation-states." In the early 2000s, Robinson (2004) also argues that the nature of globalization rests upon the transnational capitalist class' hegemony over national and local fractions of capital in most countries. However, he does partially acknowledge that national states are components of a larger "transnational state apparatus" that promotes globalization, although in Lenin's conceptualization "imperialism is essentially associated with a system of relations and contradictions between nation states" (Liodakis, 2003, 4).

Several new-Marxists (Galtung, 1971; Doyle, 1986) have relatively emphasized nation-states as major actors in imperialism theory. For them, imperialism involves the extension of power or authority over others in the interests of domination and results in the political, military, or economic dominance of one country over another (Wasko, 2003). In other words, "imperialism would be conceived of as a dominant relationship between collectivities, particularly between nations, which is a sophisticated type of dominant relationship" (Galtung, 1971, 81). Imperialism or empire can be defined, therefore, as "effective control, whether formal or informal, of a subordinated society by an imperial society" (Doyle, 1986, 30). It is crucial to understand "the basic mechanism of imperialism that concerns the relation between the parties that are connected, particularly between the nations, and who benefits most is an important point in the relations between nations" (Galtung, 1971, 85).

In the early 21st century, admitting that Lenin's definition has greatly influenced our understanding of global capitalism, we should update theoretical arguments in order to reengage with Lenin's theory of imperialism today (Fuchs, 2010b). One way to do this is to take Lenin as a theoretical impetus for the contemporary theorization of platform imperialism.

CULTURAL IMPERIALISM FROM LENIN'S FOURTH CHARACTERISTIC

Since the notion of modern imperialism has been primarily advanced by Marxist theorists beginning in the early 20th century, media scholars have developed imperialism theory in the contexts of several different areas, including culture and technology. Media theoreticians (H. Schiller, 1969; Guback, 1984; Fuchs, 2010a) have especially developed Lenin's fourth point of imperialism, primarily focusing on the major role of big companies supported by nation-states that dominate the economy. As Lenin (1917) argued, these big corporations, cartels, syndicates, and trusts first divided the home market among themselves and obtained more or less complete possession of the industry in their own country. "But under capitalism the home market is inevitably bound up with the foreign market. As the export of capital increased, and as the foreign and colonial connections and spheres of influence of the big monopolist associations expanded in all ways, things naturally gravitated towards an international agreement among these associations, and towards the formation of international cartels" (Lenin, 1917, 266).

Information industries and services, including both audiovisual and information and communication technologies (ICTs) industries, are no exception to this unequal economic geography (Fuchs, 2010a). We can say that theories of communication imperialism and cultural domination have described Lenin's fourth characteristic of imperialism in relation to media and culture: the domination of the information sphere by large Western corporations (H. Schiller, 1969; Galtung, 1971; Said, 1993; Fuchs, 2010a). Such concepts focused on the ownership and control, structure, and distribution of media content (and the media industries) in one country by another country (Boyd-Barrett, 1977; Fuchs, 2010a) or primarily by the U.S. (H. Schiller, 1976). This updated version is suited for theoretically describing Lenin's dimension of corporate economic domination in the attempt to apply imperialism theory to informational capitalism. Indeed, as Boyd-Barrett (1998, 158) indicates, "the concept of media imperialism is indebted to the works of Marx, Lenin and Luxemburg."

More specifically, several theorists claimed the cultural industry became an integral part of the advanced capitalist system in the 1930s. As Adorno (1991) points out, the culture industry has long played an architectonic role in the transformation of human and natural potential into the modern barbarism of late capitalism. Adorno and Horkheimer (1944) considered the culture industry as a main phenomenon of late capitalism, one which encompassed all products and form of light entertainment, from Hollywood films to television programs. For them, all these forms of popular culture are designed to satisfy the growing needs of mass capitalistic consumers for entertainment. "The extension of capitalist social relations and their identitarian logic to the production, distribution, and consumption of cultural goods not only destroys the emancipatory possibilities traditionally harbored by art and culture, thus sabotaging human capacities for experience and critical though, but also blinds individuals somatically, cognitively, and libidinally to the exchange relations itself" (Gunster, 2004, 23). Similar to many sectors, such as finance and manufacturing, the culture industry has been dominated by a few Western countries, the U.S. in particular, since the early 20th century; therefore, several media scholars have focused on the nature and degree of dominance.

In media studies, in particular, imperialism discourse has been intensified with the notion of cultural imperialism, referring to a global situation in which powerful culture industries and actors located almost exclusively in the West, and especially in the U.S., dominate other local, national, and regional cultures and actors (Demont-Heinrich, 2008). This domination is understood as being largely the outcome of fundamental historical inequalities which have resulted in the bulk of political and economic power being concentrated in the West. The result is a global homogenization of culture built mostly but not exclusively around Western and American cultural forms—e.g., Hollywood action films, American television sitcoms, U.K. style reality television programs, CNN style broadcast news programs, McDonald's, etc. (Demont-Heinrich, 2011). In an early thesis on these trends, communication scholar Herbert Schiller (1976) identified the dominance of the U.S. and a few European nations, including the U.K., in the global flow of media products as an integral part of Western imperialism.

The debate over imperialism in media studies further intensified beginning in the mid-1970s with the call by nations of the Third World for a New World Information and Communication Order (NWICO). In the decade following the end of World War II, many former colonies in Latin America, Africa, and Asia became independent. These countries formed the Non-Aligned Movement (NAM) in 1955 (Herman and McChesney, 1997). They initially pursued predominantly economic approaches to promote their own development; however, these nations questioned Western paradigms of development and sought alternative approaches. On the heels of this was the call for a NWICO to address imbalances in the political economy of the media and information systems (Mosco, 2009). The NWICO campaign was part of a broader struggle at that time by Third World nations to formally address the global economic inequality that was seen as a legacy of imperialism.

Based on the NWICO system, several media scholars, including H. Schiller (1976), debated the dominant power in international cultural exchange when the international communication system mainly expanded by supplying television programs and motion pictures. They argued that "the international communication system was characterized by imbalances and inequalities between rich and poor nations, and that these imbalances were deepening the already existing economic and technological gaps between countries" (UNESCO, 1980, 111–115). H. Schiller (1976) identified the dominance of the U.S. and a few European nations in the global flow of media products as an integral component of Western imperialism, and he dubbed it cultural imperialism in the following way:

> "the concept of cultural imperialism describes the sum of processes by which a society is brought into the modern world system and how its dominating stratum is attracted, pressured, forced, and sometimes bribed into shaping social institutions to correspond to, or even promote, the values and structures of the dominant center of the system (1976, 9–10).

Building on Schiller's work, Tunstall (1977) and Guback extended the meaning of dominance in international cultural exchange. For example, Guback (1984, 155–156) argued that "the powerful U.S. communication industry, including film and television as well as news, exerts influence, sometimes quite considerable, over the cultural life of other nations."

Over the decades, several empirical studies seemed to confirm this early cultural imperialism thesis by showing the one-way flow of goods from Western to non-Western countries. The authors of these studies defined cultural imperialism as the conscious and organized effort taken by the Western, especially U.S., media corporations to maintain commercial, political, and military superiority. Those Western multinational corporations exerted power through a vast extension of cultural control and domination, and thus saturated the cultural space of most countries in the world, which was claimed to have eliminated and destroyed local cultures by installing a new dominant culture in their place (Jin, 2007).

The Role of the Nation-State in Cultural Imperialism

What is important in the cultural imperialism thesis is the major role taken by the U.S. government. As discussed, media scholars have developed cultural imperialism primarily based on Lenin's fourth characteristic of imperialism, which emphasized the primary role of big corporations, in this case major U.S. media and cultural companies. However, the push by the large cultural, media, and information industries corporations into markets and societies around the world was also propelled by strong support from the U.S. government. The U.S. government's initiative and support for its culture industry has a long history. This strategy has emphasized the importance of information-based products, making the U.S. State Department a powerful government agent on behalf of the cultural sector (Miller et al., 2001). Given that much of the enormous revenues generated by the U.S. cultural industry have come from foreign markets, "the liberalization of the global cultural market is very significant for the U.S. government" (Magder, 2004, 385).

The U.S. government has indeed extensively supported domestic cultural industries, in particular Hollywood, by driving other countries to open their cultural markets, which means that the U.S. government has been deeply involved in the cultural trade issue by demanding that other governments should take a hands-off approach in the cultural area. The U.S. government acknowledges that the American motion picture and television production industries remain some of the most highly competitive around the world, although some local film industries such as Bollywood, Japanese, and Korean challenge Hollywood dominance (Jin, 2011). Most Western media TNCs get the majority of revenues from their home markets and then from a few core economies, including Western Europe and Japan (Flew, 2007). However, it is certain that the foreign markets are significant overall for the U.S. government and cultural industries.

Several non-Western economies have been targeted by the U.S. due in large part to the increasing role of emerging markets, including China, Russia, Korea, Brazil, and India. For example, *Avatar*—a Hollywood movie released in 2010—had overseas income of $915 million which significantly outpaced comparable domestic action, more than doubling its $430.7 million domestic take in the U.S. and Canada (*The Hollywood Reporter*, 2011). *Avatar* garnered gross box office receipts of $204 million in the Chinese film market alone, making China the film's top overseas box office money maker (*Associated Press: AP*, 2011b). In 2011, three movies (*Transformers: Dark of the Moon, Kung Fu Panda 2*, and *Pirates of the Caribbean: On Stranger Tides*) came in at Numbers 1, 2, and 3 on the Top Ten charts in China, grossing $345 million. Another three American films, the total reached $490 million, against four domestic productions, which took in $261 million (Jensen, 2012) indicates that China is gradually replacing Japan in becoming Hollywood's number one overseas box office revenue contributor.

U.S. film and television program exports in current dollar terms were valued at slightly over $1 billion in 1985 and $2 billion in 1990. However, the U.S. exported about $9.17 billion worth of film and television programs to the world in 2001, and the exports soared to $16.2 billion in 2012. During the period 1985–2012, foreign exports of U.S. films and television programs increased by as much as 16.2 times. The importing of foreign films and television programs increase from $195 million to $2,648 million during the same period (U.S. Department of Commerce, 2013) (see Figure 2.1). Europe was the largest audiovisual market for the U.S. in the early 21st century, although the U.S. has increased its exports to non-Western European countries. When the U.S. exported $4.98 billion worth of television programs and films to the world in 1996, Western European countries comprised the largest market at 60.8 percent, and it was almost the same in 2003 (61.9 percent). However, it substantially dropped to 50.5 percent in 2011 (U.S. Department of Commerce, 2000, 2006, 2012, 2013).

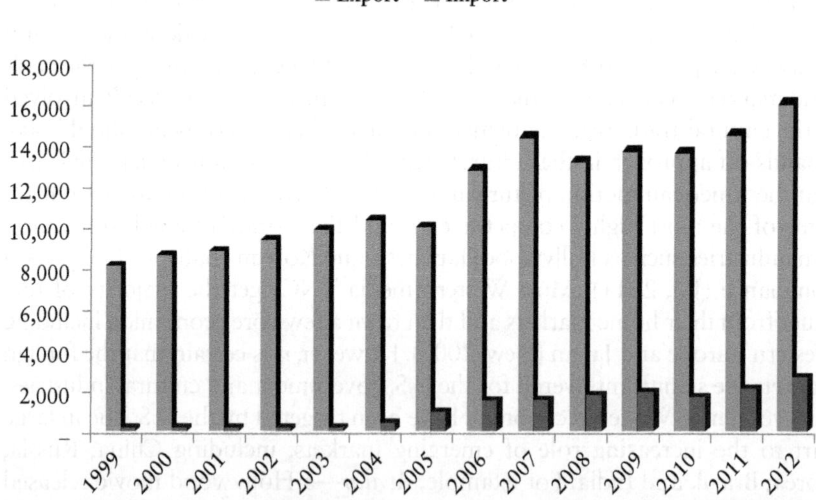

Figure 2.1 U.S. Film and Television Tape Distribution (unit: millions of dollars). Source: U.S. Department of Commerce (2013). U.S. International Services. http://www.bea.gov/international/international_services.htm

In spite of the fluctuations of Asian cultural markets, this means that countries outside Western Europe will in a few years become the major markets for the U.S. cultural industries. For example, as one of the emerging economies, the Asian audiovisual market gradually increased from 12.8 percent in 1992 to 17.1 percent in 2001, and again to 18.8 percent of the total U.S. exports in 2012 with an increasing number of broadcasting channels and movie screens in the region, partially because of the rapid growth of the Chinese market alongside several existing local markets, including Korea and Japan (U.S. Department of Commerce, 2000, 2002, 2012, 2013).

The restructuring of the global film sector was conducted through the use of larger power relations and patterns after World War II, with initial moves beginning prior to WWII. Since World War II, U.S. policy has generally supported the liberalization of international trade—that is, the elimination of artificial barriers to trade and other distortions, such as tariffs, quotas, and subsidies that countries use to protect their domestic industries from foreign competition (Congressional Budget Office, 2003). The U.S. government sought and eventually secured the liberalization of the audiovisual sector in the first General Agreement on Tariffs and Trade (GATT) negotiations in 1947. As Western countries began to settle on the arrangements that would govern the post-war world, cinema was high on the list of outstanding issues, and Hollywood wanted to restore its overseas markets (Magder, 2004). The U.S. government alongside major film/TV corporations has intensified its dominance in the global cultural market, and cultural imperialism has been one of the primary practices of Lenin's imperialism in different contexts in the 20th century, of course, until recent years.

Increasing Role of Transnational Corporations in Cultural Imperialism

Western TNCs have especially focused on domestic cultural markets with their capital as well as their cultural goods in the era of globalization. The U.S. media giants have firmly demanded that East Asian countries fully open their market to U.S. capital, as well as cultural products. They desire deregulation, privatization, and commercialization of the media industry in developing countries for easy penetration. Unlike during the period from the 1960s to the 1980s, the U.S. has used delicate strategies to penetrate the world in recent years. The U.S. media giants tend to make use of local cultural resources in order to promote their products, being influenced not so much by any particular regard for national cultures as by market forces (Jin, 2007). As Croteau and Hoynes (1997) argued, global media enterprises have been forced to adapt to local cultures and to link up with local partners in order to sustain their expansion. This does not mean that global media giants give up their roles as cultural imperialists. Instead, the U.S. media giants have adopted a strategy known as 'think globally, act locally' to maintain and/or expand their dominance effectively. The U.S. also uses indirect means to penetrate the world. For instance, the U.S. manages international agencies, including the International Monetary Fund (IMF), which have an impact on the Third World. Therefore, the U.S. is a driving force behind the IMF. On a general level, "the IMF attempts to reduce government involvement in business decisions to support the style of capitalism long advocated by the U.S., which is centered on free markets" (H. Schiller, 1999, 190).

In particular, the transnational corporations have gradually become highly influential institutions in the national cultural industry in many other countries. For example, since the late 1990s, TNCs are making inroads into the non-Western broadcasting sector by cooperating with local cable and satellite operators. Foreign financial companies and communication mega-companies—the two major sources of foreign capital—invested in Asia and Latin America because they believed the broadcasting business would be as lucrative there as elsewhere, resulting in the intensification of U.S. force in the national cultural market.

The new media sector, including platforms, is not much different. As detailed in Chapter 3, Facebook has rapidly increased its revenue for advertising in foreign countries, including several emerging markets, due to the soaring number of users in those markets. Western-based game corporations have also enjoyed profits from the global markets. By May 2007, for example, Blizzard Entertainment had sold about 9.5 million copies of the original StarCraft globally, with about 4.5 million of those copies sold in Korea (Olisen, 2007). Less than two years after its introduction in 2004, World of Warcraft, the online fantasy game, generated more than $1 billion in revenue in 2006 with almost seven million paying subscribers. "The game had more players in China, where it had engaged in co-promotions with major brands like Coca-Cola, than in the U.S." (Schiesel, 2005, B1). These new media corporations alongside cultural industries corporations have benefited from global capitalism paved by the nexus of the U.S. government and mega media TNCs.

IS IMPERIALISM DYING IN THE ERA OF GLOBALIZATION?

Since the early 1990s, two historical developments—the rapid growth of new technologies and the development of globalization—have greatly influenced the concept of imperialism. Whereas these two agendas are not mutually exclusive, we first discuss globalization, then explain why the growth of technologies has changed the direction in tandem with the role of the nation-state.

To begin with, as globalization theory has evolved over the last decade or so, contemporary theories of imperialism and global capitalism can be categorized on a continuum that describes the degree of novelty of imperialism (Fuchs, 2010a). At the end of the continuum there are theoreticians who argue that imperialism, including cultural imperialism, no longer exists today and that a post-imperialistic empire has emerged. What they emphasize is that the discrepancy between the core and the periphery cannot explain the complexity of globalization.

Since the mid-1980s, however, the cultural imperialism thesis has come under increasing criticism from diverse perspectives. Some media scholars have argued that in the current global media environment, which is characterized by a plurality of actors and media flows, it is no longer possible to sustain the notion of Western media domination (Ang, 1985; Straubhaar, 1991; Chadha and Kavoori, 2000; Sparks, 2007). They argue that the notion of dominance in culture has not been clarified. In addition, they claim that several non-Western countries, including Mexico, Brazil, and Korea, have developed their own popular cultures and exported them to other countries, resulting in the increasing role of non-Western countries in the global flow of cultural products.

Several media scholars have indeed made a case against the cultural imperialism thesis. Straubhaar (1991) emphasizes that national cultures can defend their ways of life and, in some respects, even share their images with the rest of the world. Sparks (2007, 119) also points out that "in the place of a single, U.S.-based production center dominating the whole of the world trade in television programs, it was increasingly argued that technical and economic changes were rendering the world a more complex place, in which there were multiple centers of production and exchanges flowing through many different channels." Meanwhile, Morley (2006, 36–40) argues that cultural imperialism has four significant issues and limitations, including (1) the complexities of flows in international communication; (2) the recent strategy of glocalization, (3) the effects of cultural protectionism, and (4) the impact of active audiences on media. What he emphasizes is that the international communication and media flows became more complex than in the past, and resulted in a new model of cultural imperialism.

Several other scholars also convincingly stress the discontinuity between globalization in the 21st century and in times past (Hardt and Negri, 2000; Robinson, 2007; Negri, 2008). Hardt and Negri (2000) point out that imperialism, which was an extension of the sovereignty of the European nation-states beyond their own boundaries, is over because no nation could ever be a world leader in the way modern European nations were in the midst of 19th and early-20th centuries versions of globalization. What they argue is that the old notion of imperialism has been replaced by a global capitalist system where national states have lost most of their power and influence. Hardt and Negri develop the term *empire* instead of *imperialism* to describe the contemporary form of the global order, and they argue that empire is a system of global capitalist rule that is altogether different from imperialism:

> "in contrast to imperialism, empire establishes no territorial center of power and does not rely on fixed boundaries or barriers. It is a decentered

> and deterritorializing apparatus of rule that progressively incorporates the entire global realm within its open, expanding frontiers."
>
> (Hardt and Negri, 2000, xii–xiv)

They argue that the world market under the influence of the information revolution is globalizing beyond the capacity of nation-states to affect it (Foster, 2001). "The sovereignty of nation states is vanishing, and is being replaced by a newly emerging global sovereignty known as Empire arising from the coalescence of a series of national and supranational organisms united under a single logic of rule," with no clear international hierarchy (Hardt and Negri, 2000, xii, cited in Foster, 2001).

As Robinson (2007, 7–8) also argues, "capitalism has fundamentally changed since the days of Lenin due to the appearance of a new transnational capitalist class, a class group grounded in new global markets and circuits of accumulation, rather than national markets and circuits." For Robinson (2004, 5), "world capitalism is a phase of capitalist development that is characterized by the transition from the nation state phase of world capitalism to a transnational phase." "Transnational capital has become the dominant, or hegemonic, fraction of capital on a world scale" (Robinson, 2004, 21). Robinson therefore claims, "the imperialist era of world capitalism has ended" (2007, 24). He believes that TNCs are much different than national corporations because TNCs have been free from nation-states.

More importantly, in the midst of the globalization process, some theoreticians claim that the core-periphery dichotomy described by Lenin and new Marxists does not work anymore because it is too simplistic. Hardt and Negri (2000, xii) especially argue that "theories of imperialism were founded on nation states, whereas in their opinion today a global empire has emerged, and imperialism no longer exists with the demise of nation-states," although they do not explain in detail why they think that Lenin limited his concept of imperialism to the extension of national sovereignty over foreign territory (Fuchs, 2010b). When Lenin, followed by several political economists, developed the notion of imperialism, imperialism was indeed an extension of the sovereignty of the European nation-states beyond their own boundaries. Imperialism or colonialism in this sense is perhaps dead (Foster, 2001).

In particular, Arrighi (2007) argues that China-led East Asia has emerged as the most dynamic center of world-scale accumulation processes, resulting in the decline of U.S. hegemony. The declinist's point of view insisted that U.S. global hegemony was reaching exhaustion due to imperial overstretch and a decreasing American share of overall world production. This thesis was complemented by the idea of the diminishing importance of the nation-state, which makes some scholars claim that the nation-state is disappearing, and therefore, the dominant power of the U.S. is no longer a verifiable idea (Steinmetz, 2005). In fact, "the nation state-centeredness of their own narrow definition of imperialism as the expansive process of the power of the nation state through policies of export of capital, export of labor power and constitution-occupation of areas of influence" (Negri, 2008, 34) bears little resemblance to Lenin's definition (Fuchs, 2010b, 841) because Lenin's emphasis was on finance capital, which is capital controlled by banks and employed by industrialists.

These criticisms, however, did not reflect recent trends of the transnationalization of cultural industries, as well as growing U.S. dominance in the global cultural market (Jin, 2007). As discussed, major media corporations in Western countries have diversified their dominance in developing countries with their capital and cultural products. Although America's cultural hegemony had decreased for a while in Asia, Western countries' dominance through capital and industry has greatly increased when developing countries lift their bans on foreign ownership and foreign investment as part of their globalization. The panacea of technology may reduce imperialism and domination to vestiges of the past; however, technology will always be the reality of human hierarchy and domination (Maurais, 2003; Demont-Heinrich, 2008), and digital technologies have buttressed U.S. hegemony.

REVIVAL OF IMPERIALISM: FROM INFORMATION TO PLATFORM IMPERIALISM

Since the early 21st century, those predictions of the end of American hegemony and state-based imperialism have started to look like wishful thinking (Steinmetz, 2005). As discussed previously, that globalized capital has escaped the control of the territorial state rendering it powerless and irrelevant, "giving way to a new form of stateless 'sovereignty that is everywhere and nowhere', has indeed become a fashionable argument, both within the Left as well as within the mainstream academic and policy circles" (Bose, 2007, 97).

However, economic interdependence and decolonization do not mean the demise of nation-states, nor automatic deterritorialization. Opposed to this popular view in the era of globalization, several scholars argue that contemporary capitalism is just as imperialistic as imperialism was 100 years ago or that it has formed a new kind of imperialism (Wood, 2003; Harvey, 2007; Fuchs, 2010a). As Ellen Wood (2003, 129) points out:

> "the new imperialism that would eventually emerge from the wreckage of the old would no longer be a relationship between imperial masters and colonial subjects but a complex interaction between more or less sovereign states. While the U.S. took command of a new imperialism governed by economic imperative, however, this economic empire would be sustained by political and military hegemony."

The stress is, therefore, on continuity rather than fundamental change (Wood, 2003; Harvey, 2003, 2007). Harvey (2003, 26–27) emphasizes that "capitalist imperialism focuses on the flow of economic power across and through continuous space through the daily practices of trade, commerce, capital flows, labor migration, technology transfer, flows of information, cultural impulses and the like." Unlike the emphasis on the coercive power of nation-states that Hardt and Negri focus on, "the harmonization of capitalist space relies on the soft power of consent and the emulation of models of development" (Winseck and Pike, 2007, 8). Although contemporary aspects of imperialism cannot be considered in the same way as were set out in Lenin's understanding of imperialism, contemporary critical scholars believe that "the notion of imperialism still functions as a meaningful theoretical framework to interpret the world which was globalized neoliberally" (Fuchs, 2010a, 34). These critical theoreticians commonly agree that the continuing hegemony of the U.S. is a central element in the formation of the new imperialism, including cultural imperialism and information imperialism. It certainly applies to the current form of platform imperialism because the U.S. is much more powerful than it really is in this field (Sutcliffe, 2006).

As for the role of TNCs, Herbert Schiller revised his text in his article published in 1991. In Schiller's vision (1976), the global cultural market was a world of primarily one-way cultural flow where America (primarily as a nation) dominated international trade in film and television. In his later paper (H. Schiller, 1991, 15), he made a slightly different argument with an emphasis on the role of transnational corporations as part of great powers;

> "the domination that exists today, though still bearing a marked American imprint, is better understood as transnational corporate cultural domination. Philips of the Netherlands, Daimler-Benz of Germany, Samsung of Korea, and Sony of Japan, along with some few thousand other companies, are the major players in the international market."

Of course, this does not mean that American cultural domination disappears. "It is not guaranteed in perpetuity. Yet irrefutably that domination has been preeminent for the last four decades and remains so to this date, although subsumed increasingly under transnational corporate capital and control" (H. Schiller, 1991, 15). Schiller emphasizes the increasing role of TNCs; however, this does not imply the demise of the nation-state. From Hollywood majors to advertising corporations to motor vehicle companies, corporations have been transnational for several decades and have developed a very close relationship with nation-states.

Many theoreticians have especially argued that the differential power relations associated with globalization are a continuation of past forms of Western imperialism that created the persistent differentiation between the First and Third Worlds (Amin, 1999; Miller, 2010). Harshe (1997) describes globalization and imperialism as intertwined and characterized by unequal cultural and intellectual exchanges. As Grewal (2008, 7) also points out, "the assertion that globalization is imperial has lately become the subject of mainstream discussion in the U.S. and elsewhere; it is no longer a charge made by antiglobalization activists alone."

Information Imperialism

Alongside globalization, the rapid growth of ICTs has influenced the change and continuity of the notion of imperialism. The connection of imperialism and the information sector is not peculiar for a new form of imperialism. Boyd-Barrett (1980, 23) has shown that "already in the 19th and early 20th century the big news agencies Havas, Reuters and Wolff were based in imperial capitals, and their expansion was intimately associated with the territorial colonialism of the late nineteenth century." At the time of Lenin, they served as government propaganda arms in the First World War. Later, Winseck and Pike (2007) discussed, with the example of the global expansion of cable and wireless companies (e.g., Western Union, Eastern Telegraph Company, Commercial Cable Company, Anglo American Telegraph Company, or Marconi) in the years 1860–1930, that at the time of Lenin there was a distinct connection between communication, globalization, and capitalist imperialism. They argue:

> "the growth of a worldwide network of fast cables and telegraph systems, in tandem with developments in railways and steamships, eroded some of the obstacles of geography and made it easier to organize transcontinental business. These networks supported huge flows of capital, technology, people, news, and ideas which, in turn, led to a high degree of convergence among markets, merchants, and bankers."
>
> (Winseck and Pike, 2007, 1–2)

It is clear that the notion of imperialism has gained a new perspective in the midst of the rapid growth of new technologies. The major difference stems from several significant factors that were not considered as major elements in deciding the concepts of imperialism prior to this form, namely the rapid growth of digital technologies. Whereas the importance of the global flow in capital and culture has arguably changed, several recent theoreticians have emphasized the importance of the dominance of ICTs. Dan Schiller (1999) has specifically developed a theory of digital capitalism that emphasizes the changing role of networks for capital accumulation:

> "the networks that comprise cyberspace were originally created at the behest of government agencies, military contractors, and allied educational institutions. However, over the past generation or so, a growing number of these networks began to serve primarily corporate users. Under the sway of an expansionary market logic, the Internet began a political-economic transition toward digital capitalism."
>
> (D. Schiller, 1999, xvi)

Castells (2001) also cautions against the socially and functionally selective diffusion of technology. He identifies one of the major sources of social inequality as the differential timing in access to the power of technology for people, and thus acknowledges, in contrast to the laudatory rhetoric about the globalization of technological systems, that its outcome is instead that large areas of the world, and considerable segments of population, are switched off from the new technological system. As Boyd-Barrett emphasizes (2006, 21–22), "the emergence of microprocessor-based computer network technology and the U.S. dominance of ICT are crucial for U.S. economy and imperialism." Meanwhile, Fuchs (2010a, 56) points out, "media and information play a pivotal role in the new concept of imperialism, which the U.S. has dominated based on its advanced digital technologies, although they are subsumed under finance capital in the 21st century." Whereas there are certainly different emphases, what these critical scholars commonly focus on is the increasing role of information and communication technologies—hardware, in most cases—in the process of capital accumulation favoring a few Western countries.

Towards Platform Imperialism

With the swift transfer of power to platforms, the situation has recently changed, although of course, not without periodic setbacks for traditional ICT companies. Previously powerful ICT corporations have increasingly been subordinated to platforms due to the platforms' ascendant role and power in digital media economies. For example, in August 2011, Google acquired Motorola Mobility for $12.5 billion in order to give the platform giant a presence in smartphone hardware while also bringing it thousands of new patents (Efrati and Ante, 2011). Almost at the same time, Hewlett-Packard Co., the world's largest personal computer maker, is simultaneously exploring a spin-off of its PC business as profits slide by buying U.K. software firm Autonomy Corp. for about $10.25 billion (Worthen et al., 2011).

Before these mergers, two major platforms, Google and YouTube, already became one mega platform giant when Google bought YouTube for $1.65 billion in 2006 because Google wanted to be the world's information leader and made itself universally accessible and useful through YouTube as well (*BBC News*, 2006). In 2006, News Corporation acquired MySpace, a platform of virtual communities and personal pages that by mid-2006 contained over 100 million pages and 77 million subscribers. Rupert Murdoch emphasized at a shareholder's meeting on October 20, 2006, that "technology is liberating us from old constraints, lowering key costs, easing access to new customers and markets, and multiplying the choices we can offer" (News Corporation, 2006, cited in Castells, 2008). Although News Corporation's purchase of MySpace failed to create the expected synergy, bids to purchase social media have soared as telecommunication corporations vehemently invested in Internet-related corporations in the early 21st century.[2]

As analyzed in detail in Chapter 3, it is presumptuous to say that the hardware era is gone. However, these several recent developments and the increasing role of U.S.-based platforms in capital accumulation and culture, as exemplified with Facebook and Google, are arguably clear examples of the rise of platform imperialism. Unlike hardware-driven information imperialism, platforms are about software and primarily the users because they are major customers and producers. Information imperialism means that the customers mainly buy the hardware only one time for several years; therefore, the sale of hardware from the U.S. to non-Western countries has been the most significant indicator. However, platform imperialism means that the customers continue to access the product after either purchasing or subscribing to these platforms, and their access continuously becomes a commodity to be sold to advertisers and corporations. It is not possible to separate applications and operating systems from the smartphone as a gadget, for example, the smartphone users consistently install several applications to benefit from these applications, including apps for gaming, weather reports, and email services. Compared to the previous forms of imperialism, therefore, the role of global users has also been crucial for both platform owners and the countries that invent these platforms.

Meanwhile, platform imperialism is not only about material, but also ideological issues because platform developers clearly impose their symbolic hegemony to the majority of developing countries that buy and use platforms, and therefore, provide their labor to benefit platform inventers and countries owning these platforms. Although American imperialism in culture and ICTs also meant ideological dominance influencing other countries to adopt American consumerism and democracy, the current form of symbolic hegemony is much greater than the previous form of ideological dominance due to the significance of platform technologies in people's daily lives, as discussed in later chapters.

The U.S., which had previously controlled non-Western countries with its military power, capital, and later cultural products, now dominates the world with platforms. The U.S. has, on a large scale, benefited from these platforms. This means that the U.S. has always utilized its imperial power, not only with capital, but also with technology, culture, and ideologies, to control the majority of the world. As Steinmetz (2005) argues, the current form of imperialism is not territorial in contradiction to colonialism as a territorial one, because a few Western countries do not occupy actual territories but the global markets with their advanced technologies and culture in the 21st century. We may not see the old form of territorial occupation in our society; however, the non-territorial dominance remains, and the U.S. is expanding its dominant power with diverse means, and in this case, with platform technologies and culture.

Again, John Foster (2001, 9) has already argued that "today's imperialism, represented by the U.S., is somehow lessened by the fact that there is little direct political role of foreign territories." However, now the means are different, but the global reach of imperialism is even greater. As we see in later chapters (Chapter 3 and 5), the U.S. currently controls foreign territory in the form of platforms, alongside its state power, as discussed with the case of the Google affair between the U.S. and China. The U.S. is the most powerful nation because its dominant power in the realm of platforms is seemingly unlimited, and its imperial interests backed by transnational corporations are virtually without limits.

CONCLUSION

This chapter has analyzed the evolutionary development of various notions of imperialism towards platform imperialism. It examined whether Lenin's analysis continues to explain what is happening in the world today in the 21st century. Since the new concept of imperialism functions through platform technologies, which were not seen in Lenin's imperialism, it has been crucial to understand whether these technologies play a primary role in changing the notions of imperialism.

At a glance, the massive switch to the digital economy has provided a surplus of capital for several emerging powers, including China, India, and Korea, with which to challenge the longer-term U.S. dominance, unlike the old notion of imperialism developed by Lenin (Boyd-Barrett, 2006, 24). These emerging countries have presumably competed with Western countries, and they are supposed to build a new global order with their advanced digital technologies. As Arrighi (2007) argues, China may especially become a new hegemony in the era of global capitalism. However, there are some doubts about whether non-Western ICT corporations have reorganized the global flow and constructed a balance between the West and the East. The panacea of technology may reduce imperialism and domination to vestiges of the past; however, technology will always be the reality of human hierarchy and domination (Maurais, 2003; Demont-Heinrich, 2008), and, again, platform technologies have buttressed U.S. hegemony.

In particular, non-Western countries could not construct a balanced global order, because Google, Facebook, and iPhones have reinforced the dominance of the U.S. Regardless of the fact that a few East Asian countries have developed their own platforms, the use of these platforms is limited within their countries, instead of penetrating the global markets. It is U.S.-based platforms that have penetrated the global market and expanded their global dominance. Therefore, it is safe to say that American imperialism has been continued with platforms. As in the time of Lenin between the late 19th century and the early 20th century, there has been a connection between platform and capitalist imperialism. Platforms have functioned as a new form of distributor and producer that the U.S. dominates.

Although several theoreticians argue that globalization has deterritorialized the world, resulting in the diminishing role of imperial states, the nation-states have strongly supported platform producers and distributors. In the late 20th century, a round of regional and global trade agreements subordinated national policy to supranational agreements favoring unrestricted mobility of capital, deregulation, privatization, and unfettered markets. However, in the media and technology areas, the developments are inseparable from the governments. While several platforms driven by a handful of private corporations have increased their dominance, the U.S. government and its counterpart governments have been involved in international negotiations in the 21st century. This implies that the nation-states have always been the strongest supporters of private corporations. While TNCs have developed and advanced new technologies, the U.S. government and other governments have been major players in the globalized world because they need to support the growth of their own platforms. "With globalization, capital might crack the shell of the nation-state" (Dyer-Witheford, 1999, 138).

Platform technologies are not separate from the government because they are primary engines for the digital economy. It is crucial to remember that the classical Marxist accounts of the 19th century era of free trade and its supersession by the era of inter-imperial rivalry also confusingly counterposed states and markets like contemporary discussions of globalization in the context of neoliberal free market policies. In both cases there is a failure to appreciate the crucial role of the state in making free markets possible and then in making them work (Panitch and Gindin, 2003; Wood, 2003).

Overall, platforms can be situated within more general capitalist processes that follow familiar patterns of asymmetrical power relations between the West and the East. A critical interrogation of the global hegemony of platforms proves the dominant position of the U.S. and that it has intensified an increasingly unequal relationship between the West and the East at an alarming rate. In the 21st century, the world has become further divided into a handful of Western states which have developed platforms and a vast majority of non-Western states which do not have advanced platforms.

NOTES

1. In the journal special issue (*tripleC*) titled Marx Is Back, for example, Christian Fuchs and Vincent Mosco (2012, 127) argue that "with the new global crisis of capitalism, we seem to have entered new Marxian times." They claim that the surging interest in Karl Marx's work in the early 21st century is an indication of the persistence of capitalism, class conflicts, and crisis.
2. MySpace, the long-suffering Web site that News Corporation bought in 2006 for $580 million, was sold in June 2011 to the advertising network Specific Media for roughly $35 million (Steller, 2011).

REFERENCES

Adorno, T. (1991). *The Culture Industry: Selected Essays on Mass Culture*, J.M. Bernstein (ed.). London: Routledge.

Amin, S. (1999). Capitalism, imperialism, globalization. In R.M. Chilcote (ed.), *The Political Economy of Imperialism*, 157–168. Boston: Kluwer Academic.

Ang, I. (1985). *Watching Dallas: Soap Opera and the Melodramatic Imagination*. London: Routledge.

Arrighi, G. (2007). *Adam Smith in Beijing: Lineages of the Twenty-First Century*. London: Verso.

Associated Press (AP) (2011b). Apple suit: Samsung copies our devices. 4 May.

AP (2012). Facebook set to begin trading after $16 billion offering. 22 May.

BBC News (2006). Google buys YouTube for $1.65bn. 10 October. http://news.bbc.co.uk/2/hi/technology/6034577.stm.

Bodle, R. (2010). Assessing social network sites as international platforms. *The Journal of International Communication,* 16(2), 9–24.

Bose, P. (2007). 'New' imperialism? On globalisation and nation-states. *Historical Materialism* 15: 95–120.

Boyd-Barrett, O. (1998). Media imperialism reformulated. In D. Thussu (ed.), *Electronic Empires: Global Media and Local Resistance*, 157–76. London: Arnold.

Boyd-Barrett, O. (2006). Cyberspace, globalization and empire. *Global Media and Communication* 2(1): 21–41.

Boyd-Barrett, O. (1980). *The International News Agency*. London: Constable.

Boyd-Barrett, O. (1977). Media imperialism: Towards an international framework for the analysis of media systems. In J. Curran and M. Gurevitch (eds.), *Mass Communication and Society,* 116–135. London: Edward Arnold.

boyd, d. (2007). Why youth (heart) social network sites: The role of networked publics in teenage social life. In D. Buckingham (ed.), *Youth, Identity, and Digital Media*, 119–142. Cambridge, MA: MIT Press.

Callinicos, A. (2007). *Social Theory*. Cambridge: Polity.

Castells, M. (2001). *The Internet Galaxy: Reflections on the Internet, Business, and Society.* New York: Oxford University Press.

Castells, M. (2008). Communication, Power and Counterpower in the Network Society (II). Telos 75.

Chadha, K. & Kavoori, A. (2000). Media imperialism revisited: Some findings from Asian case. *Media, Culture, and Society* 22(4): 415–432.

Cohen, N. (2008). The valorization of surveillance: Towards a political economy of Facebook, *Democratic Comunique* 22(1): 5–22.

Congressional Budget Office (2003). The Pros and Cons of Pursuing Free-Trade Agreements. http://www.cbo.gov/ftpdoc.cfm?index=4458&type=0&sequence=0.

Croteau, D. & Hoynes, W. (1997). *Media/Society: Industries, Images, and Audiences*. London: Pine.

Demont-Heinrich, C. (2008). The death of cultural imperialism—and power too? *International Communication Gazette* 70(5): 378–394.

Doyle, M. (1986). *Empires*. Ithaca, NY: Cornell University Press.

Dyer-Witheford, N. (1999). *Cyber-Marx: Circles and Circuits of Struggle in High-Technology Capitalism*. Champaign, IL: University of Illinois Press.

Efrati, A. & Ante S. (2011). Google's $12.5 billion gamble. *The Wall Street Journal*. 16 August.

Ess, C. (2009). *Digital Media Ethics*. Cambridge: Polity Press.

Feenberg, A. (1991). *The Critical Theory of Technology*. London: Oxford University Press.

Foster, J. (2001). Imperialism and empire. *Monthly Review* 57(7): 1–9.

Flew, T. (2007). *Understanding Global Media*. New York: Palgrave.

Fuchs, C. (2010a). New imperialism: Information and media imperialism. *Global Media and Communication* 6(1): 33–60.

Fuchs, C. (2010b). Critical globalization studies and the new imperialism. *Critical Sociology* 36(6): 839–867.

Fuchs, C. (2011a). *Foundations of Critical Media and Information Studies*. London: Routledge.

Fuchs, C. (2011b). A contribution to the critique of the political economy of Google. *Fast Capitalism* 8(1). http://www.fastcapitalism.com/.

Fuchs, C. & Mosco V. (2012). Introduction: Marx is back—the importance of Marxist theory and research for critical communications studies today. *tripleC: Communication, Capitalism & Critique. Open Access Journal for a Global Sustainable Information Society* 10(2): 127–140.

Galtung, J. (1971). A structural theory of imperialism. *Journal of Peace Research* 8(2): 81–117.

Gillespie, T. (2010). The politics of platforms. *New Media and Society* 12(3): 347–364.

Grewal, D. (2008). *Network Power: The Social Dynamics of Globalization*. New Haven: Yale University Press.

Guback, T. (1984). International circulation of U.S. theatrical films and television programming. In G. Gerbner and M. Siefert (eds.), *World Communications: A Handbook*, 155–156. New York: Longman.

Gunster, S. (2004). *Capitalizing on Culture*. Toronto: University of Toronto Press.

Hardt, M. & Negri, A. (2000). *Empire*. Cambridge, MA: Harvard University Press.

Harrison, S. (2007). Lenin on Imperialism. http://www.massline.org/PolitEcon/ScottH/LeninOnImperialism.pdf.

Harshé, R. (1997). *Twentieth Century Imperialism: Shifting Contours and Changing Conceptions*. New Delhi: Sage.

Harvey, D. (2003). *The New Imperialism*. New York: Oxford University Press.

Harvey, D. (2007). what ways is the new imperialism realty new. *Historical Materialism* 15(3): 57–70.

Herman, E. & McChesney. R. (1997). *The Global Media: The New Missionaries of Corporate Capitalism*. New York: Cassell.

Hesmondhalgh, D. (2010). User-generated content, free labour and the cultural industries. *ephemera theory & politics in organization* 10(3/4): 267–284.

Hoegg, R., Martignoni, M., Meckel, M. & Stanoevska-Slabeva, K. (2006). Overview of business models for Web 2.0 communities Proceedings of GeNeMe 2006.

The Hollywood Reporter (2011). Avatar' still dominating overseas box office. January 10. Accessed November 17, 2012. http://www.hollywoodreporter.com/news/avatar-still-dominating-overseas-boxoffice-19321.

International Commission for the Study of Communication (1980). *Many Voices, One World: Communication and Society Today and Tomorrow*, Paris: UNESCO.

Jin, D.Y. (2014). Critical analysis of user commodities as free labor in social networking sites: A case study of Cyworld. *Continuum: Journal of Media and Cultural Studies*.

Jin, D.Y. (2007). Reinterpretation of cultural imperialism: Emerging domestic market vs. continuing U.S. dominance. *Media, Culture and Society* 29(5): 753–771.

Jin, D.Y. (2011). *Hands On/Hands Off: The Korean State and the Market Liberalization of the Communication Industry.* Cresskill, NJ: Hampton Press.

Lenin, V. (1917). Imperialism, the highest stage of capitalism. In H. Christman (ed.), *Essential Works of Lenin*, pp. 177–270. New York: Dover.

Liodakis, G. (2003). The New Stage of Capitalist Development and the Prospects of Globalization. Paper presented for the Conference: Economics for the Future Cambridge. 17–19 September, 2003.

Magder, T. (2004). Transnational media, international trade and the ideal of cultural diversity. *Continuum: Journal of Media and Cultural Studies* 18(3): 385–402.

Marx, K. (1867). *Capital.* vol. I. London: Penguin.

McDonough, T. (1995). Lenin, imperialism, and the stages of capitalist development. *Science and Society* 59(3): 339–367.

Miller, C. (2010). Why Twitter's CEO demoted himself. *The New York Times.* 1 November.

Miller, T. (2010). Holy trinity: Nation pentagon, screen. In A. Roosvall and I. Salovaara-Moring (eds.), *Communication the Nation: National Topographies of Global Media Landscape*, 143–162. Nordicom.

Miller, T., McMurria, G., & Richard, M. (2001) *Global Hollywood.* Bloomington: Indiana University Press.

Morley, D. (2006). Globalization and cultural imperialism reconsidered: Old questions in new guises. In J. Curran and D. Morley (eds.), *Media and Cultural Theory*, 30–43. New York: Routledge.

Mosco, V. (2009, 2nd ed.). *The Political Economy of Communication.* London: Sage.

Negri, A. (2008). *Reflections on Empire.* Cambridge: Polity.

New, W. (2011). Palestinian membership in UNESCO could raise questions for US at WIPO. Intellectual Property Watch. Retrieved March 2, 2012, from http://www.ip-watch.org/2011/10/21/palestinian-membership-in-unesco-could-raise-questions-for-us-wipo/.

Olisen, K. (2007). South Korean gamers get a sneak peek at StarCraft II. *AP*, 21 May.

Pang, L. (2006). *Cultural Control and Globalization in Asia: Copyright, Piracy, and Cinema.* London: Routledge.

Panitch, L. & Gindin, S. (2003). Global capitalism and American empire. In L. Panitch and S. Gindin (eds.), *The Socialist Register 2004: The New Imperial Challenge*, 1–43. New York: Monthly Press.

Robinson, W. (2004). *A Theory of Global Capitalism: Production, Class and State in a Transnational World.* Baltimore, MD: Johns Hopkins University.

Robinson, W. (2007). Beyond the theory of imperialism: Global capitalism and the transnational state. *Societies Without Borders* 2: 5–26.

Rothenberg, M. (1995). Lenin on the state. *Science and Society* 59(3): 418–436.

Said, E. (1993). *Culture and Imperialism.* New York: A.A. Knopf.

Schiesel, S. (2005). An online game, made in America, seizes the globe. *The New York Times.* September 5, B1.

Schiller, D. (1999). *Digital Capitalism: Networking the Global Market System.* Cambridge, MA: MIT Press.

Schiller, H. (1969). *Mass Communications and American Empire.* Oxford: Westview Press.

Schiller, H. (1976). *Communication and Cultural Domination.* White Plains, NY: International Arts and Sciences Press.

Schiller, H. (1991). Net yet the post-imperialist era. *Critical Studies in Media Communication,* 8(1): 13–28.

Schiller, H. (1999). *Living in the Number One Country.* New York: Seven Stories Press.

Socialbaker (2011). Facebook reaches 600 million users as of January 2011. Retrieved September 3, 2011, from http://www.socialbakers.com/blog/100-facebook-reaches-another-milestone-600-million-users/.

Sparks, C. (2007). *Globalization, Development and the Mass Media.* London: Sage.

Steinmetz, G. (2005). Return to empire: The new U.S. imperialism in comparative historical perspective. *Sociological Theory* 23(4): 339–367.

Steller, B. (2011). News Corporation sells MySpace for $35 million. *The New York Times,* 29 June. http://mediadecoder.blogs.nytimes.com/2011/06/29/news-corp-sells-myspace-to-specific-media-for-35-million/?_r=0.

Straubhaar, J. (1991). Beyond media imperialism: Asymmetrical independence and cultural proximity. *Critical Studies in Mass Communication* 8(1): 39–70.

Sutcliffe, B. (2006). Imperialism old and new: A comment on David Harvey's the new imperialism and Ellen Meiksins Wood's empire of capital. *Historical Materialism* 14(4): 59–78.

Tech Coders.com (2012). Platforms for Software Development. Retrieved March 2, 2012, from http://www.techcoders.com/platforms-for-software-development.html/.

The Economist (2005). A Survey of Patent and Technology: A Market for Ideas. 20 October.

Tunstall, J. (1977). *The Media Are American: Anglo-American Media in the World.* New York: Columbia University Press.

U.S. Department of Commerce (2010). *Survey of Current Business.* Washington DC: U.S. Department of Commerce.

U.S. Department of Commerce (2011). *Survey of Current Business.* Washington DC: U.S. Department of Commerce.

U.S. Department of Commerce (2013). U.S. International Services. Washington DC: U.S. Department of Commerce. http://www.bea.gov/international/international_services.htm.

van Dijck, J. (2012). Facebook as a tool for producing sociality and connectivity. *Television and New Media* 13(2): 160–176.

Wasko, J. (2003). *How Hollywood Works.* London: Sage.

Winseck, D. & Pike, R. (2007). *Communication and Empire.* Durham, NC: Duke University Press.

Wood, E. (2003). *Empire of Capital.* London: Verso.

Worthen, B., Scheck, J., & Chon, G. (2011). H-P explores quitting computers as profits slide. *The Wall Street Journal.* 19 August.

Part II

Platform Politics

3 Construction of Platform Imperialism

INTRODUCTION

Over the past two decades, innovation has become one of the most significant business norms in society. Platforms, including social network sites and smartphones, have become the most innovative technologies and among the most relevant features of contemporary culture. In the 21st century, these platforms have fundamentally changed people's daily activities. Several SNSs, including Facebook and Twitter, have millions of young users spending immense time and energy to update their personal profiles with a blog-type interface in which their latest postings or photos appear on top of the SNS. These SNSs allow people to present themselves and establish or maintain connections with others (Ellison, Steinfield, and Lampe 2007; Boyd 2007; Hargittai 2008). Smartphones which were introduced only a few years ago have also changed people's lives with their touch screens and multiple applications.[1]

The rapid growth of these platforms has also greatly influenced the corporate sphere and changed the notion of imperialism. From the 17th century onwards, imperialism became increasingly associated with capitalist production, and platform technologies clearly exemplify the international and economic systems, which is the essence of Marxist theories of imperialism (Sutcliffe, 2006). As Japanese Mixi (SNS), Chinese Baidu (search engine), Weibo (microblogging), and Korean Galaxy III and V (smartphone) exemplify, several platforms have successfully penetrated their national markets and even the global market. With the success of these platforms, some people might consider that these non-Western countries play a primary role in the field of platform technologies and culture. However, the major players are U.S.-based platforms, and they reign supreme in the platform market.

This chapter empirically analyzes the construction of platform imperialism with the growth of platforms around the world. It examines the capitalization of platforms and their global expansion as the most significant form of capital accumulation in the digital age. The chapter articulates the ways in which only a few Western countries, in particular the U.S., have dominated not only the development of platform technologies but also the global penetration of these new technologies. Given that the U.S. has continued its power with platforms, it especially endeavors to make a contribution to the platform imperialism discourse as a form of new imperialism, focusing on the role of transnational corporations. In other words, we primarily investigate whether platforms and their owners, such as Facebook, Google, and Apple, alongside the nation-state, play a key role in the construction of platform imperialism.

We finally argue whether platform imperialism is useful for explaining the current power relations between the U.S. and non-Western countries. This chapter especially focuses on whether the U.S. has been dominant in the computational functions of platforms, which is one of the three major components consisting of platform imperialism. This means that the discussions in this chapter alone cannot construct platform imperialism discourse, but they provide the starting point for understanding the formation of new imperialism, alongside discussions in following chapters which emphasize several key areas, such as the role of the nation-state, intellectual property rights, and symbolic hegemony.

PLATFORMS AS CONVERGING TECHNOLOGIES

Convergence has been a buzzword since the 1990s. In the information and communication technologies (ICT) sector, the development of computers and networks in the 1960s and 1970s facilitated the usage of convergence. In the late 1990s and the early 21st century, convergence even further becomes one of the central developments taking place across the media, telecommunications, and information sectors of the communications industry (Mosco and McKercher, 2006). Media convergence is not simple and has multiple meanings (Jin, 2013). For some scholars, convergence is synonymous with media consolidation. For others, convergence describes what happens when a new, multifunction device, such as a telephone/cable/internet modem, does jobs that previously would have required two or more appliances (Schnaars et al., 2008, cited in Thornton and Keith, 2009). Essentially, to converge means to come together. In the context of communication technologies, one talks about the coming together of several discrete technologies to create a hybrid technology (Mosco and McKercher, 2006).

> "technological convergence typically means the integration of the devices that these industries use as well as the information they process, distribute, and exchange over and through these devices. By integrating computers and telecommunications, the Internet is now an iconic example of technological convergence. This form of convergence is linked to, and partly responsible for, the convergence of once separated industries into a common arena providing electronic information and communication services."
>
> (Mosco and McKercher, 2006, 734)

Henry Jenkins (2006, 2–3) points out that "media convergence can be categorized in three major areas: the flow of content across multiple media platforms, the cooperation between multiple media industries, and the migratory behavior of media audiences who will go almost anywhere in search of the kinds of entertainment experience they want." Other scholars (Baldwin et al., 1996; Wirtz, 2001) also view media convergence from three different perspectives: the consolidation through industry alliances and mergers, the combination of technology and network platforms, and the integration between services and markets. These concepts are not mutually exclusive due to the close relationship between media structure and content, and as is commonly agreed, convergence cannot be done without the integration of production between the old and new media (Jin, 2013).

Previously, the Internet was the most innovative; therefore, it was the symbol of media convergence, not only technological but also corporate convergence. Through the Internet, people can do multiple functions at the same time with no additional gadgets. Many people moved from traditional mass media, such as newspapers and television to the Internet because people use the Internet to read newspapers, watch television news, and listen to radio music. As Robert McChesney (2013, 2–3) points out, "the Internet itself has already experienced several lifetimes in the course of two decades, from Usenet days to the World Wide Web and AOL and then broadband followed by Google and now wi-fi, iPads, smartphones, and social media." Until the early 21st century, therefore, media and telecommunications corporations tried to get Internet corporations, which drove significant corporate integration (Jin, 2013).

The situation has greatly changed with platforms, because the platform becomes a symbol of convergence. To begin with, when Steve Jobs introduced the iPhone in January 2007, it became especially significant because it blended three products into one: "an iPod, with the highest-quality screen Apple had produced; a phone, with cleverly integrated functionality, such as voice-mail that came wrapped as separately accessible messages; and a device to access the Internet, with a smart and elegant browser, and with built-in map, weather, stock, and e-mail capabilities. It was a technical and design triumph for Apple, bringing the company into a market with an extraordinary potential for growth, and pushing the industry to a new level of competition in ways to connect us to each other and to the Web, whereas enjoying increasing number of applications" (Zittrain, 2008,1).

What is significant about media convergence, as in the case of iPhone, is that it directly implies the modern day capitalism, in addition to its technological convergence. Apple provides one of "the most carefully policed software platforms in history," as Steve Johnson (2010) points out. Every single application has to be approved by Apple before it can be offered to consumers, and all software purchases are routed through Apple's cash register. Most of the development tools are created inside Apple, in conditions of C.I.A.-level secrecy. The iPhone software platform has been, out of the gate, the most innovative in the history of computing with more than 150,000 applications having been created for it in less than two years. The iPhone has transformed into an e-book reader, a flight control deck, a musical instrument, a physician's companion, a dictation device, and countless other things that were impossible just 24 months before its release (Johnson, 2010). iPhone actualized digital convergence, and media corporations, venture capitalists, and inventors began to contemplate what they could do through this form of convergence.[2]

As the case of iPhone shows, the convergence of digital technologies also means a new form of convergence because it is accompanied by patents. Two or three decades ago, a machine might have five or ten patents. Today, the smartphone has about 5,000 patents. For example, from 2000 until September 2012, Apple filed 1,298 patents addressing hand-held mobile radio telephone technologies. The vast majority of these have been filed following the 2007 launch of the iPhone. Prior to 2007, Apple filed just 17 patents in this category (Thomson Reuters, 2012). As explained in Chapter 5, when Google paid an astonishing $12.5 billion to purchase Motorola Mobility in 2011, it did so because the search engine giant would acquire Motorola's vast array of 17,000 patents on phone technology and because it would turn Google into a mobile-phone maker (*AP*, 2011c).

In essence, interconnected technologies and large integrated companies create the convergence it takes to make a revolution (Mosco, 2008). This new trend of acquiring multimedia and multifunctional networks has facilitated the convergence process (D. Schiller, 2007). Convergence therefore refers to not only the integration of different technologies (mostly applications) and the integration of industries across different business sectors and different industries but also to the integration of patents in the case of platforms. Alongside the convergence of different patents in a platform, platform convergence has become one of the most active in the digital economy and culture.[3]

Finally, in the 21st century, the focus has changed to platform corporations, as Google acquired YouTube and News Corporation purchased MySpace. ICT corporations have primarily purchased new media, not cultural content corporations, and in particular, Internet and/or platform-related corporations. Previously, several non-U.S. media corporations, such as Bertelsmann in Germany, Vivendi in France, and Sony in Japan, bought several U.S. media content corporations, such as broadcasting and film firms, in the midst of the convergence boom. However, the early 21st century does not feature these forms of integration anymore because the majority of Internet properties and platforms are invented and owned by U.S.-based transnational corporations. This means that U.S. platform owners, such as Google, Microsoft, and Apple, continue to increase their market shares in the global markets, not only through increasing the number of users and/or subscribers, but also through continuing corporate convergence, which cannot be changed anytime soon.

THE AMERICAN DOMINANCE IN PLATFORMS

The debate on imperialism has been a long-standing subject since the late-1960s. Imperialism, again, involves the extension of power or authority over others in the interest of domination and results in the political, military, or economic dominance of one country over another (Wasko, 2003). The dominant position of Western-based agencies in culture in many countries is apparently a post–World War II phenomenon, and "is closely associated with the expansion of American capital and the emergence of transnational corporations as the dominant producers in industries such as processed food, soft drinks, pharmaceuticals, cars, household appliances, soaps, cosmetics, energy, and so on" (Bonney, 1984, 35–36).

Under capitalist relations of production, the decisive factor in the success or failure of corporations, and industries as a whole, is profitability, and that in turn depends upon growth—increase in market share, expansion of existing markets, and the development of new markets. Through the long boom of the 1950s and 1960s, many large corporations based in the U.S. (and in Western Europe and Japan) established themselves in numerous foreign countries to exploit local markets and, in the case of the Third World, to take advantage of cheap labor. In doing so, they needed to export not only capital and expertise but also marketing and advertising skills and techniques (Bonney, 1984). Although Western dominance has somewhat decreased in a few countries, Western countries' dominance through capital and industry has greatly increased in developing countries.

According to Alexa.com (2012), over the three-month period between September and November of 2012, among the top 100 global sites on the Web based on page views and visits, 48 websites were owned by U.S. corporations and 52 websites were owned by non-U.S. Internet firms. Other than the U.S., 16 countries had their own websites on the list, and among them China had the largest number of websites (18), followed by Japan (6), Russia (5), India (4), and the U.K. (4). A few non-Western countries, including Indonesia, Turkey, Brazil, and Mexico, also had one website each. This data seems to show that the U.S. is not a dominant force in the Internet market, although it is still the country that has the largest number of Internet corporations (48 percent in the global market).

However, when we consider the origins of the websites, the story is not the same because the websites that belong to these non-Western countries are of U.S.-origins they include Google, Facebook, Twitter, Yahoo, and Amazon. As Table 3.1 shows, other than a handful of countries, including China and Russia, developing countries have no websites that they originally created and operated themselves. Based on the origin of the websites, U.S. companies comprised 72 percent of the list—much higher than the 48 percent with no consideration of origin. This means that one country controls about three-fourths of the Internet market, and there is no sign of this trend changing in the near future.

Table 3.1 The Top 100 Sites on the Web in 2012

Rank	*Websites*	*Country*	*Country Origin*	*Major Business Models*		
				Advertising	Other Businesses	Non-Profit
1	Google	U.S.	U.S.	X		
2	Facebook	U.S.	U.S.	X		
3	YouTube	U.S.	U.S.	X		
4	Yahoo	U.S.	U.S.	X		
5	Baidu.com	China	China	X		
6	Wikipedia	U.S.	U.S.			X
7	Windows Live	U.S.	U.S.	X		
8	Twitter	U.S.	U.S.	X		
9	QQ.com	China	China	X		
10	Amazon	U.S.	U.S.	X	Product and service sales	
11	Taobao.com	China	China	X		
12	LinkedIn	U.S.	U.S.	X		
13	Blogspot.com	U.S.	U.S.	X		
14	Google India	India	U.S.	X		
15	Yahoo Japan	Japan	U.S.	X		
16	Sina.com.cn	China	China	X		
17	Google.de	Germany	U.S.	X		
18	yandex.ru	Russia	Russia	X		
19	MSN	U.S.	U.S.	X		
20	WordPress.com	U.S.	U.S.		Blog services, anti-spam technology, and hosting partners	
21	Google.com.hk	China	U.S.	X		
22	Google.co.jp	Japan	U.S.	X		
23	Bing	U.S.	U.S.	X		
24	eBay	U.S.	U.S.	X	Produce sales	
25	Google uk	U.K.	U.S.	X		
26	Google fr	France	U.S.	X		
27	VK.COM	Russia	Russia	X		
28	Microsoft	U.S.	U.S.		Product sales	
29	Babylon	U.S.	U.S.	X		
30	Welbo.com	China	China	X		
31	Googleusercontent	U.S.	U.S.	X		
32	163.com	China	China	X		

(*Continued*)

Rank	Websites	Country	Country Origin	Major Business Models		
				Advertising	Other Businesses	Non-Profit
33	tumblr.com	U.S.	U.S.	X		
34	Apple	U.S.	U.S.	X		
35	T mail.ru	Russia	Russia	X		
36	soco.com	China	China	X		
37	Pinterest	U.S.	U.S.	X		
38	Google Brazil	Brazil	U.S.	X		
39	Tmall.com	China	China	X		
40	Google Espanol	Spain	U.S.	X		
41	PayPal	U.S.	U.S.	X		
42	Google.ru	Russia	U.S.	X		
43	Goole.it	Italy	U.S.	X		
44	xhamster.com	U.S.	U.S.		Pay-per-view/ Subscription	
45	Craigslist	U.S.	U.S.		Charging fees for job and apartment rental postings in some cities	
46	sohu.com	China	China	X		
47	Blogger.com	India	U.S.	X		
48	fc2.com	Japan	Japan	X		
49	go.com	U.S.	U.S.	X		
50	imdb.com	U.S.	U.S.	X		
51	BBC Online	U.K.	U.K.			X
52	xvideos.com	U.S.	U.S.		Pay-per-view/ Subscription	
53	ASK	U.S.	U.S.	X		
54	yonku.com	China	China	X		
55	Google Mexico	Mexico	U.S.	X		
56	Hao123.com	China	China	X		
57	Google.ca	Canada	U.S.	X		
58	Flickr.com	U.S.	U.S.	X		
59	odnoklassniki.ru	Russia	Russia	X		
60	Conduit.com	U.S.	U.S.	X		
61	Adobe	U.S.	U.S.		Product sales	
62	CNN Interactive	U.S.	U.S.	X		
63	ifeng.com	China	China	X		
64	AVG	U.S.	U.S.		Product sales	

(*Continued*)

Rank	*Websites*	*Country*	*Country Origin*	*Major Business Models*		
				Advertising	Other Businesses	Non-Profit
65	to.co	U.S.	U.S.		Pay-per-view/ Subscription	
66	Amazon.co.jp	Japan	U.S.	X	Product and service sales	
67	Tudou.com	China	China	X		
68	LiveJasmin.com	U.S.	U.S.	X		
69	Pornhub.com	U.S.	U.S.		Pay-per-view/ Subscription	
70	Amazon.de	Germany	U.S.	X	Product and service sales	
71	The Pirate Bay	U.S.	U.S.	X		
72	AOL	U.S.	U.S.		Subscription	
73	rakuten.co.jp	Japan	Japan	X		
74	ESPN	U.S.	U.S.	X		
75	ebay.de	Germany	U.S.	X	Produce sales	
76	The Huffington Post	U.S.	U.S.	X		
77	Google.co.id	Indonesia	U.S.	X		
78	zedo.com	U.S.	U.S.	X		
79	Alibaba.com	China	China	X		
80	mywebsearch.com	U.S.	U.S.	X		
81	Google Turkey	Turkey	U.S.	X		
82	adf.ly	India	U.K.	X		
83	stock overflow	U.S.	U.S.	X		
84	blog spot.in	India	U.S.	X		
85	Red Tube.com	U.S.	U.S.	X		
86	Google.au	Australia	U.S.	X		
87	Amazon.co.uk	U.K.	U.S.	X	Produce and service sales	
88	About.com	U.S.	U.S.	X		
89	360buy.com	China	China	X		
90	sogou.com	China	China	X		
91	instagran.com	U.S.	U.S.	X		
92	Alipay.com	China	China	X		
93	eBay.uk	U.K.	U.S.	X	Produce sales	
94	New York Times	U.S.	U.S.	X		
95	Google Polska	Poland	U.S.	X		

(*Continued*)

Rank	*Websites*	*Country*	*Country Origin*	*Major Business Models*		
				Advertising	Other Businesses	Non-Profit
96	livedooor.com	Japan	Japan	X		
97	Netflix	U.S.	U.S.		Pay-per-view/ Subscription	
98	uol.com.br	Brazil	Brazil	X		
99	Imgur.com	U.S.	U.S.	X		
100	dailymotion.com	France	France	X		

Data source: alexa.com 2002: the top 500 sites on the web, http://www.alexa.com/topsites, accessed November 31, 2012.

Although it is not significant, the proportion of the U.S.-based platforms has increased. As of September 2014, among the top 100 global sites on the Web based on page views and visits, 52 websites were owned by U.S. corporations and 48 websites were non-U.S. Internet firms. Other than the U.S., China had the largest number of websites (16), followed by Japan (5), Russia (5), India (4), the U.K. (4), and Germany (3). A few non-Western countries, including Indonesia, Iran, Turkey, Brazil, and Mexico, also had one website each. The websites that belong to these non-Western countries are of U.S.-origins, including Google, Yahoo, and Amazon. Therefore, based on the origin of the websites, U.S. companies comprised 74 percent of the list—much higher than the 52 percent with no consideration of origin. As can be seen in Table 3.2, among the top 10 sites on the Web, Google, Facebook, YouTube, Yahoo, Twitter, and Amazon are all U.S.-based platforms. The 2014 data shows that the U.S. becomes a dominant force in the digital market (52 percent in the global market), and the U.S. has extended its dominance with several big platforms. In the early 21st century, the hegemonic power of the U.S. has been intensified with the rapid growth of platform technologies, which shows the new form of dominance.

Table 3.2 The Top 30 Sites on the Web in 2014

Rank	*Websites*	*Country*	*Country Origin*	*Major Business Models*		
				Advertising	Other Businesses	Non-Profit
1	Google	U.S.	U.S.	X		
2	Facebook	U.S.	U.S.	X		
3	YouTube	U.S.	U.S.	X		
4	Yahoo	U.S.	U.S.	X		
5	Baidu.com	China	China	X		
6	Wikipedia	U.S.	U.S.			X

(*Continued*)

Rank	*Websites*	*Country*	*Country Origin*	*Major Business Models*		
				Advertising	Other Businesses	Non-Profit
7	Twitter	U.S.	U.S.	X		
8	Amazon	U.S.	U.S.	X		
9	QQ.com	China	China	X		
10	LinkedIn	U.S.	U.S.	X		
11	Taobao.com	China	China	X		
12	Live.com	U.S.	U.S.	X		
13	Google India	U.S.	U.S.	X		
14	HAO123	China	China	X		
15	Blogspot	U.S.	U.S.	X		
16	Sina.com.cn	China	China	X		
17	Weibo	China	China	X		
18	Yahoo Japan	Japan	U.S.	X		
19	Tmall	U.S.	U.S.	X		
20	Sohu.com	China	China	X		
21	Yandex	Russia	Russia	X		
22	Bing	U.S.	U.S.	X		
23	Pinterest.com	U.S.	U.S.	X		
24	VK.COM	Russia	Russia	X		
25	Wordpress	U.S.	U.S.	X		
26	Google.de	Germany	U.S.	X		
27	Ebay	U.S.	U.S.	X		
28	360.CN	China	China	X		
29	Instagram	U.S.	U.S.	X		
30	Google Japan	Japan	U.S.	X		

Source: alexa.com. http://www.alexa.com/topsites. Accessed on September 10, 2014.

In the 2012 data, 88 of these websites, including Google, Yahoo, and YouTube, accumulate capital primarily by (targeted) advertising, and they prove that U.S.-origin platforms are symbols of global capitalism. In fact, among the top 100 list websites, only two websites (Wikipedia and BBC Online) are operated with a non-profit model. Ten websites make revenues through other business models, including pay-per-view and subscription, although a few websites (Amazon and eBay) have developed several business models, such as product and service sales and marketing. Among these, Craigslist.com makes money through a handful of revenue streams. Craigslist.com charges some fees to post a job listing in several U.S. cities, and charges fees to list an apartment rental in New York, U.S. The revenues cover only the operating expenses; the company has not made a profit since its inception (Patrick, 2012).

Meanwhile, WordPress.com is run by Automatic which currently makes money from the aforementioned upgrades, blog services, Akismet anti-spam technology, and hosting partnerships. What is most significant about the contemporary Internet is the swift growth of capitalist platforms, such as Facebook, Google, and Twitter. As Baran and Sweezy (1968) argued, in a capitalism dominated by large corporations operating in oligopolistic markets, advertising especially becomes a necessary, competitive weapon. Whether Western or non-Western, these websites and platforms are major engines appropriating advertising for global capitalism.

There are many U.S.-based platforms that have increased their global influence. Three major American-based platforms—Google, Facebook, and YouTube (also owned by Google)—made up the top three websites in both November 2012 and September 2014. Except for the two Chinese-based platforms (Baidu.com and QQ.com), again, the other 8 platforms in the top 10 were all American-based platforms. Among these, Google is the world's most accessed web platform: 46 percent of worldwide Internet users accessed Google in a three-month period in 2010 (Fuchs, 2011b). Among search engines only, Google's dominant position is phenomenal. As of November 2012, Google accounted for as much as 88.8 percent of the global search engine market, followed by Bing (4.2 percent), Baidu (3.5 percent), Yahoo (2.4 percent), and others (1.1 percent) (Kamasnack, 2012). In July 2014, Google still accounted for 88.15 percent of the worldwide market share, followed by Bing (4.61 percent), Yahoo (4.01 percent), and Baidu (0.55 percent) (Statista, 2014a).

Of course, there have been some exceptions. Although Google is an indisputable global leader in the realm of search engines, Google cannot be the major player in a few countries, including China, Korea, Japan, and Russia. These countries have developed their local search engines and successfully competed with global search engines. For example, due to the strong presence of domestic search engines, including Naver and Daum, Google is not a dominant player in the Korea's search engine market. According to Internet Trend (2013), between January 1, 2013, and October 31, 2013, the market share of Naver accounted for as much as 76.75 percent of its domestic search engine market, followed by another domestic search engine Daum (13.9 percent) in its domestic market. However, Google's share consisted of only 3.86 percent, down from 5.86 percent during 2012. Koreans use local portals to enjoy several apps, including mobile games, weather, and news; Google and Yahoo have focused on information searches, which made them invisible.[4]

In China, Google launched google.cn in 2006, agreeing to some censorship of search results to enter the country to meet the requirements of the Chinese government. In China, Google's market share stood at 15.8 percent in 2012, down from 27 percent in June 2010. Local web search engine Baidu's market share increased from 70 percent as of June 2010 to 79.5 percent in 2012 (Lee, 2010; Lau, 2010; La Monica, 2012; Statista, 2014b). Due to the fact that Baidu is limited mainly to Chinese language users, it cannot surmount Google's global market share.

Several locally based SNSs, such as Mixi (Japan), KaKao Talk (Korea),[5] QQ (China), and VK (originally VKontakte, a European social network site that Russian-speaking users use around the world[6]), are competing with American-based SNSs. For example, Russian Cyberspace, including the Commonwealth of Independent States (CIS) such as Azerbaijan, Armenia, and Georgia, known as RUNET, is a self-contained linguistic and cultural environment with well-developed and highly popular search engines, web portals, social network sites, and free e-mail services. Within RUNET, Russian search engines dominate with Yandex (often called the Google of Russia), beating out Google (Deibert et al., 2010, 17–19). The market share of Yandex was 60.3 percent in November 2012, whereas Google's share was 26.6 percent in November 2012, according to LiveInternet (2012). However, outside these few countries, the majority of countries in the world have increased their usage of Facebook and Twitter. These Western-based platforms have managed to overtake some local incumbent SNSs and search engines in the past few years (Jin, 2012).

More significantly, the globalization of local-made social network sites has not been successful. For example, since 2005 Cyworld, which has been the largest social network site in Korea, has tried to penetrate other countries as part of its globalization strategy. It has tried to penetrate both developed countries, such as the U.S., Germany, and Japan, and developing countries, including China, Taiwan, and Vietnam. Many people were interested in Cyworld's globalization strategy because they wanted to see whether local-made SNSs could compete with Western-made SNSs in the global markets. The trial was mostly unsuccessful. Cyworld retreated from Germany less than two years after its service started, just as it gave up its service in the U.S. in 2010 (Park, 2008). Likewise, Cyworld had to leave the Japanese and Taiwanese markets partially because it did not attract people who were not already familiar with the concepts that were embedded in Cyworld.

Overall, the U.S. has continued an asymmetrical relationship of interdependence between a few developed countries and the majority of developing countries up to the present time. In most platform areas where profits can be generated, private interests, especially "American-based corporations, have been able to convert beachheads into monopoly fortresses and generate endless profit" (McChesney, 2013, 151). SNSs have gained tremendous attention as popular online spaces for both youth and adults in recent years, but American-based SNSs, including Facebook and Twitter, have rapidly penetrated the world and enjoyed an ample amount of capital gains.

AMERICAN EMPIRE IN PLATFORMS

Facebook, which was founded in the U.S. in 2004, is organized around linked personal platforms based on geographic, educational, or corporate networks. Given that the general concept of platform means any base of technologies on which other technologies or processes are built, Facebook is a platform that plays an advanced role in aggregating several services. When Netscape became a platform in the 1990s, their flagship product was the web browser, and their strategy was to use their dominance in the browser market to establish a market for high-priced products (O'Reilly, 2005). Windows is the same. Microsoft's Windows operating system continues to be used on more than 90 percent of desktop computers (90.62 percent as of January 2014), followed by Mac OS (7.7 percent) and Linux (1.59 percent) (NetMarketShare, 2014). Microsoft ended its service on Windows XP in August 2014 and asked the customer to buy Windows 8, now Windows 8.1. This means that these old platforms sell their products to continue their leading position in the market.

However, for Facebook, 'usage' is more important than other functions. "People as consumers and producers flock to Facebook to socialize with their friends and acquaintances, to share information with interested others, and to see and be seen" (boyd, 2011, 39). The site can be understood as an online communication platform that combines features of e-mail, instant messaging, photo-sharing, and blogging programs, as well as a way to monitor one's friends' online social activity. Since May 2007, members have been able to download and interact with Facebook applications, programs, and accessories developed by outside companies that now have access to Facebook's operating platform and large networked membership (Cohen, 2008).

Facebook is indeed maintaining its rate of growth and generating thousands of new user registrations every day. The number of total users has grown from 585 million in December 2010 to 1 billion in October 2012, which means over 400 million new user registrations took place in less than two years (Facebook, 2012a; Socialbakers, 2012). As of June 30, 2014, the number of active monthly users was 1.31 billion. These numbers are significant because they have contributed to the high valuation assigned to the company as well as the usefulness of a network. Facebook's value reached \$50 billion in January 2011 (McGirt, 2007; Rushe, 2011). Right after its public offering on May 18, 2012, the capital value of Facebook was as much as \$104 billion (AP, 2012). One and a half years later on November 7, 2013, Twitter, the microblogging network, also started its trading in the stock market through its public offering. Twitter's IPO values were \$14.1 billion, which was the second largest Internet offering in the U.S., behind Facebook's \$16 billion IPO and ahead of Google Inc.'s 2004 IPO (*Reuters*, 2013).

Interestingly enough, before its public offering, Zuckerberg emphasized that "Facebook's social mission was to make the world more open and connected," and he stated that "the primary goal was not making money" (Channel 4 News, 2012). This might be true, and it will not always be easy to separate economic and social values as motives, but the public offering of Facebook clearly proves that the development of new technology cannot be understood without its value embedded in design for commodity exchange, as van Dijck (2012) points out. At the very least, the technological designs of online spaces and operating systems constitute a contested terrain where the imposition of designers' values and preferences are at odds with the values and preferences of the intended user base (Bodle, 2010).

Due to the increasing number of users, the usefulness of a network also increases at an accelerating rate. As Robert Metcalfe states, the value of a telecommunications network is proportional to the square is of the number of connected users of the system (Briscoe et al., 2006).[7] Facebook's astonishing increase in the number of users consequently improves the quality of its algorithm in both networking and commodifying the users, leaving other social network sites, including MySpace (now almost defunct) with less attractive and effective social media.

Facebook has rapidly expanded its dominance in many countries. According to the World Map of Social Networks, showing the most popular SNSs by country, which is based on Alexa and Google Trends for Websites traffic data (2012), Facebook is the market leader in 130 out of 137 countries analyzed (94.8 percent) as of July 2014. Facebook is up from 92 percent in June 2012, 87 percent in June 2010, and 78 percent in December 2009 (Vincos Blog, 2012). Facebook has outnumbered Iwiw in Hungary, Nasza-Klasa in Poland, Hi5 in Mongolia, and Orkut (Google) in Paraguay and India since June 2010 (in terms of the number of national users).

Although several local-based SNSs are still market leaders in Asian countries, such as China, Japan, and Korea, as well as Russia, which is very significant because these are some of the largest IT markets, Facebook has otherwise managed to overtake local incumbent SNSs, and has rapidly penetrated the majority of countries in the world. At the end of April 2013, the U.S. was the largest country in terms of the number of users with 146.8 million users. However, other countries also rapidly increased their number of users. India surpassed Brazil (69 million) to become the second largest country with 114.8 million users, followed by Indonesia (63.2 million) and Mexico (35.7 million) (Statista, 2014c).

Likewise, in Korea, Facebook has rapidly increased its user base to compete with Cyworld. Cyworld was created as a personal information management system in 1999. Cyworld has enticed Korean youth to choose it as their primary SNS. It has taken over the reins to dominate Korean the market. It was hardly an overnight success, of course, and it was later revitalized in 2001 as a full-blown SNS with the launch of its template-based homepage service, called mini-hompy, in the midst of the rapid penetration of high-speed Internet (Choi, 2006). The rapid growth of Cyworld has indeed relied heavily on the increasing number of young people who actively dedicate their time and energy to make and continue their connections with others. Almost half of Korean people (24 million) are connected through Cyworld,

Table 3.3 Facebook Users in April 2013 (unit: millions)

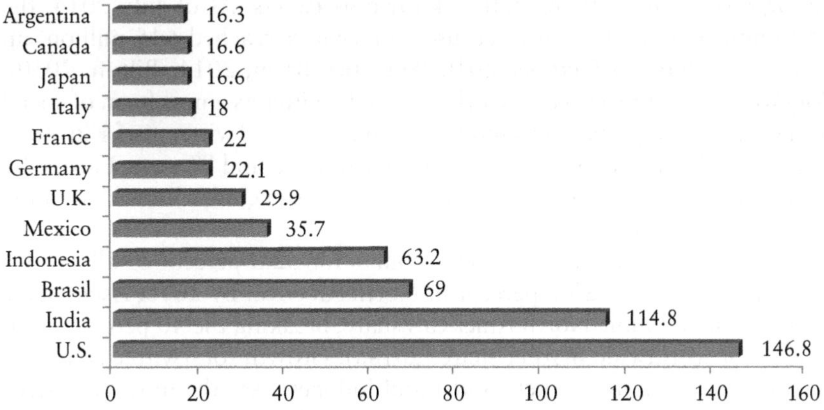

Argentina	16.3
Canada	16.6
Japan	16.6
Italy	18
France	22
Germany	22.1
U.K.	29.9
Mexico	35.7
Indonesia	63.2
Brasil	69
India	114.8
U.S.	146.8

Axis: 0 20 40 60 80 100 120 140 160

Source: Statistia (2014c). Leading countries based on number of Facebook users as of April 2013 (in millions) http://www.statista.com/statistics/268136/top-15-countries-based-on-number-of-facebook-users/

and more than 90 percent of 20 to 29 year olds use the site regularly (H. Kim, 2009).

The popularity of Cyworld among Korean youth is staggering considering the growth of Facebook in the Korean SNS market. As of December 2010, the number of Facebook users reached 3.5 million (the penetration rate is 7 percent); and it soared to 9.4 million users (18.8 percent) in November 2012 (Socialbakers, 2012). That says that fewer than 7 percent of Koreans used Facebook at the end of 2010 due to the dominant position of Cyworld. Most recent figures show that Facebook had 11 million monthly active users (the penetration rate is 22%) in Korea in June 2013 and approximately 90 percent of total users connected to Facebook on their smartphones.

As a reflection of Korea being the world's most wired country with the rapid growth of smartphones, increasingly Facebook users are rapidly switching their platform from Facebook toward smartphones (*Business Korea*, 2013). Korean youth heavily access their smartphones daily, resulting in the change of their preferred SNS, from local-based Cyworld to U.S.-based Facebook.[8] Facebook has encroached on the Korean market, mainly because the opinion leaders, including college professors and researchers, have switched to Facebook from Cyworld (Socialbakers, 2012). Facebook has positioned itself as the leader of interactive, participant-based, online media, or Web 2.0, the descriptor for websites based on user-generated content that create value from the sharing of information between participants (O'Reilly, 2005; Hoegg et al., 2006, 1).

Twitter has also experienced explosive growth over the last several years. Twitter, which was launched in July 2006 in the U.S., is an online SNS and microblogging service that allows users to post and read text-based messages of up to 140 characters, known as tweets. As of July 2014, the total number of active registered users of Twitter reached 645 million, up from 175 million in October 2010 (Statistics Brain, 2014; Bilton, 2010). Non-Western countries have swiftly adopted Twitter as a new form of social media. From a regional standpoint, the number of Twitter users in Asia-Pacific has already eclipsed those in North America and Western Europe by a wide margin—even considering that the figures exclude China due to the country's ban on the site.

In 2014, the Asia-Pacific region accounts for 32.8 percent of all Twitter users, compared with 23.7 percent in North America. By 2018, Asia-Pacific will more than double North America's share, breaking the 40 percent mark in terms of worldwide market share (2014a). Growth for Twitter is heavily weighted in emerging markets. India and Indonesia see the most consistent growth patterns throughout our forecast period, both experiencing increases well above 50 percent in 2014. Large growth rates frequently reflect a small installed base, but not in the cases of these two countries. India and Indonesia rise to have the third- and fourth-largest Twitter populations in the world in 2014, with 18.1 million and 15.3 million users, respectively—both surpassing the U.K. for the first time this year for the number of users (eMarketer, 2014a). In fact, remarkably, users from Jakarta in Indonesia were the most active within all cities ranked by the number of posted tweets in 2012. As a reflection of its critical role during the emergency situation, millions of new users joined in the wake of the March 2011 earthquake and tsunami in Japan and during election campaigns (Lee, 2013).[9]

What is significant is that non-Western countries are able to advance their use of Twitter primarily because they also have a large number of smartphone users. For example, the number of registered users of Twitter rapidly increased with the development of smartphones in Korea. As of November 2013, there were 7 million Twitter users in Korea (Lee, 2013). Since the growth in the number of smartphone users is steep, the amount of Twitter users is expected to grow. China developed Weibo in 2011, which is a hybrid of Twitter and Facebook, and it has become one of the most popular SNSs. However, the majority of users of Weibo were still limited to mainland China, Hong Kong, and Taiwan, meaning locally created SNSs cannot penetrate global markets yet due to the language barrier and the lack of brand power.

In fact, while the popularity of social network sites varies from country to country partially based on linguistic differences, Facebook (and Twitter) expands its global penetration because it offers support for multilingualism through a pop over menu that provides mechanical translations into approximately 70 languages (Bodle, 2010). Even with the ability to translate, English remains the dominant language on Facebook. Other local-based SNSs, which primarily use their own languages, find that they cannot penetrate other countries. As of November 2012, the number of English users of Facebook was recorded at 359.8 million, followed by Spanish users (142.8 million) (Socialbakers, 2013). Facebook reflects the dominance of English as the most used language on the Internet. However, whereas the dominance of English on the Internet could be surpassed by Mandarin Chinese, which is currently the second most used language (Internet World Stats, 2011), this is not the case with Facebook because Chinese barely made the top 10 languages list as of November 2012. This means that the dominant position of platforms can be intensified with the global language, English.

The dominant positions of Facebook, Twitter, and Google have been considered as clear examples of platform imperialism. Whereas these sites can offer participants entertainment and a way to socialize, the social relations present on a site like Facebook can obscure economic relations that reflect larger patterns of capitalist development in the digital age. The connection of SNSs to capitalism is especially significant. SNS users provide their daily activities as free labor to network owners, and thereafter, to advertisers. Their activities are being watched and counted and eventually appropriated by large corporations and advertising agencies (Jin, 2012). As we will discuss in later chapters, as the number of SNS users has soared, advertisers, including corporations and advertising agencies, have focused more on SNSs as alternative advertising media. Facebook has especially increased its profits from foreign countries.

In the case of smartphones, as fully discussed in Chapter 5, it is significant to know that operating systems, whether iPhone or Android, are symbols of the American empire. iPhones and Android phones seem to be everywhere, and they have formed an exclusive hegemonic power in the smartphone industry, just as Windows and Mac have in personal computers. According to the research firm IDC (2013), Android, which was invented in 2003 and integrated by Google, has been the world's best-selling smartphone platform and had a 79.3 percent share of smartphones worldwide during the second quarter of 2013, up from 57.5 percent in the third quarter of 2011. During the same period, Apple's iOS slightly decreased from 13.5 percent to 13.2 percent, followed by Windows Phone (3.7 percent), Blackberry (2.9 percent), and others (1 percent). This means that Android and iOS comprised almost 92.5 percent of the market share in the second quarter of 2013. Only two platforms, both of which are based in the U.S., have dominated the global market, which has not been seen before.

Growth was bolstered by strong Android product performance from a number of vendors, including Samsung and LG in Korea, HTC in Taiwan, and ZTE and Huawei in China (Canalys, 2011). Samsung, HTC, and others are also paying a fee, between $10 and $15 for each Android smartphone they sell, to Microsoft that owns some of the Android patents (Halliday, 2011). Digital technologies and culture have become among the most significant venues for many in the 21st century. The issue is that the U.S. has still expanded its dominance in digitally-driven technologies and culture due to platforms as in the case of popular culture, such as films and music.

The U.S. has been able to intensify its dominance in the intellectual property (IP) sector due to its advanced position in developing software, which is crucial for platforms. Although several non-Western countries have advanced their own software and platforms, the lop-sided interaction between Western and non-Western countries remains unchanged and perhaps is even more magnified today than in the past. In particular, the formation of U.S. hegemony in intellectual property rights has been extended through the efforts of international intellectual property regimes, such as WIPO (Lu and Weber, 2009).

ASYMMETRICAL POWER RELATIONSHIPS

Several U.S.-based platforms driven by a handful of private corporations have increased their dominance in the midst of neoliberal globalization. As Grewal (2008, 4) emphasizes, "the prominent elements of globalization can be understood as the rise of network power." The notion of network power consists of the joining of two ideas: first, that coordinating standards are more valuable when greater numbers of people use them, and second, that this dynamic as a form of power backed by Facebook, which is one of the largest TNCs, can lead to the progressive elimination of the alternatives, as Lenin (1917) and H. Schiller (1991) emphasized. Facebook, as the market leader in the SNS world, has eliminated competitors as the number of users exponentially soars. "In the digital era, one of the main sources of social inequality is the access to technology" (Castells, 1996, 32–33). Even when the issue is no longer that of lack of material access to technology, a power distribution and hegemonic negotiation of technologically mediated space is always at play (Gajjala and Birzescu, 2011). The powers that can be marshaled through platforms are not exclusively centered in the U.S.

However, as Lenin argued, the conflicts for hegemony between great powers, in this case U.S.-based SNSs and local-based SNSs, have been evident, and Facebook and Twitter have become dominant powers. In other words, a few U.S.-based platforms dominate the global order, which has resulted in the concentration of capital within major TNCs and start-ups. This is far from a globalization model in which power is infinitely dispersed. Capital and power are not the form of monopoly. However, a handful of U.S.-owned platforms have rapidly expanded their dominance in the global market, which has caused the asymmetrical gap between a few Western countries and the majority of non-Western countries.

As platforms rapidly become global, they contain the limitation and constraints consistent with the global diffusion of ICTs generally. The spread of networked media across borders can bring unintended consequences, including new forms of imperialism (Ess, 2009; Bodle, 2010). Whereas the diffusion of new technologies has advanced society by providing new opportunities as a public sphere tool, platform technologies have become a new corporate sphere for a few Western countries and transnational corporations headquartered in the U.S.

Platforms function as some of the most significant tools for capital accumulation for a handful of owners located in the U.S. As platform inventors and producers, several platform corporations, such as Google, Apple, and Facebook, have become primary actors in the digital economy. They especially garner revenues not only within the U.S. but also from many developing countries. The major revenue source is advertising both nationally and globally. However, they also develop other forms of resources for revenue generation, such as social games and financial rent as discussed in Chapter 6. The reality is that these few U.S.-based platforms have benefited from the rapid growth of global platform users as laborers.

In addition, platform owners have heavily pursued another capitalization process by forcing intellectual property rights. The idea of platform imperialism refers to an asymmetrical relationship of interdependence in platform technologies and culture between the West, primarily the U.S., and many developing countries. This includes the two great powers of nation-states and transnational corporations. But platform imperialism is not only about the forms of technological disparities but also the forms of intellectual property, symbolic hegemony, and user commodity. These issues encourage the concentration of capital in the hands of a few U.S.-based platform owners, resulting in the expansion of the global divide, which following chapters analyze.

In other words, unlike other forms of imperialism, the newly constructing platform imperialism needs to be understood as unequal power relations among countries backed by intellectual property, which is strongly favoring the U.S. government and transnational corporations because commercial values are embedded in platforms. As in the case of Harvey's notion of the new imperialism (2007), the platform imperialism that is evolving in the early 21st century entails construction under the single hegemony of the U.S. The inner connection between the rise of platform imperialism within the struggle of neoliberal globalization, as in the case of the post-9/11 U.S. politics, is vitally important in understanding the contemporary global order in which platforms are highly involved. Previously war, military coercion, and subversions had always been central to imperial practices (Harvey, 2007); however, the situation has changed fundamentally because territories are not the major issue in the networked society.

CONCLUSION

This chapter analyzed the increasing dominance of Western-based, and in particular American-based, platforms globally. It examined the evolutionary development of various theories of imperialism and examined whether we might be moving towards a situation of platform imperialism. Since the new concept of imperialism functions through digital technologies, first information and second platform technologies in the 21st century, it is crucial to understand whether such technologies play a primary role in changing the notions of imperialism.

At a glance, again the massive switch to the digital economy has provided a surplus for several emerging powers, including China, India, and Korea, with which to challenge the longer-term U.S. dominance, unlike the old notion of imperialism developed by Lenin (Boyd-Barrett, 2006, 24). These emerging-power countries have developed their own SNSs, search engines, and smartphones, and presumably competed with Western countries. They are supposed to build a new global order with their advanced digital technologies. On the one hand, the era of platforms has shown the increasing international hierarchy mainly because American-based platforms are dominating the world. The degree of the influence has not been seen in other fields and/or industries due to the increasing role of a few platforms invented in the U.S. Due to the significance of these platform technologies, several countries, including Korea, Japan, Taiwan, and China, have invested in these cutting-edge technologies and industries.

There are doubts as to whether non-Western platform corporations have reorganized the global flow and constructed a balance between the West and the East because the majority of countries in the world have adopted American-based platforms, resulting in the construction of platform imperialism. Unlike previous American dominance in both culture and capital, the influence of the U.S. in platforms has expanded because other countries cannot invent their own platforms due to the lack of skills, talents, and capital.

In the era of platforms, the U.S. has not been a sole player, but its dominance in the global markets has not been contested. As a matter of fact, in history there have been no other comparable cultural products and technologies in which the U.S. became such a dominant power. In the realm of culture, many countries have developed their own popular cultures and exported them to neighboring countries. In the media and telecommunications industries, the U.S. has been the largest segment and the largest investor; however, several developed countries, including the U.K., France, Germany, and Japan, have several major media and telecommunications corporations.

As Cassar (2013, 334) observes, regarding the relationship between East and West, Gramsci believed that the West needs an inferior East in order to legitimize its own position of power. Moreover, the East further legitimizes such a position by having an economic inferiority as compared to the West. Edward Said eventually constructs his theory of Orientalism on the same principles adopted by Gramsci to explain the relationship between the industrial North and the primitive South. Such an image is also exemplified in many ICT sectors.

However, platforms are not the same because the U.S.-based social network sites, search engines, and smartphones have undoubtedly been the most active and significant in the global markets. In other words, the U.S. alone has intensified its monopolistic hegemony in the realm of platforms, which cannot be seen in other areas. As discussed in Chapter 4, the U.S. government, therefore, has vehemently supported the growth of U.S.-based platforms by using its state power.

In particular, when the debates reach platforms, non-Western countries have not, and likely cannot, construct a balanced global order, because Google (including its Android operating system), Facebook, Twitter, and Apple's iPhones (and iOS) are indices of the dominance of the U.S. in the digital economy. These platforms have penetrated the global market and expanded their global dominance. Therefore, it is safe to say that American imperialism has been continued with platforms. As in the time of Lenin between the late 19th century and the early 20th century, there has been a connection between platform and capitalist imperialism. Platforms have functioned as a new form of distributor and producer that the U.S. dominates. Arguably, therefore, we are still living in the imperialist era.

A critical interrogation of the global hegemony of platforms proves that the dominant position of the U.S. has intensified an increasingly unequal relationship between the West and the East. In the 21st century, the world has become further divided into a handful of Western states, in particular the U.S., which have developed platforms and a vast majority of non-Western states which do not have advanced platforms. Therefore, it is certain that American imperialism has been renewed with platforms, like the old form of American imperialism supported by politics, economy, and military, as well as culture.

At the time of Lenin, there was certainly a connection between communication—cable and telegraph systems—globalization, and capitalist imperialism (Winseck and Pike, 2007, 1). In the 21st century, again, there is a distinct connection between platforms, globalization, and capitalist imperialism. Unlike the old notion of imperialism, though, the contemporary concept of imperialism has supported huge flows of people, news, and symbols, which, in turn, leads to a high degree of convergence among markets, technologies, and major TNCs in tandem with nation-states. Platforms can be situated within more general capitalist processes that follow familiar patterns of asymmetrical power relations between the West and the East, as well as between workers and owners, commodification, and the harnessing of user power.

NOTES

1. Whereas several countries developed and introduced their own early smartphones locally, this book identifies the iPhone made by Apple in 2007 as the

starting point of the smartphone era due to its huge impact on the global mobile industry. For example, Korea and Taiwan have rapidly developed their own smartphones right after the introduction of iPhones, and a few previous major corporations, including Nokia and Motorola, have rapidly decreased their market shares in the global market because they did not respond to the iPhone-era.

2. The most significant platform convergence in tandem with digital capitalism happens in the mobile advertising market. As global mobile ad spending increased 105.0 percent to total $17.96 billion in 2013, Facebook and Google accounted for a majority of mobile ad market growth worldwide. Combined, the two companies saw net mobile ad revenues increase by $6.92 billion, claiming 75.2 percent of the additional $9.2 billion that went toward mobile in 2013. The two companies are consolidating their places at the top of the market, accounting for more than two-thirds of mobile ad spending in 2014 (eMarketer, 2014b). The major platforms, Facebook, Google, and smartphone, are intertwined to capitalize user activities, and the benefits as usual go to the U.S.
3. Of course, we also need to understand the changing pattern in media convergence in the early 21st century because media corporations have also pursued de-convergence as a primary business model instead of continuing media convergence. As News Corporation has become two independent corporations—News Corporation encompassing newspaper and publishing and 21st Century Fox encompassing cable, filmed entertainment, and network television—since June 2013 (BBC News, 2013), several big media behemoths have spun-off or split-off their corporations into a few independent corporations and/or sold-off some of their corporations, due to the failure to achieve the expected synergy effects (Jin, 2013).
4. Naver and Daum are technically not search engines, but portals. Portal refers to a web system that provides the functions and features to authenticate and identify the users and provide them with an easy, intuitive, personalized, and user-customizable web-interface for facilitating access to information and services that are of primary relevance and interests to the users. To the organization that sets up the portal, it is a system that provides versatile functions for the organization to catalogue or organize collections of different and multiple sources of information and service resources for dissemination to many users according to their specific privileges, needs and interest. Hence, the main purpose of setting up a portal is to bring the vast information and service resources available from many sources to many users in an effective manner. See Computer Centre (2013).
5. KaKao Talk as a virtual machine platform has played a significant role in the rising smartphone-mediated youth culture in Korea. KaKao Talk allows its users to send and receive messages, photos, videos, and contact information for free. It enables users to access numerous free apps that can supplement KaKao Talk's messenger features. Since its release in March 2010, the number of subscribers has rapidly increased, reaching 42 million in March 2012 and 100 million in July 2013 (Chung, 2013). KaKao Talk was acquired by Daum, which is the second largest web portal in Korea in 2014.
6. VK was established in 2006 by Pavel Durov, a Russian entrepreneur, who is still the co-owner alongside the Mail.ru Group, the Russian Internet giant that owns a 39.9 percent stake in Vkontakte (East-West Digital News, 2012).

7. This is known as Metcalfe's law, and Metcalfe's law characterizes many of the network effects of communication technologies and networks such as the Internet, social network, and the World Wide Web, although it is controversial in its effectiveness.
8. The strength of Cyworld has been the mini-hompy, which is a three dimensional virtual space. The mini-hompy is a small cyber space that users get when they become members. Through their mini-hompy, they express themselves to others. The mini-hompy is fully customizable with wallpapers, furniture, and background music. It acts as a user's virtual home. However, the mini-hompy is not the best thing for Korean youth who are using smartphones instead of PC-based Internet. Cyworld has gradually given way to Facebook in the Korean SNS market.
9. Growth has slowed in Korea and Japan, a red flag for Twitter since both countries are wealthy and have high rates of mobile device usage—now the predominant way Twitter is accessed. New mobile applications from companies such as Korea's KaKao Corp. and Japan's Line Corp. have experienced explosive growth, making them potent competitors for eyeballs and advertising (Lee, 2013). KaKao Talk allows its users to send and receive messages, photos, videos, and contact information for free. It reached 70 million users in Korea in December 2012. Twitter is growing in Korea, but it is relatively difficult to penetrate the local market due to Korea's own KaKao Talk brand, since local search engines (portals) Naver and Daum are much more familiar to Koreans than Google. Korea, therefore, is exceptional in the process of U.S.-dominance in the realms of several platforms. However, it is only one case and does not represent the entirety of developing countries.

REFERENCES

Alexa.com (2012). Top 500 Sites on the Web. Accessed November 17, 2012. http://www.alexa.com/topsites.

Associated Press (AP). 2011a. Apple suit: Samsung copies our devices. May 4.

AP (2011b). Avatar boosts Chinese box office to $1.5B. January 10.

AP (2011c) Google launches high-stakes bid for Motorola Mobility. 15 August.

AP (2012). Facebook set to begin trading after $16 billion offering. May 22.

Baldwin, T.F., McVoy, D.S. & Steinfield, C. (1996). *Convergence: Integrating Media, Information, and Communication*. Thousand Oaks, CA: Sage.

Baran, Paul & Sweezy, Paul M. (1968). *Monopoly Capital: An Essay on the American Economic and Social Order*. New York: Monthly Review Press.

BBC News (2013). News Corp to split in two on 28 June. 24 May. http://www.bbb.co.uk/business-22651197?print=ture.

Bilton, Nick (2010). Why Twitter's CEO demoted himself. *The New York Times*. October 31. Accessed May 1, 2012. http://www.nytimes.com/2010/10/31/technology/31ev.html?pagewanted=all&gwh=5A1E5339D68D86CCA0B79715D72E2BA3.

Bodle, Robert (2010). Assessing social network sites as international platforms. *Journal of International Communication* 16(2): 9–24.

Bonney, B. (1984). Transnational advertising agencies and the local industry. *Media International Australia* 31: 34–39.

Boyd-Barrett, Oliver (1980). *The International News Agency*. London: Constable.

Boyd-Barrett, Oliver (1998). Media imperialism reformulated. In Daya Thussu (ed.), *Electronic Empires: Global Media and Local Resistance*, 157–76. London: Arnold.

Boyd-Barrett, Oliver (2006). Cyberspace, globalization and empire. *Global Media and Communication* 2(1): 21–41.

Boyd-Barrett, Oliver (1977). Media imperialism: Towards an international framework for the analysis of media systems. In James Curran and M. Gurevitch (eds.), *Mass Communication and Society,* 116–135. London: Edward Arnold.

boyd, d. (2007). Why youth (heart) social network sites: The role of networked publics in teenage social life. In D. Buckingham (ed.), *Youth, Identity, and Digital Media*. pp. 119–142. Cambridge, MA: MIT Press.

Business Korea (2013). Connections to Facebook: 990% of Facebook users in Korea connect on their mobile phones. 15 October. http://www.businesskorea.co.kr/article/1272/connections-facebook-90-facebook-users-korea-connect-their-mobile-phones.

Canalys (2011). Android takes almost 50% share of worldwide smart phone market. 1 August.

Cassar, R. (2013). Gramsci and games. *Games and Culture* 8(5): 330–353.

Castells, Manual (1996). *The Rise of the Network Society*. Cambridge, MA: Blackwell.

Channel 4 News (2012). Facebook's not only for money says Zuckerberg. Accessed April 29, 2012. http://www.channel4.com/news/facebook-set-for-biggest-ever-internet-flotation, February 2.

Choi, J.H. (2006). Living in Cyworld: Contextualizing cy-Ties in South Korea. In A. Bruns and J. Jacobs (eds.), *Uses of Blogs*, 173–186. New York: Peter Lang.

Cohen, N.S. (2008). The valorization of surveillance: Towards a political economy of Facebook, *Democratic Comunique,* 22(1), 5–22.

Computer Centre (2013). What is Portal? http://www.its.hku.hk/news/ccnews100/portal.htm.

Demont-Heinrich, Christof (2008). The Death of Cultural Imperialism—and Power too? *International Communication Gazette* 70(5): 378–394.

Demont-Heinrich, Christof (2011). Cultural imperialism versus globalization of culture: Riding the structure-agency dialectic in global communication and media studies. *Sociology Compass* 5(8): 666–678.

East-West Digital News (2012). Vkontakte's IPO postponed indefinitely: Shareholder Mail.ru Group yields control to founder. Accessed January 2, 2013. http://www.ewdn.com/2012/05/30/vkontaktes-ipo-postponed-indefinitely-shareholder-mail-ru-group-yields-control-to-founder/.

The Economist (2005). A survey of patent and technology: A market for ideas. October 20.

Efrati, Amir & Ante, Spencer (2011). Google's $12.5 billion gamble. *The Wall Street Journal*. August 16. Accessed November 21, 2011. http://online.wsj.com/article/SB10001424053111903392904576509953821437960.html.

Ellison, N.B., Steinfield, C., & Lampe, C. (2007). The benefits of Facebook "friends:" Social capital and college students' use of online social network sites. *Journal of Computer-Mediated Communication,* 12(4). http://jcmc.indiana.edu/vol12/issue4/ellison.html.

eMarketer (2009). Social network ad spending: 2010 Outlook. http://www.emarketer.com/Report.aspx?code=emarketer_2000621.

eMarketer (2010). Advertisers to spend $1.7 billion on social networks in 2010. Press Release. August 16.

Ess, Charles (2009). *Digital Media Ethics*. Cambridge: Polity Press.

Facebook (2012a). Newsroom. Accessed September 17, 2012. http://newsroom.fb.com/content/default.aspx?NewsAreaId=20.

Facebook (2012b). Form S-1 Registration Statement. New York: SEC. Accessed November 17, 2012. http://www.sec.gov/Archives/edgar/data/1326801/000119312512034517/d287954ds1.htm.

Fuchs, C. (2010). Class, knowledge, and new media. *Media, Culture and Society*, 32(1), 141–150.

Fuchs, Christian (2010a). New imperialism: Information and media imperialism. *Global Media and Communication* 6(1): 33–60.

Fuchs, Christian (2010b). Critical globalization studies and the new imperialism. *Critical Sociology* 36 (6): 839–867.

Fuchs, Christian (2011a). *Foundations of Critical Media and Information Studies*. London: Routledge.

Fuchs, Christian (2011b). A contribution to the critique of the political economy of Google. *Fast Capitalism* 8 (1). Accessed August 17, 2012. http://www.fastcapitalism.com/.

Hargittai, E. (2008). Whose space? Differences among users and non-users of social network sites. *Journal of Computer-Mediated Communication* 13: 276–297.

Internet Trend (2013). Search engine. http://www.internettrend.co.kr/trendForward.tsp.

Gajjala, Rrdhika & Anca Birzescu (2011). Digital imperialism through online social/financial networks. *Economic and Political Weekly*, 95–102.

Galtung, Johan (1971). A structural theory of imperialism. *Journal of Peace Research* 8(2): 81–117.

Google (2012). Facts about Google's acquisition of Motorola. Accessed March 29, 2012. http://www.google.com/press/motorola/.

Gramsci, A. (1971). *Selections from The Prison Notebooks*, Quintin Hoare and Geoffrey Nowell-Smith (eds. and trans.). New York: International Publishers.

Grewal, David (2008). *Network Power: The Social Dynamics of Globalization*. New Haven: Yale University Press.

Hoegg, Roman, Martignoni, Robert, Meckel, Miriam, & Stanoevska-Slabeva, Katrina (2006). Overview of business models for Web 2.0 communities Proceedings of GeNeMe 2006.

Internet World Stats (2011). Internet world users by language. http://www.internetworldstats.com/stats7.htm.

Jenkins, H. (2006). *Convergence Culture*. New York: New York University Press.

Jin, Dal Yong (2007). Reinterpretation of cultural imperialism: Emerging domestic market vs. continuing U.S. dominance. *Media, Culture and Society* 29(5): 753–771.

Jin, Dal Yong (2011). Critical analysis of U.S. cultural policy in the global film market: Nation-states and FTAs. *International Communication Gazette* 73(8): 651–669.

Jin, D.Y. (2013). *De-convergence of Global Media Industries*. London: Routledge.

Johnson, S. (2010). Rethinking a gospel of the web. *The New York Times*. 10 April.

Kamasnack (2012). Nov 2012 update. Search engine market share. Accessed November 17, 2012. http://www.karmasnack.com/about/search-engine-market-share/.

Kim, H.S. (2009). Cyworld starts 10 years ago. *Seoul Shinmun*, 12 April.

La Monica, Paul (2012). Baidu: Is China's Google better than Google? *CNN Money*. February 13. Accessed November 17, 2012. http://money.cnn.com/2012/02/13/technology/thebuzz/index.htm.

Lau, Justin (2010). Baidu profits from Google's China woes, *Financial Times*. July 22. Accessed November 1, 2011. http://www.ft.com/cms/s/2/c8fe238e-9542-11df-b2e1-00144feab49a.html.

Lee, Y.K. (2013). Twitter is cooling off in Korea and Japan. AP. 7 November.

Lee, Micky (2010). Revisiting the 'Google in China' question from a political economic perspective. *China Media Research* 6(2): 15–24.

Lenin, Vladimir (1917). Imperialism, the highest stage of capitalism. In *Essential Works of Lenin*, 177–270. New York: Dover.

Lenin, Vladimir (1964). *State and Revolution*. vol. 25.

LiveInternet (2012). Report from search engines. Accessed November 25, 2012. http://www.liveinternet.ru/stat/ru/searches.html?slice=ru;period=week.

Lu, Jia & Weber, Ian (2009). Internet software piracy in China: A user analysis of resistance to global software copyright enforcement. *Journal of International and Intercultural Communication* 2(4): 296–317.

Marx, K. (1867). *Capital*, vol. 1 London: Penguin.

Maurais, Jacques (2003). Towards a new linguistic order. In Jacques Maurais and Michael Morris (eds.), *Languages in a Globalizing World*, 13–36. Cambridge: Cambridge University Press.

McChesney, R. (2013). *Digital Disconnect*. New York: The New Press.

McGirt, Ellen (2007). Facebook's Mark Zuckerberg: Hacker, dropout, CEO. Accessed September 17, 2012. http://www.fastcompany.com/magazine/115/open_features-hacker-dropout-ceo.html.

Morley, D. (2006). Globalization and cultural imperialism reconsidered: Old questions in new guises. In James Curran and David Morley (eds.), *Media and Cultural Theory*, 30–43. New York, Routledge.

Mosco, V. & McKercher, C. (2006). Convergence bites back: Labour struggles in the Canadian communication industry. *Canadian Journal of Communication* 31: 733–751.

Mosco, V. (2008). Current trends in the political economy of communication. *Global Media Journal Canadian Edition* 1(1): 45–63.

New, William (2011). Palestinian membership in UNESCO could raise questions for US at WIPO. *Intellectual Property Watch*. Accessed March 2, 2012. http://www.ip-watch.org/2011/10/21/palestinian-membership-in-unesco-could-raise-questions-for-us-wipo/.

O'Reilly, T. (2005). What is Web 2.0. Available at http://oreilly.com/web2/archive/what-is-web-20.html.

Panitch, Leo & Gindin, Sam (2003). Global capitalism and American empire. In Leo Panitch and Sam Gindin (eds.), *The Socialist Register 2004: The New Imperial Challenge*, 1–43. New York: Monthly Press.

Park, D.W. (2008). Cyworld will retreat from the U.S. market in December. *Korea Economic Daily*. 2 November.

Patrick, K. (2012). How Craigslist makes money. *The Houston Chronicle*. Accessed January 2, 2013. http://smallbusiness.chron.com/craigslist-money-27287.html.

Reuters (2013). Twitter set for volatile debut after IPO raises at least $1.8 billion. http://www.reuters.com/article/2013/11/07/us-twitter-ipo-idUSBRE99N1AE20131107.

Rushe, D. (2011). Facebook's value swells to $50 billion after Goldman Sachs investment. *Guardian*. January 3. Accessed February 22, 2011. http://www.guardian.co.uk/technology/2011/jan/03/facebook-value-50bn-goldman-sachs-investment.

Said, E. (1993). *Culture and Imperialism*. New York: A.A. Knopf.

Schiller, D. (2007). *How to Think about Information*. Urbana, IL: University of Illinois Press.

Schiller, H. (1969). *Mass Communications and American Empire*. Oxford: Westview Press.

Schiller, H. (1976). *Communication and Cultural Domination*. White Plains, NY: International Arts and Sciences Press.

Schiller, H. (1991). Net yet the post-imperialist era. *Critical Studies in Media Communication* 8(1): 13–28.

Socialbakers (2011). Facebook reaches 600 million users as of January 2011. Accessed September 3, 2011. http://www.socialbakers.com/blog/100-facebook-reaches-another-milestone-600-million-users/.

Socialbakers (2013). Top 10 fastest growing Facebook languages. Accessed November 3, 2013. http://www.socialbakers.com/blog/1064-top-10-fastest-growing-facebook-languages.

Sparkes, M. (2012). August 17. Facebook shares plummet to half price. *The Telegraph*. Accessed November 17, 2012. http://www.telegraph.co.uk/finance/markets/9483295/Facebook-shares-plummet-to-half-price.html.

Statista (2014). Worldwide market share of leading search engines from January 2010 to July 2014. http://www.statista.com/statistics/216573/worldwide-market-share-of-search-engines/.

Statistic Brian (2013). Twitter statistics. http://www.statisticbrain.com/twitter-statistics/.

Stern, L. & Taylor, K. (2007). Social networking on Facebook, *Journal of the Communication, Speech and Theatre Association of North Dakota* 20: 9–20.

Sutcliffe, B. (2006). Imperialism old and new: A comment on David Harvey's the new imperialism and Ellen Meiksins Wood's empire of capital. *Historical Materialism* 14(4): 59–78.

Thomson Reuters (2012). Inside the iPhone patent portfolio. September.

Thornton, L. & Keith, S. (2009). From convergence to webvergence: Tracking the evolution of broadcast-print partnerships through the lens of change theory. *Journalism and Mass Communication Quarterly* 86(2): 257–276.

van Dijck, José (2012). Facebook as a tool for producing sociality and connectivity. *Television and New Media* 13(2): 160–176.

Vincos Blog (2012). World map of social networks. Accessed September 3, 2011. http://www.vincos.it/world-map-of-social-networks/.

Wasko, J. (2003). *How Hollywood Works*. London: Sage.

Wirtz, B.W. (2001). Reconfiguration of value chains in converging media and communications markets. *Long Range Planning*, 34(4): 489–506.

Zittrain, J. (2008). *The Future of the Internet*. New Haven, CT: Yale University Press.

4 Platform Politics in Nation-States

INTRODUCTION

In the field of technology, nation-states have been the most significant actors in the invention and diffusion of information and communication technologies (ICTs), However, with the increasing role of transnational corporations and venture capitals as developers and funding providers in the midst of globalization, the role of the nation-state has been challenged. Whereas the rise of the Internet and later social media is a massive shift in the way ICTs impact our lives and social interactions, these new developments inevitably lead to the question of whether the advance in new technologies impacts our political entities. It is common to encounter speculation about the decline or demise of the nation-state in academic conferences and media.

Many people contemplate that the decreasing role of the government is going to happen sometime soon. However, it is also true that in the era of platforms, many governments, in both developed and developing countries, vehemently support the growth of platform technologies, mainly because "technology is central to growth and growth is central to capitalism" (McChesney, 2013, 47). TNCs have developed and advanced new technologies, and the U.S. government and other governments have been major players in the globalized world because they need to support the growth of their own platforms. As usual, the nation-states have always been the strongest supporters of private corporations, and it is not different in the field of platform technologies.

This chapter examines the major role of the nation-state in the era of platform technologies, with the case of Google but not excluding other platforms. On the one hand, it investigates the primary role of the nation-state in the platform industries as a strong supporter in the global scene. In particular, it articulates how the U.S. government has cultivated the free flow of information norm in global affairs in the era of social media. On the other hand, it analyzes an interplay between the government and transnational corporations so that it develops the discourse of the role of the government in the era of neoliberal globalization. So that several key policy agendas such as intellectual property rights and the digital divide can be fully discussed in later chapters, in this chapter we focus on the ways in which the nation-state has supported and influenced platform corporations in forming their close relationship. The chapter eventually analyzes whether neoliberal ideologies, emphasizing a small government regime in economy, culture, and technology, have completely altered state-interventionism in the midst of neoliberal globalization with the case of U.S.-based platforms.

CHANGING ROLES OF NATION-STATES IN THE INFORMATION AND COMMUNICATION INDUSTRIES

The debates on the implications of the role of nation-states on technology have been a long-standing subject within globalization research (Miller, 2004; Fuchs, 2010). The pivotal role of the nation-state in the growth of technology is not new. Since the origin of nationalism started with the rise of printing press in the 15th century in the midst of the demise of feudalism, technology and the nation-state have closely worked together to be primary players in human history. As Benedict Anderson (1983, 6) pointed out, "the nation is an imaged political community, because the members of even the smallest nation never know most of their fellow-members, meet them, or even hear of them." However, with the invention of the printing press, the situation dramatically changed because through newspapers people in Europe started to learn about their fellow members (Thussu, 2006). The territorial and social space has become known to people at the same time. This means that people were able to understand the notion of the nation-state through the invention of a new technology.

Since then, the nation-state and technology have become close partners in developing human society. The nation-states and their relationships to technologies are key factors in determining the growth of technologies because the nation-state has initiated several key information and communication technologies, such as radio and the Internet. The governments support new technologies through legal and financial arms as well. As evidenced by the invention of the Internet, the government has become one of the most significant research and development (R&D) providers, and it has supported new media firms through several legal measures, increasingly with intellectual property rights.

Nevertheless, with the invention of a few new technologies, including satellite in the 1960s, people started to consider whether the old notion of the nation-state still works, primarily because new technologies lead the deterritorialization process. New technologies have facilitated rapid interconnectivity not only among people but also among countries. New technologies blur territories, which is the most significant indicator in deciding the national sovereignty. Hans Morgenthau (1966, 9) argued, "modern technology has rendered the nation state obsolete as a principle of political organization; for the nation state is no longer able to perform what is the elementary function of any political organization: to protect the lives of its members and their way of life."

The debate on the role of the nation-state more formally started in the early 1990s with the end of the Cold War, the commercial use of the Internet, and the rapid growth of neoliberal globalization theory. This is because the power of state-centric political and military rivalries to dominate international relations diminished, and national borders cannot stop the flow of information and other information technology developments (Göksel, 2004). On the one hand, the Internet-related corporations, which have facilitated the deterritorialization process, have no particular interests in the growth of the nation-state but are instead transfixed on their own profits through the borderless, and therefore, territory-less global society. The bottom line is that "communication technologies are being designed more to defend the investment of multimedia conglomerates than to further the goal of creating open and transparent mediaspaces" (Winseck, 2002, 810). On the other hand, since the 1990s when globalization became one of the most significant theoretical frameworks in analyzing the contemporary society, the notion of the nation-state has ignited controversies regarding its role as a primary player. With the massive involvement of transnational corporations in the realm of economy and culture, the world order of nation-states is undergoing significant change, ushered in by a globalizing age (Appadurai, 1996; Hardt and Negri, 2000; Kumar, 2010). With globalization, "capital might crack the shell of the nation-state" (Dyer-Witheford, 1999, 138).

Although the Internet and globalization do not abrogate sovereignty, they certainly weaken it. States are no longer monopolists (Engel, 2000). Therefore, some theorists argue that the nation-state loses its power as a meaningful unit in the global economy and culture of today's borderless world as neoliberal globalization theory evolves (Morley and Robins, 1995; Ohmae, 1996; Sinclair, 2007). The Japanese economist Kenichi Ohmae (1996) argued that the nation-state is losing its relevance as a unit of economic activity in today's borderless global economy amidst neoliberal globalization.

In fact, the idea behind neoliberalism, which has been primarily developed since the early 1980s, is the creation of policies that maximize the role of markets and profit making while minimizing the role of nonmarket institutions, through deregulation and privatization. Where states were once the masters of markets, now it is the markets which, on many crucial issues, are the masters over the governments of states (Strange, 1996). In other words, the rise of neoliberal globalization challenged the idea of an activist state and gave primacy to the private sector (Holroyd and Coates, 2012). As Friedman (1982, 2–3) argued, "the government's power must be limited while the private companies operate their maximum freedom in a free market." That means governments should remain primarily to better serve the corporate interests while reducing any activities that might undermine the role of business. What they commonly argue is that in capitalism, the nation-state plays no significant role in the economy. This ideological tide of neoliberalism that has swept over most of the world in the past two decades has had a profound impact on public policies, including cultural policies.

Many countries have made significant changes to their administrative machinery to accommodate this ideological shift, including more support for measures intended to harness market forces, more contracting out of government services, and more emphasis on self-help instead of reliance on government services (Jeannotte, 2010). As McChesney (2008) points out, "neoliberalism has unleashed national and international politics maximally supportive of business domination of all social affairs." He emphasizes that "the centerpiece of neoliberal policies is invariably a call for commercial communication markets to be deregulated."

Hardt and Negri (2000, xii–xiv) claim that the sovereignty of the nation-states is over because no nation would be a world leader in the way modern European nations were in the midst of globalization. Hjarvard (2003) and Giddens (1999) also emphasize that the weakening role of the nation-state has resulted in the decreasing role of domestic culture and cultural identity in non-Western countries. In addition, Waisbord and Morris (2001, vii–xxi) argue that "the state has been said to find it more difficult to exercise authority over flows of information and cultural commodities." Taking an example of China, Chin (2003) argues that several Asian governments are often criticized as lacking the power to control their cultural policies and leaving everything in the hands of corporations and market decisions as a result of global de-politicization. Through a case study of Google Earth, Kumar (2010) points out that new media poses a special kind of challenge to the nation-state because these new technologies, which have created the network society, have their own sovereign entities equivalent to a nation state.

Manuel Castells (2009, 18) also admits that "the national boundaries of power relationships are just one of the dimensions in which power and counterpower operate, although this is not to say that the nation-state disappears." What Castells (2009, 21–23) emphasizes is that even if the nation-state is not fading away as a specific form of social organization, it changes its role, its structure, and its functions. It is gradually evolving toward a new form of state that he calls 'the network state' because he believes that networks became the most efficient organizational form. As these theoreticians commonly argued, neoliberal globalization indeed engineers the restructuring of national economy, which has resulted in the transnationalization of cultural industries and the weakening role of the nation-state.

However, it is crucial to remember that the classical Marxist accounts of the 19th century era of free trade and its succession by the era of interimperial rivalry also confusingly counterpoised states and markets, as is so often done in contemporary discussions of globalization in the context of neoliberal free market policies. Among both classical Marxists and neoliberal globalization theory, there have been some failures in appreciating the crucial role of the state in making free markets happen and work (Panitch and Gindin, 2003, 11; Wood, 2003), which needs to be carefully discussed.

Several theoreticians, therefore, argue that the contemporary global flow is more complex than many globalists, who argue for the decreasing role of the government, suggest (Sánchez Ruiz, 2001; D. Schiller, 2007; Wu and Chan 2007). They commonly claim that the nation-state and domestic media firms have continued to have an influential role in national culture and technology in many countries. They contend that many countries still maintain the potential to challenge Western-based TNCs and to compete in the global market, even though some local companies and nation-states are not well-equipped for the task (Wu and Chan, 2007). McChesney (2013) emphasizes that the significant role of the government remains because it has built a national infrastructure, including telecommunications, and invested in research and development projects as one of the largest funders.[1]

As Kumar (2010) aptly puts it, it is crucial to carefully interpret the changing role of the government in the midst of neoliberal globalization:

> "while prophecies about the demise of the nation state in a globalizing world frequently recur in theories of globalization, details of the mechanism through which the classical form of sovereignty is ceding ground to the new continues to require elaboration. Given that this change is an ongoing process of negotiation that is contingent on the specific actors involved in the process, it can be better understood through a close analysis of moments of contact between the nation state and the forms of power that are challenging it."
>
> (Kumar, 2010, 154–155)

What Kumar (2010) actually argues is that these moments open up sites of contestation that allow us to complicate our understanding of the morphing nature of power, and thus enable theories of the eroding nation state to move from the conjectural to the concrete.

After conducting a case study of China's regulatory policies on trans-border TV drama flow, Chin (2003) concludes that the nation-state plays a crucial role in regulating domestic cultural polices and guiding development of the transnational flow of television dramas. Admitting that China is not a democratic country, it may not be surprising to see that the Chinese government regulates the cultural and technology areas. However, since the Chinese government has also appropriated neoliberal economic policies since the mid-1990s, it is worth trying to see what the Chinese government has done as a nation-state. By considering the trade of cultural and technological commodities as if they were any other goods and evaluating their direct or indirect impacts on the economy, policy makers in several countries have sought to promote or channel investments if they are perceived to produce social benefits, especially economic benefits (Pratt, 2005).

With the recent growth of Korean popular culture and digital technologies, including digital games and smartphones in both Asian and Western markets, Jin (2014) argues that the restructuring of the Korean ICTs and cultural industries has been directed under the banner of neoliberal globalization beginning in the early 1990s. The Korean government, however, has been deeply involved in the process as a primary player instead of decreasing its role. Therefore, the Korean ICTs and cultural industries have especially become a show window that policy makers and media scholars need to carefully analyze when it comes to the role of the nation-state.

Platform technologies also are not separate from governments because they are the primary engines for the digital economy. The roles of national politics and the relationship between policy makers and domestic forces are crucial for the growth of information and communication technologies, including platforms.

PLATFORM POLITICS IN GOOGLE

The critical juncture between the nation-state and technology is hardly new, and the same logic applies in platform technologies. There are several significant cases showing the crucial role of the government in the invention and diffusion of platforms. We currently witness it with search engines, smartphones, digital games, and social network sites, both nationally and globally. To begin with, the continuing role of the governments can be clearly seen in the battles between Western and non-Western forces in the realm of search engines. In fact, the tug-of-war between the U.S. and China regarding Google in China has been an exemplary case in understanding the role of the nation-state in the era of platform.

Google started its business in 1998, and then, as one of the most significant platforms, launched Google.cn—a filtered search engine for Internet users in China in January 2006. Unlike its launch of Google in other countries, Google launched Google.cn while agreeing to some censorship of search results, as required by the Chinese government. For example, in early June 2014, the authorities in China made Google's services largely inaccessible, a move most likely related to the government's broad efforts to stifle discussion of the 25th anniversary of the crackdown on prodemocracy demonstrators in Tiananmen Square on June 3 and 4, 1989. In addition to Google's search engines being blocked, the company's products, including Gmail, Calendar, and Translate, were affected (Levin, 2014). As this incident proves, taking its major role as a gatekeeper, the Chinese government, from the beginning, has regulated the Western search engine, resulting in the growth of domestic search engines. The Chinese government also greatly plays a key role because it blocks Facebook and Twitter.

More importantly, the U.S. government has jumped into the process in the name of human rights and national interests. As is well-documented, due to the restrictions and some cyberattacks allegedly targeting Gmail, Google warned that it might end its operations in China (*BBC News*, 2010). A global controversy surrounding Google erupted on January 12, 2010, when David Drummond (2010), Google's Senior Vice President of Corporate Development and its Chief Legal Officer, posted a statement on Google's official blog. Drummond stated that "in mid-December, we detected a highly sophisticated and targeted attack on our corporate infrastructure originating from China that resulted in the theft of intellectual property from Google." Drummond also noted that "we have evidence to suggest that a primary goal of the attackers was accessing the Gmail accounts of Chinese human rights activists." Drummond strongly stated:

> "we have decided we are no longer willing to continue censoring our results on Google.cn, and so over the next few weeks we will be discussing with the Chinese government the basis on which we could operate an unfiltered search engine within the law, if at all. We recognize that this may well mean having to shut down Google.cn, and potentially our offices in China" (2010).

The Google affair demonstrates how globalization raises the role of the nation-state in the realm of platforms. Because the economic fates of America and China are increasingly entwined, and as our contrasting political systems clash, "the two nations produce an escalating stream of communication about each other, their commercial relationship, and how their political trajectories will, in large part, shape the contours of the twenty-first century" (Hartnett, 2011, 412). This case looked like private business; however, the two governments jumped into the affairs due to several reasons, in particular commercial benefits.

The U.S. Government in the Google Affair

Several parts of the U.S. government and media have jumped into the saga between Google and the Chinese government. When White House spokesman Nicholas Shapiro referred to "recent cyber-intrusions," critics noted that the list included the August 2006 web-attack on the U.S. Department of Defense; the November 2006 targeting of the U.S. Naval War College; the August 2007 intrusion into the computers of the British Security Service, the French Prime Minister's office, and the German Chancellor's office; the October 2007 espionage at the Oak Ridge National Laboratory; and the October 2008 hacking into the Skype accounts of expatriate Chinese dissidents. In fact, computer security experts indicated that such Chinese cyber-intrusions have targeted computers in 103 countries, amounting to a massive, globalized campaign (Hartnett, 2011).

Indeed, in the wake of China's alleged attacks on Google services, several U.S. media, including *New York Times,* framed it as "cyber-warfare" and claimed that China was engaging in "vast electronic spying operations" targeting U.S. military intelligence, international corporate research, and political dissidents around the globe. The episode and the resulting flap highlight an important point about China. That point is that Beijing is increasingly devoting itself to cyber-warfare. This is a cheap way to counter American dominance in traditional military fields. If the U.S. and China ever jostle with force, Beijing may hit us not with missiles but with cyber-infiltrations that shut down the electrical grid, disrupt communications, and tinker with the floodgates of dams (Kristof, 2010).

The Google affair entered a new phase of concern when *The Washington Post* reported that in order to investigate the cyber-intrusions, Google had turned for help to the FBI and the National Security Agency (NSA). The National Security Agency is widely understood to have the government's biggest and smartest collection of geeks—the guys that are more skilled at network warfare than just about anyone on the planet. So, in a sense, it's only natural that Google would turn to the NSA after the company was hit by an ultra-sophisticated hack attack (Shachtman, 2010).

As *Wired* correctly observes, the NSA and its predecessors have a long history of spying on huge numbers of people, both at home and abroad. According to *The Guardian* (Ball, 2013), the National Security Agency has continued to conduct the same old tactic. For example, as of October 2013, it monitored the phone conversations of 35 world leaders after being given the numbers by an official in another U.S. government department. Using a source, *The Guardian* reported that the confidential memo reveals that the NSA encourages senior officials in its "custom" departments, such as the White House, State, and the Pentagon, to share their "Rolodexes" so the agency can add the phone numbers of leading foreign politicians to their surveillance systems. The document notes that one unnamed U.S. official handed over 200 numbers, including those of the 35 world leaders. These were immediately tasked for monitoring by the NSA. During the Cold War, the NSA worked with corporations like Western Union to intercept and read telegrams. During the war on terror years, the NSA teamed up with the telecommunications companies to eavesdrop on customers' phone calls and internet traffic from the telcos' switching stations (Shachtman, 2010). The world's largest intelligence gathering outfit, the NSA was tarred with having done much of the dirty work of the Bush administration's post-9/11 surveillance programs (Hartnett, 2011).[2] As Andrejevic (2013, 1) points out, "the resulting flood of information is, in part, a function of the technological developments that have made it possible to automatically collect, store, and share fantastic amounts of data. However, making sense of this information trove at the all-too-human receiving end can pose a problem," as is well proven in the case of the NSA. The NSA as a powerful state agency has used the carrot-and-stick approach in dealing with ICT corporations, including platform firms over the last several decades.

Google and other leading technology firms were furious at the Chinese government for engaging in cyber-espionage, thievery, and surveillance. The CCP was furious over allegations of cyber-espionage, U.S. arms sales to Taiwan, and U.S. support for the Dalai Lama. The Obama administration was furious over Chinese attacks, but unable to do anything about them. And the U.S. Left, once again demonizing the most basic practices of national security, was reverting to typical anti-everything-ism to announce that instead of making good sense, a Google-NSA alliance amounted to a harbinger of the coming techno-fascism (Hartnett, 2011, 416–417).

As the *Washington Post* reported (Nakashima, 2010), the world's largest Internet search company and the world's most powerful electronic surveillance organization are teaming up in the name of cybersecurity. Under an agreement that is still being finalized, the NSA would help Google analyze a major corporate espionage attack that the firm said originated in China and targeted its computer networks, according to cybersecurity experts familiar with the matter. The objective is to better defend Google—and its users—from future attack. The partnership strikes at the core of one of the most sensitive issues for the government and private industry in the evolving world of cybersecurity: how to balance privacy and national security interest. Director of National Intelligence Dennis C. Blair called the Google attacks, which the company acknowledged in January 2010, a "wake-up call." Cyberspace cannot be protected, he said, without a "collaborative effort that incorporates both the U.S. private sector and our international partners" (Nakashima, 2010).

As discussed, several theoreticians (Hardt and Negri, 2000; Robinson, 2007) argue that the nation-state was significant in Lenin's imperialism; therefore, they claim that imperialism, which relied on sovereign nation-states, no longer exists in the midst of the globalization process.

In the 21st century, however, whereas TNCs have developed and advanced new technologies, nation-states, both the U.S. government and other governments, including China, support the growth of their own platforms. These new political agendas certainly construct the new form of imperialism in tandem with platforms. The U.S. government, based on its state power, has greatly supported American-based platform owners in global politics. The involvement of the U.S. government and the Chinese government in the wake of China's attacks on Google services has become a recent case in this regard.

In the midst of the conflicts between the Chinese government and Google, the Chinese government has restricted Google discussion topics that the government finds objectionable, such as independence drives in the regions of Tibet and Xinjiang and the banned religious movement Falun Gong. For the tens of thousands of censors employed by the Chinese government, blocking access to restricted information both at home and abroad is an ongoing struggle. Search engines are prevented from linking to sensitive content (Ramzy, 2010).

Interestingly enough, the U.S. as a nation-state has strongly supported Google in the name of humanitarianism. Recognizing that events were escalating rapidly both at home and abroad and hoping to spin the crisis to the U.S.'s advantage, President Barack Obama called upon one of his administration's most experienced and articulate spokespersons, Secretary of State Hillary Clinton, to step into the cauldron (Hartnett, 2011). She responded by delivering a speech that combined heady talk of global peace with threatening imagery, thus adding further fuel to the fire of conflict by reprising the rhetoric of belligerent humanitarianism. Clinton gave two major speeches in 2010 and 2011. While the Google affair was swirling, Secretary of State Clinton, by President Obama's call, stepped to the lectern to deliver a rousing defense of international human rights and free speech (Hartnett, 2011). Clinton gave the first significant speech on Internet freedom around the world, making it clear exactly where the U.S. stood in January 2010:

> "on their own, new technologies do not take sides in the struggle for freedom and progress, but the U.S. does. We stand for a single Internet where all of humanity has equal access to knowledge and ideas. And we recognize that the world's information infrastructure will become what we and others make of it. This challenge may be new, but our responsibility to help ensure the free exchange of ideas goes back to the birth of our republic."
>
> (U.S. Secretary of State, 2010)

In her speech, Clinton cited China as among a number of countries where there has been "a spike in threats to the free flow of information" over the past year. She also named Tunisia, Uzbekistan, Egypt, Iran, Saudi Arabia, and Vietnam (U.S. Secretary of State, 2010). As Hartnett (2011, 418) aptly puts it, "Secretary of State Clinton's belligerent humanitarianism was based on a series of assumptions about American exceptionalism: we are the world's moral leaders, its technological and corporate masters, and the only nation capable of and willing to enforce the rule of law."

China Called It Imperialism

China, of course, rejected a call by Clinton for the lifting of restrictions on the Internet in the communist country, denouncing her criticism as false and damaging to bilateral ties. China's Foreign Ministry spokesman Ma Zhaoxu said in a statement posted on the ministry's website:

> "regarding comments that contradict facts and harm China-U.S. relations, we are firmly opposed. We urged the U.S. side to respect facts and stop using the so-called freedom of the Internet to make unjustified accusations against China. The Chinese Internet is open and China is the country witnessing the most active development of the Internet."
>
> (Mufson, 2010, A14)

Ma added that China regulated the Web according to law and in keeping with its national conditions and cultural traditions. It is evident that the Chinese government understands the vast size of the Chinese Internet market, and it has taken measures to cultivate the growth of local information technology, including Google's competitor Baidu.cn. (*Global Times,* 2010). As Clinton envisioned, Chairman Jiang Zemin believed that information technology would fuel the growth in other sectors (Lee, 2010). The Chinese government has maneuvered to protect its own technology-driven corporations due to their significance for the national economy. China's aggressive investment in information technology and its strict policy against foreign investment have created a favorable business environment for local Internet companies such as Baidu.cn. The competitiveness of the top Chinese Internet sites may be due not only to their quality and usefulness, but also to state policy (Lee, 2010).

China's English-language *Global Times* characterized Clinton's speech as a disguised attempt to impose [U.S.] values on other cultures in the name of democracy. The newspaper then dragged out another snarling phrase to denounce Clinton's overtures on freedom of speech: information imperialism (*Global Times,* 2010).[3] The official rhetoric charged that Google practices "information imperialism," which threatened China's judicial sovereignty and core interests. It lumped Google in with the American government, labeling Google as a tool of American hegemony that threatened to turn China into a colony of Western values (Zhang, 2013). The writer of *Global Times* argued that "[t]he U.S. campaign for uncensored and free flow of information on an unrestricted Internet is a disguised attempt to impose its values on other cultures in the name of democracy." Drawing on the victim theme of the century of humiliation narratives, the author asserted that China's real stake in this confrontation is its refusal to be "victimized by information imperialism." Clinton's call for unfettered access to information and ideas on the Internet was viewed as an American strategy for subversion and exportation of American values (Zhang, 2013, 466). Furthermore, the president of *People's Daily Online*, He Jiazheng, published an editorial "Don't Become a Tool of Hegemony, Google." He argued that since the United States' power had declined, the United States has shifted its strategic focus from the use of military force to the Internet. During this shift Google simply became a tool of the United States' Internet hegemony (Zhang, 2013, 466).

The second round of debate between the U.S. and China occurred in February 2011. Hillary Clinton again warned repressive governments, such as China, Cuba, and Syria, not to restrict Internet freedom, saying such efforts will ultimately fail. Calling the Internet the public space of the future, Clinton enumerated all the reasons that freedom of expression must be the overriding ethos of this worldwide landscape (Goodale, 2011). As expected, the Chinese government also warned the U.S. not to use the issues to meddle in China's internal affairs. The government expressed that Internet freedom in China is guaranteed by law, and stated "we are opposed to any country using Internet freedom as a pretext for interference in Chinese affairs" (States News Service, 2011).

These events firmly prove the major role of the nation-states and the reality of the free flow of information. In the 21st century, the U.S. government has intensified its efforts to penetrate the global information market. Direct government intervention and support by the State Department have developed and expanded U.S. platforms throughout the world. The U.S. campaign for an uncensored and free flow of information on an unrestricted Internet would be a disguised attempt to impose its values on other countries in the name of democracy, as some foreign media claim:

> "In the global information order, countries that are disadvantaged could not produce the massive flow of information required, and could never rival the Western countries in terms of information control and dissemination…it must be realized that when it comes to information content, quantity, direction and flow, there is absolutely no equality and fairness. The online freedom of unrestricted access is, thus, only one-way traffic, contrary to the spirit of democracy and calculated to strengthen a monopoly."
>
> (*Global Times*, 2010)

Finally, another key factor in the confrontation between the U.S. and China surrounding Google is the bulldozer force of global capitalism. One financial observer predicts that, with its business dealings renewed in China, Google's online advertising in the People's Republic of China (PRC) could net the company between $5 and $6 billion annually, proving that the giants of neoliberal capitalism and authoritarian regimes can walk happily hand-in-hand. This means that Google and other transnational corporations will continue to feel intense pressure to partner with nondemocratic states: in an age of globalization, the laws of international capitalism trump "candid" concerns over human rights. And so, since the Summer of 2010, when similar questions about censorship, new media technologies, emerging markets, and the limits of human rights flared in India, Saudi Arabia, Kuwait, and Bahrain, no U.S. companies have pulled out of these states, and the White House has issued no statements about their compromised political systems. Instead, President Obama has announced deals with China amounting to $45 billion. And so the global market marches on: democracy, free speech, and human rights be damned (Hartnett, 2011):

> "The champions of globalizing neoliberalism and belligerent humanitarianism would have us believe that that complicated dance will eventually meander into the neighborhood of democracy. Critics of the missionary myth of free markets would have us believe instead that that strange embrace will lead the lucky few into swanky post-national bistros while consigning billions to lives of poverty. Google and other

> technophiles would have us believe that the Internet will somehow prod the CCP toward opening up the flow of ideas and information."
> (Hartnett, 2011, 429)

Google is not the only case proving the massive involvement of the U.S. government. In the midst of anti-government demonstrations through SNSs in the Middle East in recent years, for example, the U.S. government has become vehemently involved in the tug-of-war with these countries. SNSs are important tools that give voice to the governments as well as individuals; therefore, many governments have tried to utilize SNSs in different ways. Most of all, SNSs can be used to further promote government information and services. This could include setting up a LinkedIn group, a Facebook group, or a Ning community. Doing so expands the government's outreach capabilities and ability to interact (Social Networks and Government, 2011).

Therefore, the U.S. State Department has been developing Twitter accounts in Chinese, Russian, and Hindi, adding to a suite of feeds that already includes French, Spanish, Arabic, and Farsi, which is another form of the government initiative (*BBC News*, 2011). What we have to understand is that governments also take key roles as users of these platforms, perhaps the largest users. "The overwhelming materiality of power over technology in capitalist nation states—a power structure itself was practiced during the Internet shut-down in Egypt at the start of the revolution" (Aouragh, 2012, 528). Since the early 1990s, several people have insisted that the market is the solution to all problems, that private enterprise is the preferred means to achieve solid economic results, and that government is the enemy.

However, the last several decades' record is of government initiative, support, and promotion of information and communication policies. The principle—vital to the worldwide export of American cultural product and American way of life—of the free flow of information has become a universal virtue to both the information industries and the U.S. government (H. Schiller, 1999). The free flow of information had been the single most important issue in U.S. foreign policy (H. Schiller, 1976), and there is no exception in the Obama government. From the huge subsidies for the information/cultural industries to ideological initiatives, the U.S. government has become a primary actor, which also applies to platform imperialism.

In the 21st century, global economic participation depends on social media/digital media. It is the life-line of neoliberal globalization. The World Trade Organization (WTO) allows the flow of market intelligence for greater profit margins, and thus if we zoom out we can see that enforced institutionalized policies like the Free Trade Agreement (FTA) increased rather than prevented digital divides. But the most important feature of this imperialism, control, and ownership, is very prevalent through what is called 'global governance' directed by big powerful institutes that strongly privilege industrialized free market states. This consolidation can only occur through state support, to be precise (Aouragh, 2012). In the post-Cold War world, national interests still matter a great deal, and it seems that the U.S. intends to act as a hegemonic power in the midst of neoliberal globalization.

INTERPLAY BETWEEN NATION-STATES AND TRANSNATIONAL CORPORATIONS

When society looks to regulate an emerging form of information distribution, be it the telegraph or radio or the Internet, it is in many ways making decisions about what that technology is, what it is for, what sociotechnical arrangements are best suited to help it achieve that, and what it must not be allowed to become (Benkler, 2003). This is not just in the words of the policymakers themselves. "Interested third parties, particularly the companies that provide these services, are deeply invested in fostering a regulatory paradigm that gives them the most leeway to conduct their businesses, imposes the fewest restrictions on their service provision, protects them from liability for things they hope not to be liable for and paints them in the best light in terms of the public interest" (Gillespie, 2010, 356). As in the case of Hollywood, in which major film production corporations and the Motion Picture Association of America (MPAA), clearly shows, the interplay between the government and TNCs is one of the major drivers in the growth of the film industry. As the U.S. government has continuously supported Hollywood backed by the MPAA and major film producers (Wasko, 2003), ICT corporations and their representative associations have continuously developed close relationships with the government, resulting in the inseparable role of the nation-state.

In fact, Google, in its newly adopted role of aggressive lobbyist, has become increasingly vocal on a number of policy issues, including net neutrality, spectrum allocation, freedom of speech, and political transparency (Phillips, 2006; Gillespie, 2010). Platform imperialism has been developed and influenced by sometimes cooperative and at other times conflicting relationships among the government, domestic capital, and TNCs. Although TNCs are valuable players to platform technologies, the nation-states are also primary actors in international negotiations. In the 21st century, the U.S. government has intensified its efforts to control the global information market. As Panitch and Gindin (2003, 35–36) succinctly argue:

> "neoliberal globalization is the acceleration of the drive to a seamless world of capital accumulation, and the mechanisms of neoliberalism may have been economic, but in essence it was a political response to the democratic gains that had been previously achieved by subordinate classes and which had become, in a new context and from capital's perspective, barriers to accumulation."

Panitch and Gindin (2003, 35–36) argue that "once the American state itself moved in this direction, it had a new status: capitalism evolved to a new form of social rule that promised, and largely delivered, (a) the revival of the productive base for American dominance; (b) a universal model for restoring the conditions for profits in other developed countries; and (c) the economic conditions for integrating global capitalism."

In the realm of platform technologies, direct government intervention and support by the U.S. State Department have developed and expanded U.S. platforms throughout the world. The U.S. government has been actively involved in the discourse of the free flow of information, and of course, one of the primary backgrounds is Google. The company lobbied 13 government agencies in 2009, spending just under $6 million in the process. Google chiefly focused on freedom of speech on the Internet in 2010, particularly because of its highly publicized battles with the Chinese government. Google urged lawmakers to adopt policies that assure a neutral and open Internet at home and put pressure on foreign governments that censor the Web (Goldman, 2010). For Google, this diversity has contributed to its considerable presence among lawmakers. The company has lobbied on issues ranging from patent reform and cloud computing to renewable energy. From 2007 to 2010, Google increased its lobbying expenditure by more than $1 million each year. In 2010, the company spent a record $5.1 million (Chiu, 2011). When Google's second-quarter profits were below expectations in 2010, the company explained that profit margins were hit by Google's increased hiring, weakening of the Euro, and acquisition costs. Google also stated that the company is facing legal and lobbying costs as it faces increased pressure from regulators (ComputerWeekly.com, 2010).

Google's lobbying costs continue to increase. Google led in lobbying spending by 10 tech firms who pumped a combined $61.15 million into efforts to influence federal regulators and lawmakers in 2013, up 15.9 percent from the previous year, according to records filed with the Clerk of the House this week. Consumer Watchdog (2014), a nonpartisan nonprofit public interest group, analyzed the spending records and stated, "policymaking in Washington is all about how much money you can throw around. These tech guys are increasingly willing to spend whatever it takes to buy what they want." Google spent $14.06 million on lobbying in 2013, a 14.7 percent decrease from 2012 when it was the target of an antitrust investigation by the Federal Trade Commission. Other tech firms are not far behind. Microsoft spent $10.49 million on 2013 lobbying, up 29.7 percent from 2012.

What is significant is this scene is the rise of platform firms. "The rise of Google as a top-tier Washington player fully captures the arc of change in the influence business. Nine years ago the company opened a one-ma lobbying shop, disdainful of the capital's pay-to-pay culture. Since then, Google has soared to near the top of the city's lobbying ranks" (Hamburger and Gold, 2014). Most of all, Facebook, which has substantially increased in its Washington presence over the last two years, set another company record in its effort to buy influence in Washington. Spending soared 61.2

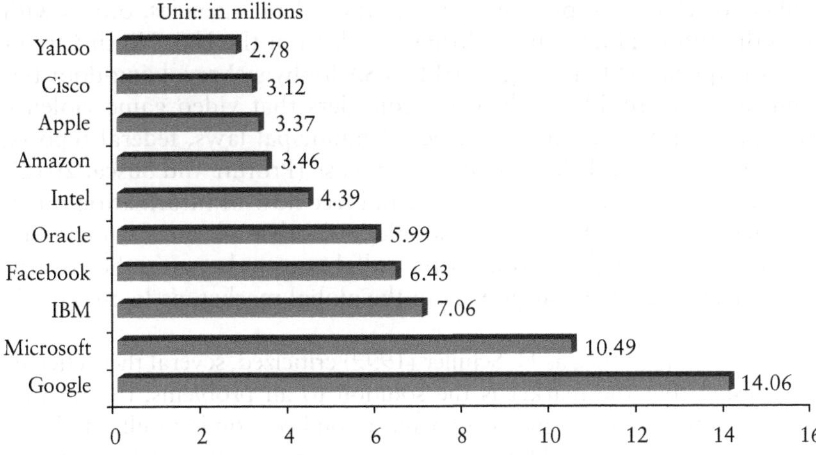

Figure 4.1 Top 10 Tech Companies in Lobbying in 2013.
Source: Consumer Watchdog (2014). Google Leads Pack as 10 Tech Firms Pump $61.15 Million into 2013 Lobbying Efforts.

percent to $6.43 million in 2013 from $3.99 million in 2012 (Consumer Watchdog, 2014) (See Figure 4.1).

The nexus of private corporations and the government is everywhere, of course. In 1994, the Interactive Digital Software Association, renamed Entertainment Software Association (ESA) in 2003, was created after politicians expressed concerns about violent video game content and its potential negative effects on children (Lubin, 2006, cited in Proffitt and Susca, 2012). The ESA, the $60.4 billion (Takahashi, 2010, cited in Proffitt and Susca, 2012) video game industry's largest and most powerful trade organization and lobbying group, also owns and operates the Entertainment Software Rating Board (ESRB), the industry panel that oversees its voluntary video game ratings. This panel and its ratings system were created as a result of similar political and social pressure related to violent video games (Lubin, 2006). The ESA represents 90 percent of video game manufacturers including divisions of massive conglomerates like Disney, Time Warner, and Sony and spends millions of dollars annually lobbying Congress and other federal agencies that influence, enforce, or create media policy.[4]

The ESA also contributes directly to political candidates; between 2004 and September 2011, the ESA spent $23.2 million lobbying the government and nearly $1.3 million on direct campaign contributions, with much of that money devoted to politicians in states where video game regulation had been proposed (Proffitt and Susca, 2012). In 2003, a *Wall Street Journal* reporter wrote that proposed restrictions on gaming companies that included labeling content had failed due in large part to "heavy lobbying, lawsuits and threats of legal action by the videogame industry" (Pereira, 2003). In 2011, the Center for Responsive Politics identified 28 lobbyists working on behalf of the ESA, including former members of Congress, previous lawyers for federal agencies, others with ties to the White House, and a former clerk from the U.S. Ninth Circuit Court of Appeals ("Lobbying," 2011). ESA lobbyists' revolving-door ties to industry are troubling when one considers that video game violence and regulation have been the subject of municipal laws, federal reports, and, most recently, a U.S. Supreme Court case (Proffitt and Susca, 2012). The U.S. campaign for an uncensored and free flow of information on an unrestricted Internet backed by Google and other platforms, including Microsoft, has been clear proof of the collaboration between the government and TNCs, two great powers in the global market, as Lenin (1917) argued.

Since the early 1990s, as H. Schiller (1999) criticized, several theoreticians have insisted that the market is the solution to all problems, that private enterprise is the preferred means to achieve solid economic results, and that government is the enemy. However, as the case of Google in China proves, as well as intellectual property rights related global politics, the last several decades' record is of government initiative, support, and promotion of information and communication policies. The principle—vital to the worldwide export of American cultural product and American way of life—of the free flow of information has arguably become a universal virtue to both the information industries and the U.S. government (H. Schiller, 1999), and this fundamental political agenda continues in the Obama government. The U.S. government has become a primary actor in tandem with TNCs, which also applies to platform imperialism.

The U.S. is not the only country to actualize the increasing role of the government in the field of digital/social technologies in the midst of neoliberal norms. The Chinese government also capitalizes on neoliberal globalization, meaning the role of China in global capitalism has rapidly increased. One needs to be very careful, though, because "China is not capitalist despite the rise of a capitalist class and capitalist enterprises" (Arrighi, 2007, 331):

> "The capitalist character of marked-based development is not determined by the presence of capitalist institutions and dispositions but by the relation of state power to capital. Add as many capitalists as you like to a market economy, but unless the state has been subordinated to their class interest, the market economy remains non-capitalist."
>
> (Arrighi, 2007, 331–332)

The Chinese state in Arrighi's view still retains a high degree of autonomy from the capitalist class and is therefore able to act in the national rather than in a class interest (Robinson, 2010).

Since the late 1970s, the Chinese state has undergone a radical transformation in order to pursue substantive linkages with transnational capitalism. Neoliberal ideas have been influential in China as the post-Mao leadership embraced the market system as a means to develop the country (Zhao, 2008). In *A Brief History of Neoliberalism*, David Harvey (2005, 120) points out that "the outcome in China has been the construction of a particular kind of market economy that increasingly incorporates neoliberal elements interdigitated with authoritarian centralized control." As The Top Sites on the Web table (Table 3.1) shows, Chinese platforms, including Baidu, QQ, and Taobao, utilize the targeted advertising capital business model, which is not different from U.S. Internet capitalism.

Of course, this does not imply that China has entirely adopted neoliberal capitalist reform. Although China's transition from a planned economy to a socialist market economy is substantial, China also poses an alternative to the Washington Consensus, which emphasizes the continuing role of the government in the market. As Zhao (2008, 37) puts it, the Chinese government has developed both "neoliberalism as exception" and "exceptions to neoliberalism" for the national economy and culture. The Chinese government has developed a market-friendly economy; however, at the same time, it continues to play a primary role in the market.

In summary, when society looks to regulate an emerging form of information distribution, be it the telegraph or radio or the Internet, it is in many ways making decisions about what that technology is, what it is for, what sociotechnical arrangements are best suited to help it achieve that, and what it must not be allowed to become (Benkler, 2003). This is not just in the words of the policymakers themselves. Interested third parties, particularly the companies that provide these services, are "deeply invested in fostering a regulatory paradigm that gives them the most leeway to conduct their businesses, imposes the fewest restrictions on their service provision, protects them from liability for things they hope not to be liable for and paints them in the best light in terms of the public interest" (Gillespie, 2010, 356).

Google, again, in its newly adopted role of aggressive lobbyist, has become increasingly vocal on a number of policy issues, including net neutrality, spectrum allocation, freedom of speech, and political transparency (Phillips, 2006; Gillespie, 2010). Platform imperialism has been developed and influenced by sometimes cooperative and at other times conflicting relationships among the government, domestic capital, and TNCs. TNCs are valuable players to platform technologies; the nation-states are also primary actors in international negotiations. A change in the way the nation-state operates is likely but such a change is not necessarily going to indicate a weakening or end to the nation-state (Hewitt-Page, 2013). As Marx stated (1867), the capitalist expansion of TNCs with the nexus with the nation-state inevitably takes the political form of imperialism, and it is further evident in the case with the development of platform imperialism.

In the era of platform, the role of the nation-state remains as one of the most significant forces. Whereas there are several important factors for the growth of technologies, including the emerging role of TNCs and venture capitals, the nation-state has always been a primary player in the development of new technologies, including the Internet. Due to the massive capital involvement in the early stage of the development, government research and development projects provide the fundamentals for several information and communication technologies. The nation-state has also supported the dispersion of ICTs through its policy measures, including the deregulation of the market in favor of the growth of new technologies. Regardless, building telecommunications infrastructure heavily relies on the government. The government intervention is not required in several parts of the global economy anymore, as in the case of foreign currency exchange; however, we can witness the increasing role of the government in national security, as the post-9/11 era exemplifies.

Platform technologies are not separated from the government because they are primary forces for the digital economy as well as national security, which ask for the continuing role of the government. While TNCs have developed and advanced new technologies, the U.S. government and other governments have also been major players in the globalized world because they need to support the growth of their own platforms. Several transnational platforms, such as Google, Facebook, Apple, and video game corporations, have massively lobbied the government in order to secure their growth both domestically and globally. In particular, when these platforms go global, the U.S. government and other governments in non-Western countries have vehemently supported their own businesses. The nation-states have always been significant in international negotiations alongside TNCs.

CONCLUSION

This chapter has analyzed the role of the government in the realm of platforms in the process of neoliberal globalization. Neoliberalism has emphasized the decreasing role of the government in order to guarantee the maximum profits of the private sector. While several countries have pursed a small government regime in actualizing neoliberal globalization, several countries have not followed this logic. Instead, some countries, including Canada, China, and Korea, have intensified the role of the government in several areas, particularly in digital/social technologies due to the significant role of platforms in their countries. The U.S. is not exceptional in the race. The U.S. has not retreated from the global markets. The U.S. government has utilized its strong stance as a global leader in politics, economy, and culture in order to continue to reign supreme in the era of social media.

The pressures of economic, cultural, and political globalization ushered in by the rapid growth of ICTs, in this case, platform technologies, have challenged the sovereignty of nation-states by weakening their ability to control major national affairs and to protect their citizens. The proponents of globalization claim that nation-states have lost their power in the realm of economy and culture. What they argue is that the national boundary is gone and cannot continue to function to shape people's cultural identities and cultural sovereignty. However, the power of the nation-state does not exist in isolation but is formed and developed through engagement in international relations (Jin, 2014). Far from the nation disappearing with globalized commerce, "hyper-nationalism and a semi-secret state presence are integral to many countries and even to the U.S. cultural industries and crucial to its empire" (Miller, 2010, 143).

As proven in the case of Google affairs between the U.S. and China, although it is seemingly a private enterprise sphere, two powerful governments must be in the front line in order to guarantee their national benefits. The U.S. government—the strongest supporter of neoliberal globalization—emphasizing a small government regime, had no hesitation to take a primary role representing the private sector as it did many times previously in the name of democracy and humanitarianism, but also capitalism. The Chinese government also jumped into the tug-of-war, as expected, in the name of nationalism. This implies that whether democratic or socialistic, the role of government remains key in the era of neoliberal globalization. Whereas several Western governments, including the U.S. and the U.K. may give away their power to the private sector resulting in the debacle of welfare states, these countries alongside nondemocratic governments have continued to be vanguards in global affairs in the name of national interests.

Despite the fact that there are challenges to state sovereignty and autonomy in the era of globalization, states hesitate to yield all control to new forces. Thus, the "end of nation state" approach by Susan Strange and Kenichi Ohmae is too deterministic. It gives the impression that it is an inescapable process. State sovereignty might be affected by the transformations taking place in the world, yet it is not intended and depends on unknown circumstances (Göksel, 2004). Globalization is not a new phenomenon.

Over the past five centuries, technological change has progressively reduced the barriers to international integration. Transatlantic communication, for example, has evolved from sail power to steam to telegraph to telephone to commercial aircraft and now to the Internet. Yet states have become neither weaker nor less important during this odyssey. On the contrary, in the countries with the most advanced and internationally integrated economies, governments' ability to tax and redistribute incomes, regulate the economy, and monitor the activity of their citizens has increased beyond all recognition. This has been especially true over the past century (Wolf, 2001). The borderless flow of technology, culture, and capital does not mean the demise of the nation-state because, for both regulation and deregulation, the government is always taking a primary role.

The proposition that "globalization makes states unnecessary is even less credible than the idea that it makes states impotent. If anything, the exact opposite is true, for at least three reasons" (Wolf, 2001, 188–189). First, the ability of a society to take advantage of the opportunities offered by international economic integration depends on the quality of public goods, such as property rights, an honest civil service, personal security, and basic education. Without an appropriate legal framework in particular, the web of potentially rewarding contracts is vastly reduced. This point may seem trivial, but many developing economies have failed to achieve these essential preconditions of success. Second, the state normally defines identity. A sense of belonging is part of the people's sense of security, and one that most people would not want to give up, even in the age of globalization. It is perhaps not surprising that some of the most successfully integrated economies are small homogeneous countries with a strong sense of collective identity. Third, international governance rests on the ability of individual states to provide and guarantee stability. The bedrock of international order is the territorial state with its monopoly on coercive power within its jurisdiction. Cyberspace does not change this: economies are ultimately run for and by human beings who have a physical presence and, therefore, a physical location. Globalization does not make states unnecessary. On the contrary, for people to be successful in exploiting the opportunities afforded by international integration, they need states at both ends of their transactions. Failed states, disorderly states, weak states, and corrupt states are shunned as the black holes of the global economic system (Wolf, 2001, 188–189).

The social media sector relies heavily on government policies and investments and provides an important illustration of how proactive government policies and internal collaboration have become central to the efforts to establish national competitiveness in the 21st century (Holroyd and Coates, 2012). The social media revolution requires extensive government involvements as both regulators and deregulators, as well as the major customers within the nation. When it goes global, the role of the nation-state is crucial because they protect the private sector with state power, and in this case, a few Western countries have vehemently supported TNCs who own social media because social media are primary engines for both the digital economy and culture.

NOTES

1. McChesney (2013, 51–52) focuses on the notions of externality and public good, which cannot be done without the continuing and leading role of the nation-state. He claims that "the more a good or service has public-good attributes, the more there is a need for the government to play a role in creating policies to encourage production of that good and to share the expense equitably."
2. The NAS has been indeed everywhere. As revealed in September 2014, for example, Yahoo might have had to pay millions of dollars per day in fines if the company kept refusing to comply with U.S. government requests for its users' Internet data, newly released documents show. In a small victory for Yahoo's legal challenges to U.S. spying, a court permitted the company to release on September 12, 2014, 1,500 pages of partly redacted documents that shed light on the scope and force of the government's surveillance methods. One document

shows the U.S. in May 2008 threatened Yahoo with a fine of $250,000 day that would double each week the company failed to turn over data. Yahoo complied on May 12, 2008, giving in to the National Security Agency's Prism electronic surveillance program that had operated without public knowledge until former agency contractor Edward Snowden exposed it in 2013. The revelations ignited a debate about the scope of U.S. spying and prompted Internet companies to take additional measures to boost the use of encryption for e-mails and other communications (Strohm, 2014).

3. *People's Daily*, the party's mouthpiece, and *Global Times*, a populist and nationalistic newspaper, offer both English and Chinese news and commentary and hone closely to the official line. Therefore, the articles and editorials in these newspapers can be considered as official statements by the Chinese government (Zhang, 2013).
4. There are hundreds of pages of campaign finance records including lobbying reports and lists of campaign contributions. All of these reports are publicly available through The National Institute on Money in State Politics website at http://www.followthemoney.org/search-results/SearchForm?Search=nea and The Center for Responsive Politics website at https://www.opensecrets.org/. Where appropriate, text citations from specific reports and records are provided.

REFERENCES

Anderson. B. (1983). *Imagined Communities*. London: Verso.

Aouragh, M. (2012). Social media, mediation and the Arab revolutions. *tripleC* 10(2): 518–536.

Ball, J. (2013). NSA monitored calls of 35 world leaders after US official handed over contacts. *The Guardian*. 25 October. http://www.theguardian.com/world/2013/oct/24/nsa-surveillance-world-leaders-calls.

BBC News (2010). Google may end China operations. January 13.

Chin, Y.C. (2003). The nation-state in a globalizing media environment: China's regulatory policies on transborder TV drama flow. *Javnost-the Public* 10(4): 75–92.

Chiu, E. (2011). Google, Facebook lead new generation of technology companies pressing government for favorable treatment. OpenScreats.org. 17 February. http://www.opensecrets.org/news/2011/02/google-facebook-lead-new-generation.html.

ComputerWeekly.com (2010). Google share price dips after profits in strong Q2 disappoint investors. 16 July. http://www.computerweekly.com/news/1280093281/Google-share-price-dips-after-profits-in-strong-Q2-disappoint-investors.

Drummond, D. (2010). A new approach to China. 12 January. http://googleblog.blogspot.ca/2010/01/new-approach-to-china.html.

Engel, C. (2000). The Internet and the nation state. In C. Engel and Kenneth H. Heller (eds), *Understanding the Impact of Global Networks on Social, Political and Cultural Values*, 213–272. Baden-Baden: Nomos Verlagsgellschaft.

Friedman, M. (1982). *Capitalism and Freedom*. Chicago: The University of Chicago Press.

Fuchs, C. (2010). New imperialism: Information and media imperialism. *Global Media and Communication* 6(1): 33–60.

Giddens, A. (1999). Runaway world: 1999 Reith lecture. Available online at http://news.bbc.co.uk/hi/english/static/events/reith_99/week1/week1.htm. Last accessed 29 May 2008.

Global Times. (2010). The real stake in free flow of Information. January 22.

Göksel, N.K. (2004). Globalisation and the state. *Center for Strategic Research*. http://sam.gov.tr/wp-content/uploads/2012/02/1.-NiluferKaracasuluGoksel.pdf.

Hamburger, T. and M. Gold (2014). Google, once disdainful of lobbying, now a master of Washington influence. 12 April. *The Washington Post*. Retrieved from http://www.washingtonpost.com/politics/how-google-is-transforming-power-and-politicsgoogle-once-disdainful-of-lobbying-now-a-master-of-washington-influence/2014/04/12/51648b92-b4d3-11e3-8cb6-284052554d74_story.html.

Hardt, M. & Negri, A. (2000). *Empire*. Cambridge, MA: Harvard University Press.

Hartnett, S.J. (2011). Google and the "Twisted Cyber Spy" affair: US–Chinese communication in an age of globalization. *Quarterly Journal of Speech* 97(4): 411–434.

Hewitt-Page, D. (2013). Technology and the nation-state: Governing social complexity. Our Kingdom: Power and Liberty in Britain. 29 May. Accessed on November 8, 2013. http://www.opendemocracy.net/ourkingdom/dylan-hewitt-page/technology-and-nation-state-governing-social-complexity.

Holroyd, C. & Coates, K. (2012). *Digital Media in East Asia: National Innovation and the Transformation of a Region*. New York: Cambria Press.

Jeannotte, S. (2010). Going with the flow: Neoliberalism and cultural policy in Manitoba and Saskatchewan. *Canadian Journal of Communication* 35: 303–324.

Jin, D.Y. (2014). The power of the nation-state amid neoliberal reform: Shifting cultural politics in the new Korean wave. *Pacific Affairs* 87(1): 71–92.

Kristof, N. (2010). Google takes a stand. *The New York Times*. 14 January. http://www.nytimes.com/2010/01/14/opinion/14kristof.html?_r=0.

Kumar, S. (2010). Google Earth and the nation state: Sovereignty in the age of new media. *Global Media and Communication* 6(2): 154–176.

Lee, M.K. (2010). Revisiting "Google in China" question from Political economic perspective. *China Media Research* 6(2): 15–24.

Lobbying: Entertainment Software Association. (2011). Center for Responsive Politics.

McChesney, R. (2008). *The Political Economy of Media: Enduring Issues, Emerging Dilemmas*. New York: Monthly Review Press.

Miller, M. (2004). A view from a fossil: The new economy, creativity and consumption—Two or three things I don't believe In. *International Journal of Cultural Studies* 7(1): 55–65.

Miller, T. (2010). Holy trinity: Nation, pentagon, screen. In Anna Roosvall and Inka Salovaara-Moring (eds.), *Communicating the Nation: National Topographies of Global Media Landscapes*. Goteborg: Nordicom.

Molloy, S. (2003). Realism: A problematic paradigm. *Security Dialogue* 34(1): 71–85.

Morgenthau, H. (1966). Introduction. In David Mitrany, *A Working Peace System*, 2nd ed., pp. 7–11. Chicago, IL: Quadrangle Books.

Morley, D & Robins, K. (1995). *Spaces of Identity: Global Media, Electronic Landscapes and Cultural Boundaries*. London: Routledge.

Mufson, Steven (2010). Chinese government sharply criticizes Clinton's speech urging Internet freedom. *The Washington Post*, January 23, A14.

Nakashima, E. (2010). Google to enlist NSA to ward off attacks. *The Washington Post.* 4 Feb. http://articles.washingtonpost.com/2010-02-04/news/36786801_1_google-attacks-uncensored-search-engine-google-applications.

Ohmae, Kenichi (1996). *The End of the Nation State: The Rise of Regional Economies.* Free Press.

Phillips, Kate (2006). Google joins the lobbying herd. *The New York Times.* March 29. Accessed March 1, 2012. http://www.nytimes.com/2006/03/28/politics/28google.html?pagewanted=all.

Pratt, A. (2005). Cultural industries and public policy: An oxymoron. *International Journal of Cultural Policy* 11(1): 31–44.

Proffitt, Jennifer & Susca, Margot (2012). Follow the money: The Entertainment Software Association attack on video game regulation. ICA Conference, Phoenix, AZ, May 2012.

Ramzy, A. (2010). The great firewall: China's web users battle censorship. *Time.* April 13. Accessed March 1, 2011. http://www.time.com/time/world/article/0,8599,1981566,00.html. Retrieved from http://www.opensecrets.org/lobby/clientsum.php?id= D000025695&year=2011.

Sánchez Ruiz, E. (2001). Globalization, cultural industries, and free trade: The Mexican audiovisual sector in the NAFTA age. In Vincent Mosco and Dan Schiller (eds.), *Continental Order: Integrating North America for Cybercapitalism*, 86–119. New York: Rowman & Littlefield.

Shachtman, N. (2010). 'Don't Be Evil,' meet 'Spy on Everyone': How the NSA deal could kill Google. *Wired.* 4 February. http://www.wired.com/dangerroom/2010/02/from-dont-be-evil-to-spy-on-everyone/.

Sinclair, J. (2007). Cultural globalization and American empire. In Graham Murdock and Janet Wasko (eds.) *Media in the Age of Marketization.* Cresskill, NJ: Hampton Press.

Stig Hjarvard (2003). *Media in a Globalized Society.* Copenhagen: Museum Tusculanum Press.

Strange, S. (1996). *The Declining Authority of States.* In *The Retreat of the State.* Cambridge University Press.

Thussu, D. (2006). *International Communication: Continuity and Change.* London: Arnold.

U.S. Secretary of State (2010). Remarks on Internet Freedom. Accessed March 1, 2012. http://www.state.gov/secretary/rm/2010/01/135519.htm.

Waisbord, S. & Morris, N. (2001). Introduction. In Nancy Morris and Silvio Waisbord (eds.), *Media and Globalization: Why the State Matters.* Lanham: Rowman & Littlefield.

Winseck, D. (2002). Netscapes of power: Convergence, consolidation and power in the Canadian mediascape. *Media, Culture and Society* 24(6): 795–819.

Wolf, M. (2001). Will the nation-state survive globalization? *Foreign Affairs* 80(1): 178–190.

Wu, H. & Chan, J.M. (2007). Globalizing Chinese martial arts cinema: The global-local alliance and the production of Crouching Tiger, Hidden Dragon. *Media, Culture and Society* 29(2): 195–217.

Yochai, B. (2003). Freedom in the commons. *Duke Law Journal* 52: 1245–1276.

Zhang, L. (2013). The Google-China dispute: The Chinese national narrative and rhetorical legitimation of the Chinese Communist Party. *Rhetoric Review* 32(4): 455–472.

5 Intellectual Properties in the Digital Economy

INTRODUCTION

In the 21st century, the rapid growth of the digital media landscape has created enormous tensions between content producers and intellectual property rights holders who are increasingly engaged in a form of culture war over access to and dissemination of information (Downes, 2006). Whereas creative and/or cultural industries have increasingly focused on the production of creativity, intellectual property (IP) rights have become a major arena of social and political conflict over the past several decades. In particular, the global diffusion of social network sites and smartphones has intensified the legal landscape due to the emphasis on patent and design, which means that the era of social media has shifted the nature of legal battles between Western and non-Western countries and their transnational corporations. Platform providers have created massive profits from hardware, software, and services protected by IP laws, including copyrights, patents, and trademarks.

The rapid growth of the era of smartphones has especially raised one of the most significant legal debates. Since Apple released iPhone in January 2007, several mobile phone makers around the world, including Samsung and LG in Korea and HTC in Taiwan, have developed their own local smartphones. During the process, these major smartphone makers have argued that other corporations copy their unique intellectual properties, including patents and design. As key instruments in intellectual property, patents and design have emerged as the new battlefield in which smartphones would be played out.

Since intellectual property has become one of the most significant revenue resources for telecommunications corporations and new media firms, several transnational telecommunications and media corporations have attempted to use legal forces, both nationally and globally, in order to maintain their global dominance in the global smartphone markets. The dramatic changes ushered in by cutting-edge technologies have increased the magnitude and relevance of the phenomenon of the diffusion of infringement of IP rights. In other words, the infringement of intellectual property has hurt corporate profits and American hegemony. Therefore, the U.S. government and transnational corporations, such as Microsoft, Apple, and Google, have worked together to strengthen IP rights in the global markets.

This chapter critically analyzes intellectual property rights, which are some of the most significant components of platform imperialism.[1] It explores the key issues in conjunction with intellectual property rights, such as the transformations in market structures, technology, and socio-cultural norms. Given that the current debates in the realm of intellectual property have primarily occurred between a handful of Western corporations, including Apple and several non-Western corporations such as Samsung, the chapter also analyzes whether the U.S. has dominated the global environment in the realm of IP rights in order to determine the power relations between the U.S. and the majority of non-Western countries.

HOW TO INTERPRET INTELLECTUAL PROPERTY IN THE PLATFORM ERA

Two of the principal forms of intellectual property rights (IPRs) are copyrights and patents. The World Intellectual Property Organization (WIPO) (2010) divides IPRs into two groups: (1) industrial property which includes inventions (patents), trademarks, industrial designs, and geographic indications of source and (2) copyrights which include literary and artistic works such as novels; poems and plays; films; musical works; artistic works such as drawings, paintings, photographs, and sculptures; and architectural designs. Copyrights protect forms of expression such as written materials and artistic works; patents protect underlying ideas used for industrial products or processes. Many clashes amount to tactical skirmishes among companies for competitive advantage—a long and familiar dynamic in copyright law. But much of the turmoil revolves around a deeper issue: What legal principles and social norms should be used to promote new creativity, especially when the Internet and other digital technologies are involved (Bollier, 2011). Of course, these two major areas in IPRs are sometimes exchangeable. For example, "where computer software receives protection, it is ordinarily under copyright law, although in recent years software developers have been granted patent protection as well" (Shadlen et al., 2005, 49).

Previously, in media studies, the majority of studies focused on copyrights due to their studies' emphasis on the protection of creativity as forms of text, audio, and video. However, with the rapid growth of new technologies, including smartphone-related technologies (both hardware and software), patents have become one of the major agendas we face. Platform technologies, such as SNSs, search engines, and smartphones have increasingly influenced the digital economy and culture. The tension between those who lead the development of platform technologies and those who use these technologies has been intensified. Particularly with the issue of technology transfer, these two forces have instigated a huge legal battle.

It was not long ago when policy makers and corporations, as well as new technology inventors started to pay attention to IP rights, in particular, patents. Since the advent of the Uruguay Round trade negotiations in 1986, international law has been trending toward the global harmonization of IP rights protections across nations at all levels of economic development. This movement is embodied in the World Trade Organization's (WTO) Trade-Related Aspects of Intellectual Property Rights (TRIPS) Agreement. Signed in 1994 at the conclusion of the Uruguay Round, which created the WTO, TRIPS sets minimum standards that all organization members must meet regarding the protection of intellectual property rights (Watson, 2011). In addition to the basic free-trade principles of national treatment and most favored-nation status, TRIPS also "has an additional important principle: intellectual property protection should contribute to technical innovation and the transfer of technology. Both producers and users should benefit, and economic and social welfare should be enhanced," according to the WTO (Watson, 2011, 253).

At the national level, "conforming to the new obligations for increased protection of intellectual property involves difficult trade-offs. Increasing protection can potentially stimulate innovation and generate higher economic output, but doing so can lead to diminished diffusion of new goods and, subsequently, higher prices and less innovation downstream" (Shadlen et al., 2005, 50). As Dan Schiller (2007, 46–47) points out, "intellectual property laws stake out and seek to enhance artificial information scarcities; they constitute not defensive but preemptive claims." In particular, patents grant to their corporate holders a third species of monopoly power, deployed far more extensively—and unevenly—than would have been true had they been used only for the useful inventions of a disinterested science (U.S. Patent and Trademark Office, Information Products Division Technology Assessment and Forecast Branch, cited in Schiller, 2007).

More specifically, the political economy of intellectual ownership and exploitation of communications follows a long line of inquiry into the effects of capitalist logic on production and culture (Hermanns, 2005). For many corporations and countries, "it is important to talk about IP laws, because in the wake of what is widely referred to as the information society, the manufacturing trades have been significantly weakened and displaced by the growing importance of trade in information-based products and services variously linked to claims and requirements of creativity, originality, and innovation" (Hermanns, 2005, 68). The ownership and protection of intellectual property is one of the most pressing issues within development debates in the early 21st century. Since the start of commercial use of the Internet in the mid-1990s, information communication and technologies have greatly contributed to the growth of the global economy. As many parts of society have substantially relied on the Internet, information and communication technologies (ICTs) have become some of the most significant components of the digital economy in many countries.

As noted in the United Nations Development Programme (UNDP) (2011, 169), "it is widely recognized that any analysis of the creative economy, which intellectual property has rapidly become part of, must consider the role of intellectual property, which is a key ingredient for the development of the creative industries in all countries. Intellectual property law is a major policy tool and part of the regulatory framework around the creative industries. If properly managed, it can be a source of revenue for both developed and developing countries." In particular, IP rights have become significant with the growth of ICTs as part of the cultural and/or creative industries. Intellectual property regimes are the sets of legal rights that result from intellectual activity in the industrial, scientific, literary, and artistic fields. They aim to safeguard creators and other producers of intellectual goods and services by granting them certain time-limited rights to control the use of those productions. These rights do not apply to the physical object in which the creation may be embodied, but instead to the intellectual creation as such. "IPRs can take the form of copyrights or geographical indications and appellations of origin, topics that will be elaborated later, but IPRs also include patents, industrial designs, trademarks, and secrets" (UNDP, 2011, 170).

International IP law received attention in the wake of neoliberalism, media deregulation and global integrative economic policies, including the North American Free Trade Agreement and the Agreement on TRIPS (McLeod, 2001; Hermanns, 2005). At the same time, "critical socio-legal studies are turning to the law's instrumental role in shaping and governing transnational relationships and interdependencies, positing correlations between these unfolding patterns and earlier readings of imperialism" (Hermanns, 2005, 73). Understanding intellectual property issues in the global scene, therefore, means that it is not only about technology transfer or the protection of creativity, but also the asymmetrical power relations between a few IP holder countries and corporations and the majority of IP users.

INTELLECTUAL PROPERTY AND INFORMATION AND COMMUNICATION TECHNOLOGIES

The increasing role of intellectual property rights in our economy is directly related to the growth of ICTs, and in particular the Internet. When the Internet began to play a key role in our society, Alan Greenspan, Federal Reserve Board Chairman of the U.S., noted in testimony to Congress in 1998, "our nation has been experiencing a higher growth rate of productivity—output per hour—worked in recent years. The dramatic improvements in computing power and communication and information technology appear to have been a major force behind this beneficial trend" (U.S. Department of Commerce, 1998, 1). The ICT sector of the U.S. economy, which includes the computer hardware, software, networking, and telecommunications industries, constituted an estimated 8.2 percent of the gross domestic product (GDP), close to twice its share of GDP a decade or so before (U.S. Department of Commerce, 1998; Samuelson, 1999).

This trend is not much different in many other countries. Several countries, including China, Japan, Taiwan, and Korea, have advanced their ICTs, and these emerging technologies have become primary drivers of the digital economy in these countries, although ICTs are not the only component of the digital economy. With some exceptions in the 2000 dot. com bubble era, the ICTs have continuously contributed to the growth of both the national and the global economy. In fact, many countries are keen about IP rights because they have increasingly contributed to the economy. The contribution of copyright-based industries to the national economy in terms of value added, GDP generation of employment and trade, cannot be ignored. According to the International Intellectual Property Alliance (IIPA), the percent contribution of copyright-based industries to GDP was $1.7 trillion ($1,765 billion), accounting for 11.25 percent of the U.S. economy. Based on the available WIPO data, the second highest in contribution of copyright-based industries to GDP is Australia (10.3 percent in 2007). Other countries like Singapore (5.67 percent in 2001), Canada (4.7 percent in 2004), Mexico (4.77 percent in 2003), and Colombia (3.3 percent in 2005) also experienced high numbers (UNDP, 2011, 180). (See Table 5.1.)

Since only a limited number of countries used the same standard produced by WIPO, it is not possible to compare several key countries, such as Japan, Korea, and China, with these countries mentioned above, but each country's data also provides a similar trend. For instance, based on a few ICT industries, including semi-conductor, telecommunications, broadcasting, and software and computer-related industries, Korea has

Table 5.1 Economic Contribution of Copyright-Based Industries to GDP

Country	*Reference Year*	*% Contribution*
U.S.	2012	11.48
Australia	2007	10.3
Hungary	2002	6.7
Russia	2004	6.1
Netherlands	2005	5.9
Singapore	2001	5.7
Mexico	2003	4.8
Canada	2004	4.7
Colombia	2005	3.3
Bulgaria	2005	2.81

Source: UNDP (2011). Creative Industry Report 2010, 180; IIPA (2013). Copyright Industries in the U.S. Economy The 2013 Report, 2.

proven the increasing role of the ICT sector in the national economy. As the main part of the digital economy, Korea's ICT sector has increased its contribution to GDP from 6 percent in 2001 to 8.6 percent in 2005 and again to 12.3 percent in 2012 (Korea Bank, 2013). This data explains the role of IP rights in the U.S. economy is much higher than in many other countries, with rare exceptions, which makes the U.S. government and corporations focus on IP rights as the primary part of the national economy. As will be discussed later, it is also evident that the U.S. has executed a rigorous global IP norm partially because it wants to protect its own digital economy, which is increasingly significant for employment as well.

Due to the significant role of ICTs in the digital economy, in the 1970s a number of developed countries started to introduce legislation which sought to protect aspects of intellectual property relating to computer software. However, it was not until the introduction of the Trade-Related Aspects of Intellectual Property Rights Agreement, which first came into effect in 1996, that a more harmonized approach toward intellectual property began to be realized (UNCTAD, 2002, 22).

The trade-offs involved in granting and protecting IPRs are particularly acute in software, given the sheer domination of the sector by firms from a single country, the U.S. (Shadlen et al., 2005, 50). According to the United Nations Conference on Trade and Development (UNCTAD), 17 of the world's 20 largest software companies, such as Microsoft, Oracle, and Electronic Arts, are North American, and U.S. firms accounted for more than 50 percent of the world's supply of software and a substantially larger share of packaged software at the end of the 1990s (UNCTAD, 2002, 6–9). And this advantage appears to be growing: "while the U.S. played host to three-quarters of the world's top software firms in 1990, it would play host to 85 percent of their counterparts by the late 1990s" (Shadlen et al., 2005, 50).

As briefly noted, the Internet has especially become significant for many countries, resulting in the acknowledgement of the important role of IP rights. Later, with the rapid growth of platforms, such as SNSs and smartphones, the emphasis has shifted toward these platforms as the primary part of the digital economy and culture due to their immense influences in our daily life and economy. Social network sites and smartphones are different. With the Internet, copyright has been the most significant aspect. However, with platforms, patent and design are becoming the most important aspect as primary parts of the digital economy. Whereas several platform developers and producers advance their technologies and designs, some of them are obviously copied by other corporations, and they have legally disputed intellectual property rights. The magnitude of IP rights has soared in the early 21st century, and transnational corporations must maintain their IP rights in order to increase their revenues in the global markets.

GROWTH IN INTELLECTUAL PROPERTY RIGHTS

Smartphones and other kinds of mobile multimedia have been gaining popularity in the early 21st century. However, it was the wildly enthusiastic reception of Apple's iPhone in mid-2007 that galvanized the smartphone market (Goggin, 2009). The dominant power of the U.S.-based SNSs and smartphone producers has created massive profits, which are protected by IP laws for the U.S. government and corporations. Statistical limitations and deficiencies in data collection have made it impossible to compile universal data on copyright rights from the creative industries. Therefore, official figures for entire global intellectual property rights are not available (United Nations Development Programme, 2011, 162).

However, royalty payments and license fees are associated with the use of intellectual property for production and consumption of goods and services—for instance, licensing services for the right to use entertainment, computer software, or other nonfinancial intangible assets. Based on available national data on creative industries at the world level, revenues associated with receipts of intellectual property rights more than doubled between 2002 and 2008. Royalty revenues rose from $83 billion to $182 billion. A similar trend is shown for imports, which increased from $91 billion to $185 billion during this same period (UNDP, 2011, 163). Although it is not conclusive, this data shows that IP rights have soared over the past several years with the rapid growth of global trade in both cultural and technological goods and services.

With relatively reliable data in the U.S., as much as three-quarters of the value of publicly traded companies in America has come from intangible assets in the early 21st century, up from around 40 percent in the early 1980s, and the economic product of the U.S. has become predominantly conceptual. IP forms part of those conceptual assets (*The Economist*, 2005) as one of the major means of capital accumulation in the digital era. Technology firms are seeking more patents, licensing more, litigating more, and overhauling their business models around intellectual property. In addition, generating IP is less capital-intensive in platforms than other aspects of the IT businesses because it relies mainly on people who have innovative ideas rather than bricks, mortar, and machinery. That makes it attractive to many start-up firms. Venture capitalists often demand that firms patent technology, both to block rivals and to have assets to sell in case the firm flounders (*The Economist*, 2005). Technological innovation drives industrial growth and helps raise living standards. Thus, the importance of IP rights and global knowledge economy in the 21st century cannot be doubted.

According to the International Monetary Fund (IMF), in 2009 the global IP marketplace was worth $173.4 billion, and within the U.S. $84.4 billion—nearly half of the global total (Millien, 2010). This implies that the U.S. has benefited from innovation and IP. Although the total amount is a little bit different from the IMF, the U.S. Department of Commerce (2010, 2011, 2012, 2013) showed that the total amount of revenues from royalties and license fees that the U.S. received from foreign countries soared from $20.8 billion in 1992 to $124.1 billion in 2012, the highest in history.[2] The royalties and license fees that the U.S. paid to foreign countries increased from $5.1 billion in 1992 to $39.8 billion in 2012. (See Table 5.2.) The net profits in 2012 were recorded as being as much as $84.2 billion; therefore, the U.S. has tried to establish a rigorous global standard in IP rights.

Table 5.2 Royalties and License Fees of the U.S. (unit: millions of dollars)

Year	*Exports*	*Imports*
1995	30,289	6,919
1996	32,470	7,837
1997	33,228	9,161
1998	35,626	11,235
1999	39,670	13,107
2000	43,233	16,468
2001	40,696	16,538
2002	44,508	19,353
2003	46,988	19,033
2004	56,715	23,266
2005	64,395	24,612
2006	70,727	23,518
2007	84,580	24,931
2008	93,920	25,781
2009	89,791	25,230
2010	107,165	33,434
2011	120,836	36,620
2012	124,182	39,889

Source: U.S. Department of Commerce (2010, 2011, 2012, 2013). *Survey of Current Business*. Washington DC: U.S. Department of Commerce.

Whereas IP rights have become one of the most significant engines for developed countries, both the cultural industries and the IT industries are vital for the U.S. economy. They are among the all-too-few U.S. industries that generate substantial trade surpluses in the midst of growing U.S. trade deficits. As Greg Papadopoulos, chief technology officer of Sun Microsystems, states, intellectual property has become more central to these U.S. industries (*The Economist*, 2005).

Of course, this does not mean that the U.S. is the only country in the scene. On the contrary, the role of non-Western countries has substantially increased. In 2001, the U.S. issued around 160,000 patents (Schiller, 2007). By using the human development report published by the United Nations Development Program, Miller (1999, A8) pointed out that as of 1999 "America and the other rich, industrialized nations hold 97 percent of all worldwide patents." However, there has been a significant change due to the increasing role of China and Korea. According to WIPO (2012, 52–53), in 2011 Japan issued as many as 238,823 patents, followed by the U.S. (224,505), China (172,113), Korea (94,720), and the EU (62,112). The list of the top 20 patent offices consists mostly of those located in high-income countries, and the combined shares of the top 5 offices for applications and grants worldwide were nearly 79 percent; but there are also a few in middle-income countries. (See Figure 5.1.)

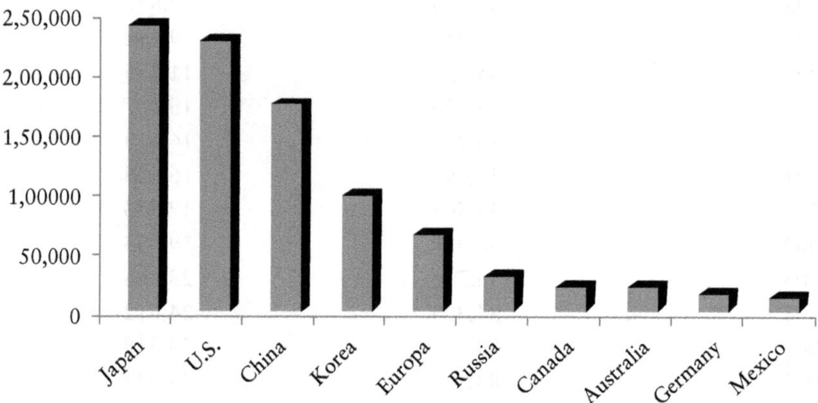

Figure 5.1 Patents Granted for the Top 10 Countries in 2011.
Source: WIPO (2012). World Intellectual Property Indications, 53.

This implies that the global scene in IP rights has changed much over the past decade. Although a handful of rich countries have still continued their significant roles in developing IP-related technologies, a few non-Western countries, including China, Korea, and Mexico, have shown promise as new players. Perhaps this data shows growing evidence of a decline in U.S. supremacy in patents. The reality is that due to the rapid growth of these non-Western countries in the IP sector, which was not seen a decade ago, the U.S. and a few rich countries have tried to intensify international IP laws through both global agencies, including the WTO and WIPO, and bilateral talks between the U.S. and some countries, such as Korea, Philippines, and Colombia. By offering government protection for a temporary monopoly license, "they have the necessary function of rewarding and therefore encouraging innovation, and patents have exploded in prominence in the digital age" (McChesney, 2013, 134).

INTELLECTUAL PROPERTY WARS IN THE ERA OF SMARTPHONES

The Growth of the Smartphone Market amidst Intellectual Property Wars

What is significant is that the legal battle between Apple and Samsung has contributed to change the major players in the global mobile markets. Until 2009, Nokia was number one, holding 38.9 percent of the market share, followed by Blackberry (19.8 percent) and Apple (14.5 percent). HTC ranked fourth (4.6 percent), and Samsung held the fifth position (3.3 percent) (IDC, 2010). Until 2009, smartphones accounted for 15.4 percent of all mobile phones shipped in 2009, up slightly from 12.7 percent in 2008. (See Table 5.2.) However, the situation has rapidly changed with the development of smartphones. Whereas many mobile makers, including Apple, have begun to produce smartphones, two of Korea's major electronics manufacturers, Samsung and LG, have suddenly increased their global penetration with several popular smartphones as well, including Galaxy 3, Galaxy 5, and Optimus. Back when Samsung still focused on feature phones in 2008 and 2009, the market share of Samsung in the global mobile markets was 3.6 percent and 3.3 percent, respectively. In 2010, however, Samsung became the second largest mobile maker with a 20.1 percent market share, and then became the number one maker and exporter with 23.4 percent in 2012, surpassing Nokia (IDC, 2012, 2013). (See Table 5.3.) Samsung claimed the top spot in the Chinese smartphone market (the world's largest market) for the first time in 2012 by nearly tripling its sales. In the smartphone market alone, excluding feature phones, Samsung accounted for 31.3 percent in 2013, followed by Apple (15.6 percent), Huawei (4.8 percent), and LG (4.8 percent) (Gartner, 2014). Samsung and Apple lost their market share during the second quarter of 2014 due to the rapid growth of Chinese smartphone makers, such as Huawei and Lenovo. Samsung's market share in the global market went down to 25.2 percent, while Apple accounted for 11.9 percent during the same time (Slashgear, 2014).[3]

What is interesting is that the battle between Samsung and Apple has greatly helped these two powerhouses as the global leaders in the smartphone industry. Through the continuing legal battles surrounding IP rights, the majority of newspapers and broadcasters have followed and reported on the processes, and the potential smartphone buyers buy either iPhone or Galaxy. As Pantech, the third largest smartphone maker in Korea, explains, in 2010 the company sold 55 percent of its smartphones in the foreign market, while selling 45 percent in the domestic market. However, in 2012 the foreign market for Pantech was 43 percent, and then it was only 30 percent in the first quarter of 2013 (*Weekly Chosun*, 2013). According to Pantech, "during the peaks of the legal battle between Samsung and Apple in the first half of 2012, the entire media reported it as if it was a live sport

Table 5.3 Top Mobile Makers in the World (unit: %)

	2009	*2010*	*2011*	*2012*	*2013*
Nokia	38.9	32.6	24.3	19.3	1t3.8
RIM (Blackberry)	19.8				
Apple	14.4	3.4	5.4	7.8	8.4
HTC	4.6				
Samsung	3.3	20.1	19.3	23.4	24.5
LG		8.4	5.1	3.2	3.8
ZTE		3.6	4.1	3.7	
Huawei					3.0
Others	19	31.9	41.8	42.6	46.4

Source: IDC, 2010, 2012, 2013, 2014a.

event. Regardless of the verdict, the two corporations enjoyed huge advertising effects. The smartphone users have rapidly shifted to only these two companies, and the second-tier corporations have dramatically lost their market share" (*Weekly Chosun*, 2013).

As IP and services are the growth engines of the modern economy, of which Microsoft was a crown jewel in the 1990s and the early 21st century (*The Wall Street Journal*, 2003), Apple is now taking the leading role, but its competitors, including Samsung, have vehemently challenged Apple's status in the social media era. "Strengthened IP rights continue to function as a prime objective of big business as a whole" (Schiller, 2007, 47).

Patent Wars Started in the Mobile Business

As platform technologies, such as smartphones, search engines, and SNSs and global trade in these platform technologies and products develop, the dramatic changes ushered in by cutting-edge technologies have significantly increased the magnitude and relevance of IP rights. There is an increasing tension between developed countries as IP owners and developing countries as IP users, particularly in platforms due to their unique roles not only as computational infrastructure, but also as the software framework that allows software to run on the platforms.

It is puzzling to contemplate Steve Jobs' fury on IP wars, because Apple had previously not been in the phone business. Perhaps one explanation lies in the fact that the lightning rod for Jobs' fury had to do with the ownership of ideas in the innovation and design process (Goggin, 2012). For Jobs and Apple, patents functioned not only as a way to protect their ideas and the investment in them—the traditional rationale of patents in intellectual property law; patents also functioned as a way to conduct politics by other means (Jaffe and Trajtenberg, 2002; Leith, 2007, cited in Goggin, 2012).

The importance of patents has grown suddenly in the smartphone industry with its emphasis on features, which have become more important.[4]

It was Nokia who struck the first blow against Apple when it filed suit in U.S. courts in October 2009, alleging that the iPhone infringed 10 of its patents to do with technologies for affording compatibility with wireless and mobile standards (Wray, 2009). "The basic principle in the mobile industry is that those companies who contribute in technology development to establish standards create intellectual property, which others then need to compensate for," said Ilkka Rahnasto, Vice President, Legal and Intellectual Property at Nokia. "Apple is attempting to get a free ride on the back of Nokia's innovation."

In March 2010, Apple adopted the same tactic itself. Apple filed 1,298 patents addressing hand-held mobile radio telephone technologies between 2000 and September 2012. The vast majority of these have been filed following the 2007 launch of the iPhone. Prior to 2007, Apple filed just 17 patents in this category. Apple has entered into 479 lawsuits to protect IP behind the technology, including in camera, user interface, and battery (Thomson Reuters, 2012). Apple sued Taiwanese handset maker HTC, alleging that it has infringed 20 patents relating to the iPhone‘s user interface, underlying architecture, and hardware. In a statement, Jobs said, "We think competition is healthy, but competitors should create their own original technology, not steal ours" (Arthur, 2010). The U.S. International Trade Commission ruled that HTC infringed on one of four patents Apple had disputed and imposed a sales ban on some of the Taiwan maker's phones.

Since then, smartphone and tablet technology has spawned a wealth of patent litigation. HTC has countersued Apple and is also fighting a patent case in Germany. Microsoft Corporation and Motorola Mobility also have lawsuits against each other (Jim and Gupta, 2011). As a mobile phone pioneer for decades, Motorola possesses a trove of basic patents essential to building most digital devices. Google acquired Motorola Mobility with its 17,000 patents and another 7,500 patents pending in 2011. Google CEO Larry Page said, "the deal will enable us to better protect Android from anticompetitive threats from Microsoft, Apple, and other companies" (Barrett, 2012). Google paid $12.5 billion for the Moto X and Moto G Smartphone manufacturer, Google's largest acquisition thus far. However, Google decided to sell its Motorola Mobility smartphone unit to China's Lenovo for about $2.9 billion, just two years after its acquisition in January 2014. Motorola has continued to lose money due to heavy competition in the smartphone market. Interestingly enough, when Google decided to sell Motorola, it decided to keep the vast majority of the 17,000 Motorola Mobility patents it acquired with the purchase. Patents have become a key battleground among tech firms—especially in the mobile area, and Google cannot give it up (Rushe, 2014).

In fact, a scramble for patents had already begun. In December 2010, four companies, including Microsoft and Apple, paid $450 million for around 880 patents and applications owned by Novell. In July 2011, those two companies and four others, including Research in Motion, maker of the Blackberry, spent $4.5 billion on 6,000 patents owned by Nortel, a bankrupt Canadian telecoms-equipment maker (*The Economist*, 2011a). Most of all, the tug-of-war between Apple in the U.S. and Samsung in Korea has been furious.

Intellectual Property Wars between Apple and Samsung

The smartphone patent wars have heated up since early 2011 with Apple's patent infringement suit. The suit includes trade dress allegations against Samsung, claiming that Samsung's Galaxy line of phones and tablets borrows too much from the Apple iPhone and other products. Galaxy products use Google Inc.'s Android operating system, the lawsuit says, which directly competes with Apple's mobile software. It also alleges that Samsung infringes on a number of Apple patents for technology and trademarking of its mobile product line (Levine, 2011). In a lawsuit filed in U.S. District Court for the Northern District of California, Apple alleges the product design, user interface, and packaging of Galaxy products "slavishly copy" Apple (AP, 2011a). Samsung Electronics Co. immediately responded and sued Apple claiming patent infringement a week after the iPhone maker filed a complaint. Samsung submitted complaints to courts in Seoul, Tokyo, and Mannheil, Germany, alleging Apple infringed patents related to mobile communications technologies. Samsung claims that Apple infringed Samsung patents related to communication standards and a technology that connects mobile phones to personal computers for wireless data transfer (Yang, 2011).

Two major verdicts showed totally opposite results. On the one hand, the nine-member jury in the U.S. court in August 2012 sided almost entirely with Apple in its patent dispute case with Samsung, awarding Apple nearly $1.05 billion in a sweeping victory over claims that the Korean electronics maker copied the designs of its iPhone smartphone and iPad tablet (Guglielmo, 2012). Later, the judge in California revisited that price tag and vacated about $450 million of that original award (Chen, 2013). On the other hand, the Court of Appeal in the U.K. concluded that Samsung did not copy Apple's iPad designs in building its Galaxy Tab product in October 2012 (Arthur, 2012). These are just two of dozens of ongoing patent lawsuits currently being waged between the tech titans across the globe as of August 2013 (Pepitone, 2013). Samsung and Apple filed over 40 patent lawsuits against each other over the last three years. However, the two companies signed a pact that ends all patent lawsuits outside of the U.S. The lawsuits end in countries including Britain, France, Spain, Germany, Italy, Korea, Japan, Australia, and the Netherlands, although they continue their legal battle in U.S. courts (Chowdhry, 2014). The settlement comes as Samsung grapples with declining demand for its smartphones and slumping earnings due to the grown of Chinese and Indian smartphone companies. As some analysts explained, "the whole industry paradigm is changing, and Apple and Samsung have no time to waste and it's time to get back to work" (Satariano and Rosenblatt, 2014).

What the two major companies were trying to say is very simple: a company must protect its intellectual property and ensure its continued innovation and growth in the mobile communications business (Yang, 2011). It has been a war of innovative ideas and designs between Apple and Samsung. It appears to be a life or death struggle between the two smartphone makers—no longer just mobile makers. When Steve Jobs unveiled the latest iPhone 4 mobile in 2010, Samsung, the world's second-largest mobile phone producer, made public its new smartphone called Galaxy S only hours after Jobs' presentation. Samsung has the ambition to beat out Apple and to dominate the lucrative world market (*Korea Times*, 2010). The tensions happen in the midst of the emergence of local-based smartphone powerhouses, which means that a few emerging markets have competed with the U.S.-based smartphone providers. The reality, however, is that the U.S. has continued to dominate the smartphone market with its advanced technologies protected by intellectual property rights. Apple's iPhones have been successful and have influenced subsequent smartphone makers and designers. However, as Porter (2012) points out, it is worth remembering patents sometimes halt the innovation process:

> "the main purpose of IP protection is to encourage innovation, a broad social good, by granting creators a limited monopoly to profit from their creations. While companies like Apple may believe they are insufficiently compensated for their inventions, the evidence often suggests otherwise. The belief that stronger intellectual property protection inevitably leads to more innovation appears to be broadly wrong. It's not that we don't need to protect intellectual property at all. But the protections must take into account that innovation is often a cumulative process, with each step piggybacking on the ideas before it."

What Porter emphasizes is that "the software that drives smartphones is composed of a vast array of ideas from multiple sources. Everybody infringes to some extent on everybody else. Overly strong intellectual property laws that stop creators from using earlier innovations could slow creation overall and become a barrier for new technologies to reach the market" (Porter, 2012).

The major reason for the intensification of IP rights is clearly because IP owners are powerful TNCs. They are people who have been around awhile, not the people who have done a lot of innovation lately. Broad patents allow dominant businesses to stop future inventions that would disrupt their business model (Porter, 2012). Apple has continued to increase its aggressiveness in defending its IP by tracking the company's initiation of patent infringement suits. As of June 2012, Apple had already filed nearly as many patent suits that year as it did in 2010 and 2011 combined. As Thomson Reuters (2012) points out, the marriage between must-have consumer technology and constant product innovation continues to grow in an ultra-competitive marketplace. Therefore, we expect IP to continue its evolution beyond solely intellectual capital protection, and into more of a strategic tool in the ever-increasing quest for market leadership. In this regard, *The Economist* (2011b) states that although the basic idea of patent is a good one, the patent system has been stifling innovation rather than encouraging it.[5]

As Tim Wu (2011, 25) clearly argues, "time after time, in every media sector, the process of change repeats itself. Whichever company establishes early technological dominance does everything in its power to maintain its first-mover advantage." Wu labels this effort the "Kronos Effect: the efforts undertaken by a dominant company to consume its potential successors in their infancy." For a while, sometimes a considerable while, the early winners succeed by pursuing short-term, profit-maximizing politics to forestall or eliminate would be competitors. They resist alternative technological approaches, even those that are clearly superior to their own. "They undercut newcomers at every turn, legally and sometimes illegally. If they recognize the threat early enough, the established dominant players may buy out the newcomer and suppress its technological breakthroughs" (Aronson, 2011, 89). Steve Job's clearly understood this logic and tried to actualize Apple's advantage as the first mover in the smartphone market with all efforts. For him, the victor would go on to prosper, whereas the loser would wilt away and die. This is how the cycle turns, and Jobs certainly understood that such first-mover-takes-all contests were the very soul of the capitalist system (Wu, 2011).

In fact, one of the major factors that encourage a monopolistic market structure is "the importance of technical standards, which become imperative if different firms and consumers are going to be able to use it effectively. Once they are set, the firm that holds the patent or even a head start is off to the races. Smart firms do what they can to make their technical system the industry standard, hence giving them the pole position and a two-lap lead in a three-lap race" (McChesney, 2013, 133). As discussed so far, the widespread use of patents is also a big factor for the intensification of the status-quo in platform technologies.

PLATFORMS AND CONTINUING U.S. DOMINANCE

We cannot deny that the IP war between Apple and Samsung has been important because it is the largest legal battle in the realm of smartphones. However, we need to understand that there are several more important issues than this legal battle. Most of all, it is significant to know that both iPhone and Android are symbols of American empire. In this case, platforms dominated by U.S. iPhones and Android phones seem to be everywhere, and they have formed an exclusive hegemonic power in the smartphone industry, just as Windows and Mac have in personal computers.

According to the research firm IDC, Android, which was invented in 2003 and integrated by Google, has been the world's best-selling smartphone platform and had a 75 percent share of smartphones worldwide during the third quarter of 2012, up from 57.5 percent in the third quarter of 2011. During the same period, Apple's iOS market share also increased slightly from 13.5 percent to 14.9 percent, followed by Blackberry, Symbian, and Windows Phone 7 (IDC, 2012). Android's domination of global smartphone markets reached a peak in the second quarter of 2014, with four out of every five smartphones running its operating system. The Android operating system reached a record of 84.7 percent during the same period, followed by Apple (11.74 percent), Windows Phone (2.5 percent), Blackberry (0.5 percent), and others (0.7 percent). This means that Android and iOS comprised almost 96.4 percent of the market share, up from 54.4 percent in the second quarter of 2011 (Strategy Analytics, 2013; IDC, 2014).

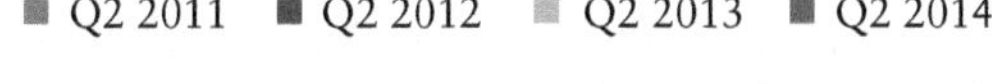

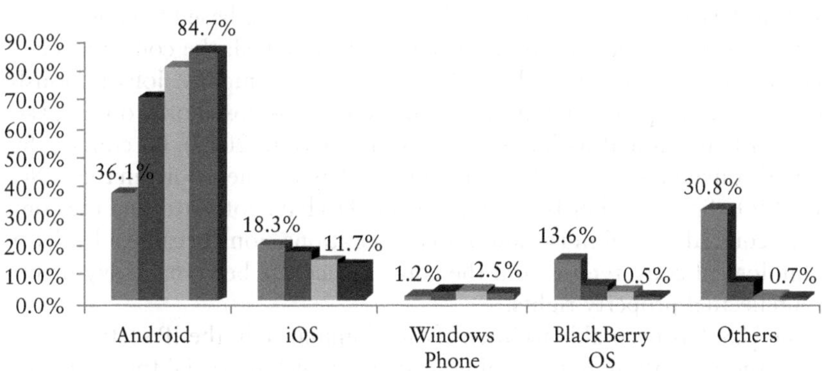

Figure 5.2 Global Smartphone Operating System Market Share in 2011–2014.
Source: IDC (2014b). Smartphone OS Market Share Q2 2014. http://www.idc.com/prodserv/smartphone-os-market-share.jsp

The dire consequence for Apple is that Apple has to use another powerful force to defeat competitors, which is through legal battles as it had done with Samsung. Having failed to compete in the marketplace, Apple and Microsoft are choosing to compete in the courts. On October 31, 2013, a consortium of companies including Microsoft, Apple, Sony, Ericsson, and BlackBerry filed lawsuits against Android manufacturers such as Samsung, HTC, LG, Huawei, Asustek, and ZTE, as well as other Android manufacturers (Koetsier, 2013).

Growth was bolstered by strong Android product performance from a number of vendors, including Samsung and LG in Korea, HTC in Taiwan, and ZTE and Huawei in China (Canalys, 2011). Regardless, only two platforms, both of which are based in the U.S., have dominated the global market, which has not been seen before. Samsung, HTC, and others are also paying a small fee, between $10 and $15 for each Android smartphone they sell, to Microsoft that owns some of the Android patents (Halliday, 2011). Digital technologies and culture have become among the most significant venues for many in the 21st century. The issue is that the U.S. has swiftly expanded its dominance in digitally-driven technologies and culture due to platforms as in the case of popular culture, such as films and music.

Samsung desperately needed to have its own operating system and developed Tizen in 2013. Samsung may use this new operating system on Galaxy SV in the near future. As discussed, every Android phone that Samsung sells is a funnel that takes the money the customers spend on apps, music, or movies and channels it into Google's pocket. Samsung wants a piece of that action, so is keen to set up its own alternative. And because Tizen phones avoid paying Google a fee to use Android, they are cheaper for Samsung to sell and are thus perfect for developing markets where phones need to be cheaper to compete (Trenholm, 2013). Whereas we cannot predict the success of the Tizen phone, since most of Samsung's high-end phones sell with Android, Tizen could provide Samsung with an alternative that would make the local-based smartphone maker less reliant on U.S.-based Google.

What Samsung pursues is what Steve Jobs pursued: the convergence of software and hardware, both made by the same company. Jobs famously sought to keep Apple's operating system exclusive—closed off from rivals—and tightly integrated with Apple hardware (Barrett, 2012). Of course, this form of convergence was vehemently pursued by Japanese Sony in the 1980s and 1990s. Sony as a hardware giant wanted to have software, and the company acquired several music and film corporations. Sony became a leader in technological convergence, and the convergence has been massively driven by intellectual property rights.

The U.S. has been able to intensify its dominance in the IP sector due to its advanced position in developing software, which is crucial for platforms. Although several non-Western countries have advanced their own software and platforms, the lop-sided interaction between Western and non-Western countries remains unchanged and perhaps is even more magnified today than in the past. In particular, the formation of a U.S. hegemony in IP rights has been extended through the efforts of international IP regimes, such as WIPO (Lu and Weber, 2009).

In fact, WIPO is unusual among the family of UN organizations in that it is largely self-financing. About 90 percent of the organization's budgeted expenditure of 618.8 million Swiss francs for the 2010–2011 biennium came from earnings from the services which WIPO provides to users of the international registration systems (PCT, Madrid system, The Hague System, etc.). The remaining 10 percent was made up mainly of revenue from WIPO's arbitration and mediation services and sales of publications, plus contributions from member states. These contributions are relatively small. The five largest contributing countries each donate about one-half percent of the organization's budget (Dignan, 2011).

In other words, WIPO is funded differently than other UN agencies because, instead of receiving direct government support, the vast majority of its funding comes from fees paid by users of its services—mainly international patent filing, and mainly from the private sector. It is known that only about 1 percent of WIPO funding is from U.S. government contributions. UNESCO, by contrast receives some 22 percent of its funding—or about $80 million by one account—from the U.S. government (New, 2011).

However, since the U.S. is the biggest source of patent fees for WIPO, which earns the majority of its revenue from patent fees, there were occasional calls from the U.S. IP industry (which pays those fees) for the U.S. government to pull out of WIPO if it could not achieve breakthroughs in advancing global IP policy, in particular the harmonization of national patent laws (New, 2011). While the U.S. government sometimes directly funds WIPO, it forces WIPO to actually internationalize U.S. versions of IP policy because the U.S. government and TNCs believe that they could increase their revenues in the IP sector by better regulating the illegal usage of American-origin intellectual properties through WIPO. Global IP dominance redefines social identities and relations in economy, politics, and culture to reinforce and perpetuate the historically constructed and highly uneven distribution of IP production and consumption. The developed world serves as host to IP owners, while the developing world houses the users (Pang, 2006).

As several platforms driven by a handful of private corporations have increased their dominance, the U.S. government and its counterpart governments have also been involved in international negotiations. This implies that the nation-states have always been the strongest supporters of private corporations. TNCs have developed and advanced new technologies, and the U.S. government and other governments have been major players in the globalized world because they need to support the growth of their own platforms. As Dyer-Witheford (1999) points out, capital might crack the shell of the nation-state, but, again, platform technologies are not separate from governments because they are the primary engines for the digital economy. Therefore, it is crucial to remember that the classical Marxist accounts of the 19th century era of free trade and its succession by the era of inter-imperial rivalry also confusingly counterpoised states and markets, as is so often done in contemporary discussions of globalization in the context of neoliberal free market policies. Among both classical Marxists and in neoliberal globalization theory, there have been some failures in appreciating the crucial role of the state in making free markets happen and work (Panitch and Gindin, 2003, 11; Wood 2003), which needs to be carefully discussed.

Finally, in addition to the multilateral pressures derived from membership in the WTO, countries also face bilateral pressures from the U.S. to increase intellectual property rights. After all, TRIPS only establishes minimal standards. Even after the Uruguay Round was completed and a new global IPR regime was integrated into the WTO, the U.S. made no secret of its intent to continue to use bilateral instruments to secure increased IP rights. Trade authorities and business constituencies in the U.S. regarded the TRIPS transition periods as excessive, and both the standards and enforcement mechanisms as too lax. Throughout the 1990s, the USTR pushed for higher levels of protection. "Developing countries were discouraged from taking advantage of the transition periods, for example, and in bilateral negotiations many countries committed themselves to higher standards, sometimes referred to as TRIPS Plus" (Shadlen et al., 2005, 56).

CONCLUSION

This chapter has analyzed the increasing role of IP rights in the era of social media. Where ICTs have become some of the most significant components of the digital economy, platform technologies and culture have opened a new era because of their huge influence in the realm of IP rights. Platform technologies, such as social network sites, search engines, and smartphones are core areas for which countries and corporations have emphasized IP rights due to the fact that they are valuable monetary assets. As Perelman (2003, 29) aptly puts:

> "The dramatic expansion of intellectual property rights represents a new stage in commodification that threatens to make virtually everything bad about capitalism even worse. Stronger intellectual property rights will reinforce class differences, undermine science and technology, speed up the corporatization of the university, inundate society in legal disputes, and reduce personal freedoms."

As Perelman outlined, intellectual property rights are in the process of corrupting society in a number of ways. Most of all, intellectual property rights will reinforce class differences. Worldwide, the rich have become richer to an unimaginable extent in recent years. Intellectual property rights also create an atmosphere of secrecy, which is inimical to scientific progress. "Purveyors of intellectual property implore the government, often with success, to mandate modifications that limit the capacity of modern technologies to violate intellectual property rights—even if they cause inconvenience to the consumers who m capitalism is supposed to serve" (Perelman, 2003, 33–36).

Historically, the division between the Organization for Economic Co-operation and Development (OECD) countries and developing countries regarding intellectual property has been based on a fundamental disparity between the "haves" and "have-nots." OECD countries view IP as monetary "assets" that deserve protection, just as financial instruments deserve protection. "The right to protection derives from the 'investment' in research and development that generates the technology assets. Developing countries have based weak enforcement policies largely on claims to "moral justice" that demand a rebalancing of global economic position, and on the apparent 'cost-free' character of preexisting technology" (Abbott, 2007, 8).

The North-South dividing line regarding IP policy was clearer when the "haves" and "have-nots" were comparatively easy to identify. However, over the past decade, a number of major developing country actors have entered a new "middle ground" which places them squarely in neither camp (this type of transition reflects also the historical pattern of countries, which today is part of the OECD). The emergence of China and India as centers of innovation is fundamentally altering the dynamic between the "haves" and "have-nots." Both these countries are presently undergoing difficult internal IP policy transformations as their interests in promoting and protecting domestic innovation achieves greater parity with their interests in making low-cost use of externally-generated innovation. Similarly, other major developing country economies, such as Brazil, are progressively more successful in selected high-technology sectors, for instance, "intermediate-sized civilian aircraft, and are increasingly seeking to identify the proper balance between more and less protective IP policies" (Abbott, 2007, 8). Given that the great preponderance of global patent ownership is in the hands of enterprises based in OECD countries, and that shifts in the pattern of patent ownership are likely to emerge slowly, more comprehensive systems of protection on the part of developing countries will result in net royalty outflows (Abbott, 2007).

The recent growth of an IP regime based on new platforms shows an asymmetrical relationship of interdependence between the West, primarily the U.S., and many developing countries. It is characterized in part by unequal technological exchanges and therefore cultural and capital flows (Jin, 2015). In the early 21st century, it is not unusual to witness the U.S. expanding its dominance in the global markets, not only with cultural products, but also with intellectual properties based on its advanced technologies. The dramatic changes marshaled in by cutting-edge digital technologies have significantly increased the magnitude and relevance of the phenomenon of the diffusion of IP rights infringement. Therefore, as global computer networks and global trade in software products and cultural genres develop, there is an increasing tension between developed countries as IP owners and developing countries as IP users. This is due to their unique roles not only as computational infrastructure, but also as software framework that allows software to run (Jin, 2013a). Admitting the significance of innovative designs as a form of open source for platforms, IP becomes important for designers and corporations because of platforms' commercial imperatives for massive capital gains (Jin, 2015).

The smartphone patent wars underscore "the difficulty we face in enacting fundamental discussion of mobile media platforms" (Goggin, 2012, 749). We could see patents as a relatively inefficient way to demonstrate the interdependent, collaborative nature of technology innovation—underscoring how adaptation happens, with PDAs blurring into early smartphones, begetting iPhones which are close relatives of Androids, and so on. Of course, manufacturers and media companies alike veer between rivalrous self-assertion of the unique inventive genius of one firm, on the one hand, and smiling partnerships and alliances (Symbian, Open Handset Alliance) on the other hand. "Yet the slew of suits over smartphone patents would be farcical if they did not so palpably enact the desire of some of the most wealthy companies in the world to seize control of the future of mobile media—with nary a nod to the claims of the three billion citizens globally who use today's technology, and who surely care about the affordance and prospects for what follows" (Goggin, 2012, 749).

Intellectual property rights have played a key role in accumulating capital in the hands of a few Western-based platform developers and owners. Whereas a few non-Western countries are developing their own platform technologies and expanding their market share in the global markets, IP rights are some of the most difficult hurdles that they have to surmount. However, as Western countries, in particular the U.S., have influenced several global agencies in order to make very strict IP norms that are favoring these countries, non-Western countries are experiencing two fundamental challenges: the development of platform technologies comparable to Western-based ones and IP laws which have resulted in capital accumulation for a few Western corporations. In the field of platform technologies, as Facebook, Twitter, Google, and smartphones (in the case of operating systems) prove, American dominance has been expanding on a large scale, which has been intensifying asymmetrical power relations between Western and non-Western countries.

NOTES

1. As discussed in Chapter 1, accepting platforms as digital media intermediaries, the idea of platform imperialism refers to an asymmetrical relationship of interdependence between the West, primarily the U.S., and many developing powers—of course, including transnational corporations. Characterized in part by unequal technological exchanges and therefore capital flows, the current state of platform development implies a technological domination of U.S.-based companies that have greatly influenced the majority of people and countries. Unlike other fields, including culture and hardware in which a method for maintaining unequal power relations among countries is primarily the exportation of these goods and related services, in the case of platform imperialism the methods are different because intellectual property and commercial values are embedded in platforms and in ways that are more significant for capital accumulation and the expansion of power.
2. Royalties and license fees are payments and receipts between residents and nonresidents for the authorized use of intangible and nonfinancial assets as well as

proprietary rights (such as patents, copyrights, and trademarks) and for the use, through licensing agreements, of produced originals of prototypes (such as films and manuscripts) (The World Bank, 2011).

3. Google's partnership with three Indian phone makers will make more trouble for Samsung. Google launched its new Android One operating system in India in September 2014, which would lead to a surge in demand for low-end Android phones. Unless Samsung changes its strategy, it will continuously lose its share in emerging markets. This implies that without controlling the operating system, hardware makers cannot sustain dominance in the platform markets. Again, the U.S.-based platform corporation will extend its market share in non-Western markets with new operating systems (Bhattadarjee, 2014).
4. The battle surrounding patent has been everywhere in the era of platform. Another major legal case is between Tyler and Cameron Winklevoss and Mark Zuckerberg. The Winklevoss brothers sued Zuckerberg because he allegedly stole their idea for a site called the Harvard Connection. In 2002, the brothers and their partner Divya Narendra discussed an idea for a social network and hired Zuckerberg to help design it. But Zuckerberg then went his own way and started Facebook, which triggered the legal battle over ownership rights. The brothers reached a settlement that included cash and stock in Facebook and was reportedly worth $20 million in cash and $45 million of private Facebook stock at a time when the company was valued at $15 billion (Szalai, 2012).
5. As for this, a recent verdict on copyright perhaps shows a very interesting lesson. On November 14, 2013, Google won dismissal of a long-running lawsuit by authors who accused the Internet search company of digitally copying millions of books for an online library without permission. U.S. Circuit Judge Denny Chin in New York accepted Google's argument that its scanning of more than 20 million books, and making "snippets" of text available online, constituted "fair use" under U.S. copyright law (Stempel, 2013). In Chin's view, Google Books expands the market for books by helping consumers discover books they would not otherwise have known existed. If the ruling is upheld on appeal, it will represent a significant triumph for Google. More important, it would expand fair use rights, benefiting many other technology companies. Many innovative media technologies involve aggregating or indexing copyrighted content. This ruling is the clearest statement yet that such projects fall on the right side of the fair use line (Lee, 2013). Regardless of the fact that some people, including book authors, do not agree, what is most significant is that the current form of sharing of book content on the Internet helps innovation, instead of hurting it because it helps the readers; therefore, it eventually helps the authors. Admitting it is still controversial. This decision at least shows the importance of openness for the development of technologies and society.

REFERENCES

Abbott, F. (2007). *The Political Economy of the WIPO Development Agenda.* In *Views on the Future of the Intellectual Property System* (ed.), International Centre for Trade and Sustainable Development. 7–12. Geneva: International Centre for Trade and Sustainable Development.

Aronson, J. (2011). Book review: The master switch: The rise and fall of information empire. *International Journal of Communication* 5: 89–94.

Arthur, C. (2010). Apple sues HTC over iPhone patents. *The Guardian*, March 2. http://www.theguardian.com/technology/2010/mar/02/apple-sues-htc-iphone-patents.

Arthur, C. (2011). BT sues Google over Android. Guardian.co.uk, December 19. http://www.guardian.co.uk/technology/2011/dec/19/bt-sues-google-over-android.

Arthur, C. (2012). Samsung Galaxy Tab 'does not copy Apple's iPad designs. *The Guardian*. October 18. Accessed November 18, 2012. http://www.guardian.co.uk/technology/2012/oct/18/samsung-galaxy-tab-apple-ipad.

AP (2011). Apple suit: Samsung copies our devices. May 4.

Barrett, P. (2012). Apple's jihad. *Bloomberg Businessweek*, 4273, 2 April, 55–63.

Bollier, D. (2011). Intellectual property in the digital age. In Ben Walmsley (ed.), *Key Issues in the Arts and Entertainment Industry*, 1–15. Oxford: Goodfellows Publishers Lt.

Canalys (2011). Android takes almost 50% share of worldwide smart phone market. August 1.

Chen, B. (2013). Jury to decide how much more Samsung must pay Apple in patent case. *The New York Times*, 11 November. http://www.nytimes.com/2013/11/12/technology/jury-to-decide-how-much-more-samsung-must-pay-apple-in-patent-case.html?_r=0.

Chowdhry, A. (2014). Apple and Samsung drop patent disputes against each other outside of the U.S. *Forbes*, 6 August. http://www.forbes.com/sites/amitchowdhry/2014/08/06/apple-and-samsung-drop-patent-disputes-against-each-other-outside-of-the-u-s/.

Dignan, L. (2011). Could world intellectual property organization be defunded? ZDNet. http://www.zdnet.com/blog/btl/could-world-intellectual-property-organization-be-defunded/62338.

Downes, D. (2006). New media economy: Intellectual property and cultural insurrection. *Journal of Electronic Publishing* 9(1). http://quod.lib.umich.edu/j/jep/3336451.0009.103/--new-media-economy-intellectual-property-and-cultural?rgn=main;view=fulltext.

Dyer-Witheford, N. (1999). *Cyber-Marx: Circles and Circuits of Struggle in High-Technology Capitalism*. Champaign, IL: University of Illinois Press.

Gartner (2014). Gartner says annual smartphone sales surpassed sales of feature phones for the first time in 2013. 13 February. http://www.gartner.com/newsroom/id/2665715.

Goggin, G. (2009). Adapting the mobile phone: The iPhone and its consumption. *Continuum: Journal of Media & Cultural Studies* 23(2): 231–244.

Goggin, G. (2012). Google phone rising: The Android and the politics of open source. *Continuum: Journal of Media & Cultural Studies* 26(5): 741–752.

Guglielmo, C. (2012). Apple wins over jury in Samsung patent dispute, awarded $1.05 billion in damages. *Forbes*. August 24. Accessed September 17, 2012. http://www.forbes.com/sites/connieguglielmo/2012/08/24/jury-has-reached-verdict-in-apple-samsung-patent-suit-court-to-announce-it-shortly/.

The Economist (2005). A survey of patent and technology: A market for ideas. October 20.

The Economist (2011a). Intellectual property: Battles over patents are becoming fiercer and more expensive. 20 August.

The Economist (2011b): Why America's patent system needs to be reformed, and how to do it. 20 August.

Halliday, J. (2011). Samsung and Microsoft settle Android licensing dispute. *The Guardian*. September 28. Accessed March 1, 2012. http://www.guardian.co.uk/technology/2011/sep/28/samsung-microsoft-android-licensing-dispute.

Hermanns, K.S. (2005). The hand that sets the table ... The political economy and self-reflexive project of intellectual property law in relation to traditional knowledge. *International Journal of Media and Cultural Politics* 1(1): 67–88.

IDC (2010). Nokia owned the global smartphone space in 2009. February 5. Press release.

IDC (2012). Worldwide mobile phone market maintains its growth trajectory. February 1. Press release.

IDC (2013). Strong demand for smartphones and heated vendor competition characterize the worldwide mobile phone market at the end of 2012. January 24. Press release.

IDC (2014). Worldwide smartphone market grows 28.6% year over year in the first quarter of 2014. 30 April. Press Release.

Jaffe, A., & Trajtenberg, M. (2002). *Patents, Citations, and Innovations: A Window on the Knowledge Economy*. Cambridge, MA: MIT Press.

Jim, C. & Gupta, P. (2011). Apple scores limited victory in smartphone patent war. Reuters, December 20. http://www.reuters.com/article/2011/12/20/us-htc-apple-patent-idUSTRE7BI24620111220.

Korea Bank (2013). IT and GDP. http://www.itstat.go.kr/stat/graphView.htm?mclass_cd=IF&detail=&startYear=2001&endYear=2012&ctrlRadio=year&x=27&y=6.

The Korea Times (2010). Smartphone war. June 9.

Koetsier, J. (2013). Judgment day for Android: Apple, Microsoft file lawsuit against Google, Samsung. *Venture Beats*. 1 November. http://venturebeat.com/2013/11/01/judgement-day-for-android-apple-microsoft-file-lawsuit-against-google-samsung/.

Lee, T. (2013). Google Books ruling is a huge victory for online innovation. 14 November. The Washington Post. http://www.washingtonpost.com/blogs/the-switch/wp/2013/11/14/google-books-ruling-is-a-huge-victory-for-online-innovation/.

Leith, P. (2007). *Software and Patents in Europe*. Cambridge: Cambridge University Press.

Levine, D. (2011). Apple sues Samsung over Galaxy products. *Reuters*. April 18.

Lu, J. & Weber, I. (2009). Internet software piracy in China: A user analysis of resistance to global software copyright enforcement. *Journal of International and Intercultural Communication* 2(4): 296–317.

McLeod, K. (2001), *Owning Culture: Authorship, Ownership and Intellectual Property Law*, New York: Peter Lang.

Miller, J. (1999). Globalization widens rich-poor gap, UN report says, *The New York Times*, 13 July, A8.

Millien, R. (2010). The US$173.4B global intellectual property marketplace? Accessed February 23, 2012. http://dcipattorney.com/2010/12/the-us173-4b-global-intellectual-property-marketplace/.

Mueller, F. (2011). Google is patently too weak to protect Android. http://fosspatents.blogspot.com/2011/01/google-is-patently-too-weak-to-protect.html.

New, W. (2011). Palestinian membership in UNESCO could raise questions for US at WIPO. Intellectual Property Watch. Accessed March 2, 2012. http://www.ip-watch.org/2011/10/21/palestinian-membership-in-unesco-could-raise-questions-for-us-wipo/.

Pang, L. (2006). *Cultural Control and Globalization in Asia: Copyright, Piracy, and Cinema*. London: Routledge.

Panitch, L. & Gindin, S. (2003). Global capitalism and American empire. In Leo Panitch and Sam Gindin (eds.), *The Socialist Register 2004: The New Imperial Challenge*, , 1–43. New York: Monthly Press.

Pepitone, R. (2013). Apple patent win: Samsung banned from selling some phones in U.S. CNN Money. 9 August. http://money.cnn.com/2013/08/09/technology/mobile/apple-samsung-itc/.

Perelman, M. (2003). The political economy of intellectual property. *Monthly Review* 54(8): 29–37.

Porter, M. (2012). Tech suits endanger innovation. *The New York Times*. 29 May. Accessed November 5, 2013. http://www.nytimes.com/2012/05/30/business/economy/tech-lawsuits-endanger-innovation.html?_r=0.

Rushe, D. (2014). Google to sell Motorola Mobility to Lenovo in $2.9 bn deal. *The Guardian*. 30 January.

Samuelson, P. (1999). Intellectual property and the digital economy: Why the anti-circumvention regulations need to be revised. *Berkeley Technology Law Journal* 14(1): 1–49.

Satariano, A. & Rosenblatt, J. (2014). Apple, Samsung agree to end patent suits outside U.S. Bloomberg. 6 August. http://www.bloomberg.com/news/2014-08-05/apple-samsung-agree-to-end-patent-suits-outside-u-s-.html.

Schiller, D. (2007). *How to Think about Information*. Urbana, IL: University of Illinois Press.

Shadlen, K., Schrank, A., & Krutz, M. (2005). The political economy of intellectual property protection: The case of software. *International Studies Quarterly* 49: 45–71.

Slashgear (2014). IDC: Samsung slides, Apple loses market share in smartphones. 29 July. http://www.slashgear.com/idc-samsung-slides-apple-loses-market-share-in-smartphones-29339144/.

Stempel, J. (2013). Google defeats authors in U.S. book-scanning lawsuit. 14 November. Reuters. http://www.reuters.com/article/2013/11/14/us-google-books-idUSBRE9AD0TT20131114.

Strategy Analytics (2013). Android captures record 81 percent share of global smartphone shipments in Q3 2013. http://blogs.strategyanalytics.com/WSS/post/2013/10/31/Android-Captures-Record-81-Percent-Share-of-Global-Smartphone-Shipments-in-Q3-2013.aspx.

Szalai, G. (2012). Winklevoss twins use Facebook settlement money to invest in new social network. *The Hollywood Reporter*. 17 September. http://www.hollywoodreporter.com/news/winklevoss-twins-use-facebook-settlement-370723.

Thomson Reuters (2012). Inside the iPhone patent portfolio. September.

Trenholm, R. (2013). Tizen tablet is a first step for Samsung's Android rival. CNET. 25 October. http://crave.cnet.co.uk/mobiles/tizen-tablet-is-a-first-step-for-samsungs-android-rival-50012598/.

United Nations Development Programme (2011). *Creative Industry Report 2010*. New York: UNDP.

United Nations Conference on Trade and Development (2002). Changing Dynamics of Global Computer Software and Services Industry: Implications for Developing Countries. New York: UNCTAD.

U.S. Department of Commerce (1998). *The Emerging Digital Economy.* Washington DC: U.S. Department of Commerce.

U.S. Department of Commerce (2010). *Survey of Current Business.* Washington DC: U.S. Department of Commerce.

U.S. Department of Commerce (2011). *Survey of Current Business.* Washington DC: U.S. Department of Commerce.

U.S. Department of Commerce (2012). *Survey of Current Business.* Washington DC: U.S. Department of Commerce.

U.S. Department of Commerce (2013). *Survey of Current Business.* Washington DC: U.S. Department of Commerce.

The Wall Street Journal (2003). Monti's wrecking crew. 7 August. http://online.wsj.com/news/articles/SB106021398070464800.

Watson, A. (2011). Does TRIPS increase technology transfer to the developing world? The empirical evidence. *Information & Communications Technology Law* 20(3): 253–278.

Weekly Chosun (2013). Samsung-Apple wars victimized Pantech. 26 August. http://weekly.chosun.com/client/news/viw.asp?nNewsNumb=002271100017&ctcd=C05.

Wood, E. (2003). *Empire of Capital.* London: Verso.

The World Bank (2011). Royalties and license fees, receipts. Accessed April 1, 2012. http://data.worldbank.org/indicator/BX.GSR.ROYL.CD.

World Intellectual Property Organization (2010). What is intellectual property? http://www.wipo.int/about-ip/en/.

World Intellectual Property Organization (2012). 2012 world intellectual property indicators. Geneva: WIPO.

Wray, R. (2009). Nokia sues Apple over alleged breach of patent. *The Guardian*, October 22. http://www.guardian.co.uk/business/2009/oct/22/telecoms-nokia.

Wu, T. (2011). *The Master Switch: The Rise and Fall of Information Empires.* New York: A.A. Knopf.

Yang, J. (2011). Samsung counter sues Apple as patent dispute deepens. *Bloomberg.* April 22. Accessed September 16, 2012. http://www.bloomberg.com/news/2011-04-22/samsung-sues-apple-on-patent-infringement-claims-as-legal-dispute-deepens.html.

Part III

Political Economy of Platform Technologies

6 User Commodities as Free Labor in the Social Media Era

INTRODUCTION

The popularization of social network sites (SNSs) in the early 21st century has generated some controversies regarding the nature of user participation as a form of labor. SNSs, including Facebook and Twitter, have added hundreds of thousands of users every day who present themselves, expand their networks, and develop relationships with others (Mansson and Myers, 2011; boyd, 2011). As these users spend immense time and energy to update their personal profiles, advertisers and corporations monetize their participation. With the convergence of SNSs with smartphones, these new forms of participation are seemingly empowering platform users. However, the evolution of SNSs has unavoidably resulted in a growing interest towards considering users as members of new participatory cultures for a corporate sphere, with target audiences whom big corporations appropriate. As van Dijck (2012, 161) aptly puts it, "even though communicative traffic on social media platforms seems determined by social values such as popularity, attention, and connectivity, they are impalpably translated into monetary values and redressed in business models [in that these platform appropriate users] made possible by digital technology."

Several previous studies examined the nature of SNS users as free labor (Coté and Pybus, 2007; Cohen, 2008; Lee, 2011; van Dijck, 2012; Fuchs, 2010, 2014) from a critical theory approach in order to extend their understandings of emerging SNSs. Some of them especially adopted audience commodity theory developed by Dallas Smythe (1977, 1981) in interpreting the current form of labor in the era of social media. They have certainly contributed to the understanding of free labor in our contemporary digital capitalism in which social media plays a key role in accumulating capital for corporations and platform developers. In particular, since platform owners, such as Facebook and Google expand to garner revenues through user activities, both nationally and globally, it is crucial to understand the dominant role of platforms in capitalizing user activities in the global scene.

This chapter develops a critical approach to SNSs with emphasis on the monetization process of SNSs with the case of Facebook, not only within a nation but also between countries. As the role of the users is one of the most distinctive characteristics of platforms, unlike previous works that largely overlooked the multiplicity of the nature of users as free labor, it discusses the commodification of Facebook and its users in broader viewpoints in order to map out the comprehensive commodification process of Facebook users. Since Facebook has developed a mixture of strategies, such as targeted advertising and selling customized metadata while retailing exclusive access to games, we need to advance diverse standpoints. Second, it contextualizes the role of users in the reproduction of capital relations by critically engaging with Smythe's audience commodity thesis, because the commodification of SNS users is especially the embodiment of the notion of audience commodity. Finally, it articulates whether or not Facebook can be placed within more general capitalist processes that show asymmetrical power relations between companies and users, as well as between Western social media and non-Western social media corporations, and if yes, the ways in which Facebook harnesses user activities.

FREE LABOR, AUDIENCE COMMODITIES, AND SOCIAL NETWORK SITES

The perception of free labor or immaterial labor has originated within the debates of autonomist Marxism since the 1990s (Dowling, 2007; Hesmondhalgh, 2010). Lazzarato (1996, 133) first defined immaterial labor as "the labor that produces the informational and cultural content of the commodity," and later many theoreticians developed the concept of immaterial labor. On the one hand, with some optimistic emphasis on collective participation, Mansson and Myers (2011) and Hardt and Negri (2004) argue that SNS users as affective users enjoy their participation in SNSs with excitement. Hardt and Negri (2004, 108) particularly claim that "immaterial labor as labor creates immaterial products, such as knowledge, information, communication, a relationship, or an emotional response." This incorporated affective labor involves human contact and interaction, and they (2004, 110–111) argue, "immaterial labor as a form of affective labor involves both body and mind that produces or manipulates affects such as a feeling of ease, well-being, satisfaction, excitement or passion." Mansson and Myers (2011, 155) also argue that "online activities are a form of affection" and "expressions of affection are used to maintain and develop relationships."

On the other hand, other theoreticians (Fuchs, 2010; Andrejevic, 2011) critically argue that user participation in SNSs is a form of exploitation because they believe that SNS users' time and energies have been utilized as not-paid-for work, known as free labor. For them, SNS users are commodified into exploited laborers (Terranova, 2000; Fuchs, 2010). Fuchs (2014, 117) especially contends that "unpaid Internet prosumer labor is a new form of labor that is connected to other forms of exploited labor." There are certainly some positive aspects of immaterial labor; however, immaterial labor can also be categorized as unpaid and exploited. For Fuchs and Sevignani (2013, 237), "this online activity is fun and work at the same time—play labor. Play labor (playbour) creates a data commodity that is sold to advertising clients as a commodity. They thereby obtain the possibility of presenting advertisements that are targeted to users' interests and online behavior. Targeted advertising is at the heart of the capital accumulation model of many corporate social media platforms."

Terranova (2000, 33) also states, "simultaneously voluntarily given and unwaged, enjoyed and exploited, free labor on the Net includes the activity of building websites, modifying software packages, reading and participating in mailing lists, and building virtual spaces on MUDs (multi-user dungeons—a multiplayer real-time virtual world game)." What Terranova (2000, 37) argues is that "free labor is the moment where the knowledgeable consumption of culture is translated into excess productive activities that are pleasantly embraced and at the same time often shamelessly exploited."[1] As Andrejevic (2011) also points out, free labor is unpaid work, but also freely given work, because the voluntary involvement of immaterial labor has eventually turned into the commodification process. For these scholars, SNS users are commodified into exploited laborers.

Whereas these two different interpretations have developed their own strong footholds, this chapter critically develops the notion of free labor in terms of its work as unpaid, because social media users are being exploited in the digital capitalism era, although social network site users perhaps do not care to be paid. In social network sites, including Facebook, users are the producers and the consumers (Fuchs, 2010). However, there is no money reward between the users and Facebook because Facebook as a company owns the major resources on Facebook and the profit. Therefore, it is significant to analyze Facebook users as free labor with a modification of audience commodity theory. The current situation is not exactly the same as when Smythe developed his notion of audience commodity; however, Smythe's work certainly provides a useful tool in understanding SNS users as unpaid workers.

As is well known, Smythe (1977) argued that commercial networks sell the audience as both products and labor. He stated that audiences were products that media, in particular commercial networks, sold to advertisers, and he recognized the significant economic relationship between the advertiser and the corporate product sponsor. The approach to audience labor theorization was evinced through Smythe's economic consideration that "watching time as a form of productive labor draws on Marx, for whom labor must be productive, must produce value" (Shimpach, 2005, 355). As Smythe argued:

> "The material reality under monopoly capitalism is that all non-sleeping time of most of the population is work time. This work time is devoted to the production of commodities in general (both where

> people get paid for their work and as members of audiences) and in the production and reproduction of labor power (the pay for which is subsumed in their income). Of the off-the-job work time, the largest single block is time of the audiences which is sold to advertisers. It is not sold by workers but by the mass media of communications" (1977, 3).

Smythe (1977, 5) also pointed out that "the owners of TV and radio stations and networks, newspapers, and enterprises which specialize in providing billboard and third class advertising are the principal producers of the commodity which advertisers buy with their advertising expenditures." He suggested that "what they buy are the services of audiences with predictable specifications who will pay attention in predictable numbers and at particular times to particular means of communication." The specifications for the audience commodities include age, sex, income level, family, location, ethnicity, ownership of home and automobile, credit card status, and social class (Smythe, 1977, 4).

There are several scholars who have developed and clarified Smythe's concept of audience commodity (Jhally, 1987; Meehan, 1990; Fuchs, 2012a) because the work of the audience is materially embedded in the capitalist application of communication technologies (Manzerolle, 2010, 455). Again, the major characteristics of work have fundamentally changed since Smythe wrote, and the idea of a fairly monolithic audience as a theoretical perspective for labor cannot foreground enough of what is going on in sites like Facebook, because these sites have been commodified in multiple ways. Arvidsson and Colleoni (2012, 138) argue that Smythe's theory of the audience commodity is based on a number of premises that do not apply to the situation of online prosumer (producer and consumer) practices; however, the current practice of the utilization of users can be analyzed by critically employing the audience commodity theory because of its characterization of free labor.

Previously, the critical theory of communication was used to misconstrue the artificial notion of the audience because they considered the audience as only consumers. By assuming the notion of a helpless audience manipulated by corporate media, critical theorists place "the source of social alienation in the realm of consumerist mass communication" (Castells, 2009, 127). However, in the era of platforms, audiences situate themselves as creators and/or producers while consuming content. This implies that it is crucial to analyze the nature of audiences as prosumers, which is now the primary area that critical theorists need to emphasize. What we need to focus on is the malleability of commodification and how new media, such as Facebook, has complicated this concept much more than the early Web 2.0 technologies. Facebook has utilized several business strategies, including looking at advertising and financial rent, although these are interconnected with each other.

ASYMMETRICAL DOMINANCE OF FACEBOOK IN THE GLOBAL SNS MARKET

In the early 21st century, several SNSs including Facebook and Twitter have utilized people's contributions, and Facebook is one of the most significant in terms of its monetization based on its popular global usage. Facebook was founded by Mark Zuckerberg in the U.S. in 2004 as an online yearbook for students at Harvard University. Facebook is a platform that plays an advanced role in aggregating several services. Since May 2007, "members have been able to download and interact with Facebook applications, programs and accessories developed by outside companies that now have access to Facebook's operating platform and large networked membership" (Cohen, 2008, 5).

Facebook provides a pre-established page format that facilitates the creation of a personal profile by registered members that includes photos, work and education history, contact information, hobbies, area of residence, and the user's favorite music, movies, TV shows, and books. These features are utilized by Facebook users to connect to their online friends. Facebook also provides a wall, which functions as a message board on which users can post messages and photos for other members. More recently, Facebook has become a place for people to enjoy social gaming, including *SongPop*, *Dragon City*, and *Angry Birds Friends*, and it competes with console and online games to attract game players.

Facebook has maintained its rate of growth and generates thousands of new user registrations every day. As of June 30, 2014, the number of active monthly users was 1.31 billion, an increase of 14 percent year-over-year. About 829 million daily active users on average visited Facebook in June 2014 (Facebook, 2013a; Facebook, 2014a). Since India, Brazil, and Indonesia have huge populations, and their penetration rates are much lower than that of the U.S., the number of users will continue to grow. Facebook users also generated an average of 4.5 billion Likes daily as of May 2013, up from 2.7 billion in August 2012, which is a 67 percent increase (Facebook, 2012b; Facebook, 2013b; Zephoria, 2014). Facebook has rapidly expanded its dominance in many countries, resulting in another form of asymmetrical power relationship between the U.S.-based media firm and corporations in the rest of the world. According to the World Map of Social Networks, showing the most popular SNSs by country, again, Facebook is the market leader in 130 countries out of 137 analyzed (94.8%) as of July 2014, up from 87 percent in June 2010, and up from 78 percent in December 2009 (Vincos Blog, 2013). In history, we have never seen this kind of huge dominance of a Western-based technology in the global market. These numbers are significant because they have contributed to the high valuation assigned to Facebook. As discussed in previous chapters, local-based SNSs are still market leaders in Japan (Mixi), China (QQ), Russia (VK.COM), and Korea (Cyworld). However, Facebook has rapidly penetrated the majority of countries around the world, and this trend will be continuing.

Meanwhile, it is impossible to disregard the influence of the market in defining the commercial meaning of this new realm of communication (van Dijck, 2012). When Facebook attracted 4,000 members on the Harvard campus in the spring of 2004, Zuckerberg was approached to monetize the site by selling advertisements. Zuckerberg, however, clearly expressed his disapproval by saying, "no, Facebook is cool and if we start selling pop-ups of Mountain Dew it's no longer gonna be cool. We don't know what it is yet, we don't know what it can be, what it will be; we just know it's cool." Zuckerberg emphasized that "Facebook's social mission was to make the world more open and connected," and he stated that "the primary goal was not making money" (*Channel 4 News,* 2012). This cool concept is ephemeral and difficult to exploit, but one thing Zuckerberg certainly understood was that conventional business models did not apply to his invention. In a world where social structure is everything, connections become the prime economic value. Zuckerberg did not want to ruin the coolness of Facebook in the first stage (van Dijck, 2012, 169–170).

As seen in Fuchs' interview with Zuckerberg for *Time* (2012b, 151), Zuckerberg said that "the goal of the company is to help people to share more in order to make the world more open and to help promote understanding between people. The long-term belief is that if we can succeed in this mission then we also [will] be able to build a pretty good business and everyone can be financially rewarded." However, starting in 2005 Zuckerberg finally began to understand the importance of Facebook's business value and shifted his position toward utilizing the capitalist system by developing the site's business model in several ways. As in many ICTs, the developer perhaps dreamed of the monetization of Facebook, which is not unusual. As discussed in Chapter 1, as one of the major components of platforms, platforms can be analyzed from the corporate sphere because "their operation is substantially defined by market forces and the process of commodity exchange" (van Dijck, 2012, 162).

What Zuckerberg learned is that Facebook can offer participants entertainment and a way to socialize, and the social relations present on a site like Facebook can obscure economic relations that reflect larger patterns of capitalist development in the digital age (Jin, 2012). After his acceptance of the value of Facebook as a tool to monetize the resources, the connection of Facebook to digital capitalism started to become significant. The number of Facebook users has soared globally, and advertisers, including corporations and advertising agencies, have focused more on Facebook as an alternative advertising medium in the social media era. Zuckerburg eventually listed Facebook in the U.S. stock market to be a symbol of a new corporate sphere garnering revenues in multiple ways.

Consequently, Facebook has become a dominant power, resulting in the concentration of capital in the hands of U.S.-based SNS start-ups. This is far from a globalization model in which power is infinitely dispersed. Unlike in Smythe's conceptualization, capital and power are not the form of monopoly in the SNS world; however, a handful of U.S.-owned platforms have rapidly expanded their dominance in the global market, which has caused the asymmetrical gap between a few Western countries and the majority of non-Western countries (Jin, 2013a), in addition to the asymmetrical relation between the corporation and users.

Valorization of Google

A very similar path can be found with Google as well. Since its inception as a private company in 1998 by Larry Page and Sergey Brin, Google has been seen as a different kind of search engine. As a search engine, Google prides itself on providing objective search results that are not biased by advertisers' money. Google separates search results from advertisers' links so that users can differentiate 'real information' from 'paid information.' The homepage of Google is simple: it only has a search box. The homepage does not contain any advertisement (Lee, 2010). But Google has outgrown its search engine. Google no longer sees itself as merely a search engine business. It stated in its 2008 annual report that "we began as a technology company and have evolved into a software, technology, Internet, advertising and media company all rolled into one" (Google, 2008, 17, cited in Lee, 2010).

As of May 2009, Google provides 23 search applications, 14 communication applications, and 3 mobile applications. In addition to the popular Google Search application, users can also search for U.S. patents with Patent Search, and to search one's computer hard disk with Desktop. Other than search applications, Google offers software for communication: Bloggers for blogging, Gmail for e-mail, and Orkut for social networking. Google organizes, and in some cases creates, information that is potentially valuable for users and profitable for advertisers. Shortly after launching the Google search engine, they realized that advertising revenue was crucial to the survival of the company (Lee, 2010, 914).[2]

As Google (2012a) reported in the S-1 filing with the U.S. Securities and Exchange Commission, its revenues increased by 32.5 percent from 2011 to 2012. Google acquired Motorola Mobility and started to sell hardware ($4,136 million) in 2012. Although it sold Motorola Mobility later, The majority of revenues still came from Google advertising, from $43,686 million in 2012 to $50,547 million in 2013 (Google, 2014a). This increase resulted primarily from an increase in advertising revenues generated by Google websites and Google Network Members' websites and, to a lesser extent, an increase in other revenues driven by hardware product sales. The increase in advertising revenues for Google websites and Google Network Members' websites resulted primarily from an increase in the number of paid clicks through its advertising programs, partially offset by a decrease in the average cost-per-click paid by advertisers. Google (2012a, 33) also clearly explained that "the increase in the number of paid clicks generated through our advertising programs was due to an increase in aggregate traffic including mobile queries, certain monetization improvements including new ad formats, the continued global expansion of our products, advertisers, and user base, as well as an increase in the number of Google Network Members."

The fact of the matter is that inequality in Google, and in platforms in general, is not experienced as coercive or unpleasant. To the contrary, because it appeals to our egos by allowing us to express ourselves, participation in Google and Facebook is creative and pleasurable. The platform thus represents a form of hegemony, a system of rule in which a minority can rule over a majority not by brute force or deception but through consensus (Mejias, 2013). From a Gramscian perspective (cited in Mejias, 2013), hegemonic power is predicated on a harmonious relationship between unequal social classes achieved through the formation of a popular discourse of inclusion: political accommodation of the underprivileged allows the ruling class to maintain its privileges by seeming to represent the interests of the ruled. "In the context of digital networks, the trope of "total inclusion" establishes hegemony by promoting the idea that the consensual acceptance of the terms of use (which spell out precisely the way in which we are to be ruled) is rewarded by the opportunity to have a presence in the network on the same terms enjoyed by everyone else" (Mejias, 2013, 8).

Despite the early euphoria over the Web 2.0 belonging to "crowds" or "communities," platforms are rapidly turning the Internet into a proprietary space where control over tools and services is firmly held by a small number of media corporations who are "pushing for control and exclusion as a means to exploit and reorient online users as consumers. As citizens further move from being traditional media audience members to online media participants, online user attention will increase in economic value. If left unchecked, its apparatus of production will intensify, further deepening and widening the commodification of communication (Milberry and Anderson, 2009, 409).

USER PARTICIPATION TOWARDS FREE LABOR

Facebook provides new opportunities for users to actively and affectively participate in the production process, while consuming Web 2.0 technologies. Web 2.0 is defined by the ability of users to produce content collaboratively. Web 2.0 is based on user-generated content that creates value from the sharing of information between participants and the business model in which users provide content, which is then leveraged into the user as free labor to be exploited (Cohen, 2008; Ritzer and Jurgenson, 2010, 19). By contributing their time and energy with a click of the keyboard and mouse, Facebook users build friendships, acquire information, and generate a feeling of ease. However, the users, blinded by their seeming empowerment to realize unfulfilled desires, overlook or fail to perceive that it is their labor that shapes the cyber space and that generates the profits that accrue for the owner of Facebook (Bonsu and Darmody, 2008).

Indeed, Facebook has massively benefited from user activities. Facebook's revenue has been soaring primarily due in large part to its ad component. As discussed in Chapter 3, Facebook's ad revenue has dramatically increased, and the proportion from the U.S. decreased—meaning Facebook has rapidly increased its profits from foreign countries. This change is primarily due to factors including a faster growth rate among international users.

More specifically, advertising is generated from the display of advertisements on the website. The arrangements are evidenced by either online acceptance of terms and conditions or contracts that stipulate the types of advertising to be delivered, the timing and the pricing. The typical term of an advertising arrangement is approximately 30 days with billing generally occurring after the delivery of the advertisement. Facebook has opened up the private data of its users to extract more value out of the site, risking a serious loss of users because of a steady erosion of privacy and trust (Nussbaum, 2010, cited in van Dijck, 2012). Transnational corporations and advertising agencies garner the opportunities presented by having a presence on Facebook, and Facebook gains increasing ad revenue. Advertisers continue to develop their ad strategy to make social networks a priority because the benefits of additional exposure to the increasing number of users are immeasurable.

Of course, the exploitation of user participation in social network sites, including Facebook, has been controversial due to both the nature of users as a class and the quantification of user participation (Jin and Feenberg, 2015). Hardt and Negri (2000, 354–359) argue that "immaterial labor is beyond measure or immeasurable." However, "the use value of a user's affective labor is constantly established through specific processes of measurement that served to quantify its corresponding exchange value" (Dowling, 2007, 126). Within SNSs' productive processes, one can conceive a form of exploitation because Facebook does not pay any wage for the labor that produces content (Cohen, 2008).

Telecommunications, media, and online publishers have utilized the younger generation—user as content-creator labor—whose major characteristics include the rapid acceptance of new technology, as well as their roles as heavy users of SNSs. Facebook has acknowledged the subtleties of free labor; therefore, it has utilized the seemingly endless time and energy of young users. Meanwhile, some argue whether user participation can be measured and sold to advertisers, and if so, who conducts the quantification of user participation. In this regard, Smythe pointed out (1977, 4–5) that "several media research corporations and media corporations themselves as well as AC Nielsen quantified audience participation in order to assure that advertisers get what they pay for when they buy audiences." In other words, "how exactly does the audience become a commodity and how is its labor appropriated by media firms" is one of the key issues, and this occurs through audience measurement, which can be considered as an attempt to define the intangible (Webster et al., 2000, cited in Bermejo, 2009). Smythe (1977, 4–5) wondered how advertisers were assured that they were getting the audience they were paying for, and he stated that "the socio-economic characteristics of the delivered audience/readership and its size are the business of A.C. Nielsen and a host of competitors who specialize in rapid assessment of the delivered audience commodity."

However, since Smythe did not clearly explain the quantification process, some scholars later clarified the concept. For example, Maxwell (1991, 31) argues that "the ratings industry produces the first formal expression of the audience as an information commodity sold to broadcasters, cable casters, advertisers, and other paying customers. The circuit of exchange is completed as this information commodity is transformed into the audience commodity sold for advertising money."

Interestingly enough, Facebook (2012b) itself reveals that it creates value for advertisers through its own monetization strategy by offering a combination of 'reach,' 'relevance,' 'social context,' and 'engagement,' which is worth understanding. To begin with, 'reach' means that advertisers can engage *with monthly* active users (*MAUs*) on Facebook based on information they have chosen to a vast consumer audience with Facebook's advertising solutions (Facebook, 2012b). Previously, by using Saleem's infographic (2010), Arvidsson and Colleoni (2012, 145) argued, "advertising is not the most important source of income for Facebook. And there is no linear relation between the number of users and the advertising revenue that Facebook has been able to attract and investor valuations of the company." However, as Figure 6.1 demonstrates, there has been a clear linear relation between the two categories, as Facebook has rapidly increased its ad revenue, from $300 million in 2008 to $6,986 billion in 2013, an increase of 63.2 percent from a previous year, primarily based on its increasing number of registered users, which are 1.23 billion active users (Edwards, 2014).

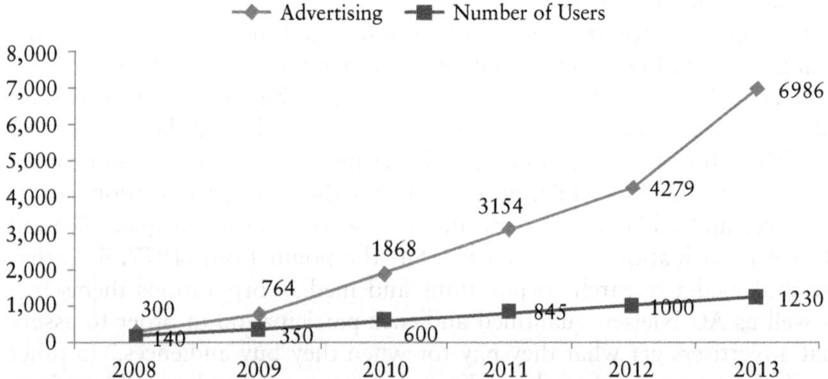

Figure 6.1 Relation between Advertising Revenues and the Number of Facebook Users (unit: millions).

Source: Combined from eMarketer (2013b); Facebook (2012b); Facebook (2013c). Facebook Reports Fourth Quarter and Full Year 2012 Results; Facebook (2012b): S-1 filing with the U.S. Securities and Exchange Commission, F 17 Facebook (2014b). Annual Report, 34.

Secondly, 'relevance' implies advertisers can specify that Facebook shows their ads to a subset of Facebook users based on demographic factors and specific interests that they have chosen to share with the company on Facebook or by using the Like button around the Web. Facebook allows advertisers to select relevant and appropriate audiences for their ads, ranging from millions of users in the case of global brands to hundreds of users in the case of smaller, local businesses (Facebook, 2012b).

Meanwhile, 'social context' implies that the recommendations of friends have a powerful influence on consumer interest and purchase decisions. Facebook offers advertisers the ability to include social context with their marketing messages. Social context is information that highlights a friend's connections with a particular brand or business; for example, that a friend Liked a product or checked in at a restaurant. Facebook believes that users find marketing messages more engaging when they include social context. Finally, Facebook emphasizes 'engagement.' This implies that Facebook believes that the shift to a more social Web creates new opportunities for businesses to engage with interested customers. Any brand or business can create a Facebook page to stimulate an ongoing dialog with users (Facebook, 2012b).

As for the nature of the exchange value embedded in the user activities as commodities, Micky Lee (2011, 445) argues, "the audience in a capitalist media system is best represented as a commodity of exchange value." In other words, Facebook has discovered that advertisers' objectives range from building long-term brand awareness to stimulating an immediate purchase. Facebook's combination of reach, relevance, social context, and engagement gives advertisers enhanced opportunities to generate brand awareness and affiliation, while also creating new ways to generate near-term demand for their products from consumers likely to have purchase intent (Facebook, 2012b).

In this sense, watching is work rendered as a quantifiable activity by ratings points that reflect units of audience power (Miller, 2003). The details of users' consumption habits become information commodities. Whenever Facebook users access information, their clicks have become quantifiable commodities to be bought and sold. Facebook users provide their daily activities as free labor to network owners, and thereafter, to advertisers, and user activities are primarily being watched and counted and eventually are appropriated by large corporations and advertising agencies.

As Lanier explains following his interview with a blogger (Gots, 2012), Facebook's business model is based on the value to advertisers of the rich data its users provide by sharing their changing interests and relationship networks in real time. As a computer scientist and artist, in *You Are Not a Gadget*, Lanier (2010, 54) previously acknowledged that "Facebook might capture extremely valuable information called the social graph, and using this information, an advertiser might hypothetically be able to target all the members of a peer group just as they are forming their opinions about brands, habits, and so on." He also emphasized that "the situation with social networks is layered with multiple absurdities, and the advertising idea hasn't made any money." His argument was based on a quick retreat of 2007's Bacon, which Facebook's facture to gather information to be sold to advertisers.

A few years later, however, Lanier believes that "the big data that Facebook and other networks gather is especially valuable because of its level of detail. It goes far deeper than registration demographics: geography, age, gender, education—enabling marketers to target you, the consumer, based on up-to-the moment details like your favorite music and what shoes you bought last week" (Gots, 2012). As Sutchiffe (2006) clearly points out, one of the most distinctive features of the notion of imperialism designed by Marxists is the concerns about the working of the productive system and the hierarchy of classes which it generates. In this sense, it is about the stability of the productive system and the dominance and exploitation of some classes over others. As Marx (1867) limited the notion of class to wage labor under the conditions of 19th century industrialism, some may argue that Facebook users cannot be categorized as a class; instead, the nature of users is beyond the notion of class, because it is a matter of gender, age, and geography among many other factors.

However, as discussed, several theoreticians, including Terranova (2000; as free labor) and Hardt and Negri (2004; as immaterial labor) already identified platform users as a new class with different concepts of labor. Regardless of the fact that these two different approaches did not agree in terms of the nature of exploitation, both commonly argue that users are a form of labor. In fact, the analysis of Facebook users is not that simple, because advertisers and Facebook itself utilized users not only based on gender and age but also on class in the process of commodification. As Fuchs (2010, 188) argues, "class relationships have become generalized. The production of surplus value and hence exploitation is not limited to wage-labor, but reaches society as a whole."

Facebook has also developed a direct marketing method. As Table 6.1 explains, advertising revenue accounted for 84.2 percent of Facebook's annual revenue in 2012, down from 98 percent in 2009. Although it is not the primary revenue resource yet, revenue from nonadvertising increased by 62.3 times between 2009 and 2012. Whereas many other Web 2.0 technologies, including YouTube, sell users' free time and energy to advertisers, Facebook utilizes their users as markets as well.

Table 6.1 Facebook's Revenue (in millions)

	2008	*2009*	*2010*	*2011*	*2012*	*2013*
Advertising	300	764	1868	3154	4279	6986
Payments and Other Fees		13	106	557	810	886
Total	272	777	1974	3711	5089	7872

Source: Facebook (2014b). Annual Report 2013. Facebook (2013c). Facebook Reports Fourth Quarter and Full Year 2012 Results; Facebook (2012b): S-1 filing with the U.S. Securities and Exchange Commission (2012), F 17.

Facebook enables payments between the users and developers on the Facebook platform. The users can purchase virtual or digital goods on the Facebook platform by using credit cards or other payment methods available on the website. The primary method for users to transact with the developers on the Facebook platform is via the purchase of virtual currency, which enables the users to purchase virtual and digital goods in games and apps. Upon the initial sale of virtual currency, Facebook records consideration received from a user as a deposit. When a user engages in a payment transaction utilizing Facebook's virtual currency for the purchase of a virtual or digital good from a platform developer, Facebook reduces the user's virtual currency balance by the price of the purchase, which is a price that is solely determined by the platform developer. Facebook remits to the platform developer an amount that is based on the total amount of virtual currency redeemed minus the processing fee that Facebook charges the platform developer for the transaction. Facebook's revenue is the net amount of the transaction, representing Facebook's processing fee for the service performed (Facebook, 2012b).

As van Dijck (2012, 171) points out, Facebook chose a mixture of strategies like targeted advertising and selling customized metadata. In the past year, "it has added integrating pay services for online games and selling exclusive access to games or apps to members of the site." Membership of a particular social network site is increasingly monetized as a direct marketing tool; for instance, Facebook gives user communities privileged access to certain selected services and goods via their features Facebook Connect and Open Graph. Platforms thus become closed membership alliances whose data represent specific marketing and advertising niches. Corporations define their customer segments through a refined system of algorithmic connections (van Dijck, 2012).

Financial Valuation of Facebook

Facebook has developed its financial valuation, which is related to "its perceived capacity for attracting future investment, or, to use a more general term, financial rent" (Arvidsson and Colleoni, 2012, 145). Right after its initial public offering (IPO) on May 18, 2012, the capital value of Facebook was as much as $104 billion (Geron, 2012). At $38 a share, Facebook was valued at $104 billion, the biggest-ever valuation by an American company at the time of offering (Raice et al., 2012). The share price nosedived from $38 to $20.11 on August 20 of the same year, around 53 percent of its IPO price. Critics claimed that the company was overvalued and had not devised a credible plan to generate revenue, and it subsequently turned out to be true (Sparkes, 2012). However, the share price steeply rebounded to $50.14 as of October 4, 2013, and rose to $76.67 as of September 10, 2014, valuing the company at $202 billion (Figure 6.2). That makes Facebook the 22nd largest company in the world, and the largest social media company. This means that Facebook's business model "can be interpreted as a symptom of a transition away from a Fordist, industrial model of accumulation where the value of a company is mainly related to its ability to extract surplus value from its workers, to an informational finance-centered model of accumulation where the value of a company is increasingly related to its ability to maintain a brand that justifies a share, in terms of financial rent, of the global surplus that circulates on financial markets," as Arvidsson and Colleoni (2012, 145) point out.

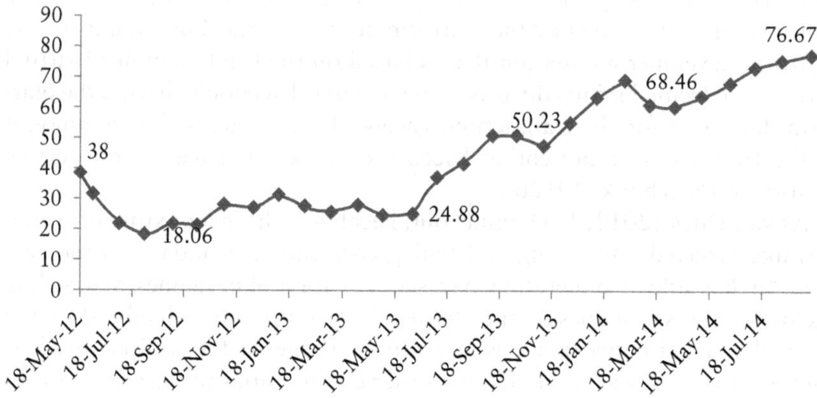

Figure 6.2 Facebook's Stock Price, May 2012–September 2014 (unit: dollars).

The capital value of Facebook is volatile, but experts predicted that it will grow over the next three years to $104.3 billion in 2017 due to the rapid growth of the digital ad market (Satell, 2013); however, it fulfilled and surpassed this prediction within only a year. With the rapid growth of smartphone consumers, Facebook has developed mobile ads, and eMarketer (2013a), a consulting company, expected Facebook to reap $965 million in U.S. mobile ad revenue in 2013, which is about 2.5 times the $391 million earned in 2012, the first year that Facebook started showing mobile ads. In 2013, Facebook's mobile advertising revenue represented approximately 45% of total advertising revenue, which is clearly far beyond the expectation (Facebook, 2014b).

Among technology companies, it ranks fourth only behind Apple ($593 billion), Google ($403 billion), and Microsoft ($383 billion), and surpasses IBM ($189 billion) and Oracle ($181 billion) (Figure 6.3). In the era of digital capitalism, Facebook attracted investments, which has been one of its significant forms of revenue. Zizek (2009, cited in Bohm et al., 2012) indeed makes this point clearly in his discussion of Microsoft. According to Zizek, there is no way that Microsoft's model of value production and profitability can be explained in terms of the productivity of the labor power it deploys. Instead, Bill Gates' business model is based on creating a form of monopolistic control over the basic infrastructure of the knowledge economy and doing everything he can to ensure that Microsoft maintains effective control over the networks and protocols of communication that are used in the communicative circuits of production in the social factory. For several observers, Facebook is the new Microsoft. It has established itself as the de-facto gatekeeper and standard of the social networking world.

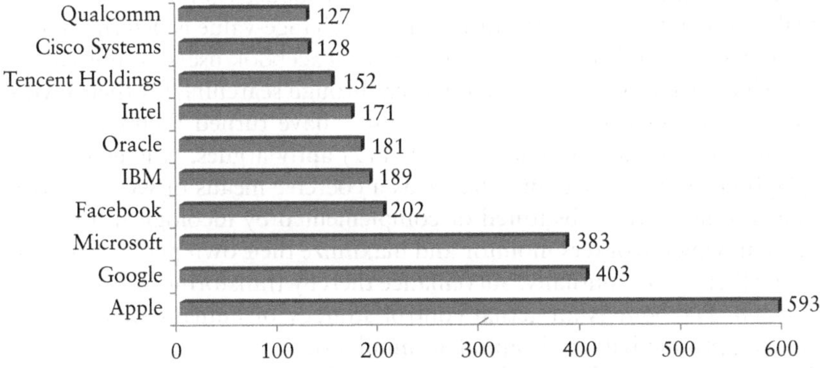

Figure 6.3 Top 10 Tech Companies by Market Value as of September 9, 2014.
Source: Bloomberg (2014). Facebook Valuation Tops $200 Billion, 9 September.

As Fuchs (2011, 231) points out, "financial capital does not itself produce profits, and it is only an entitlement to payments that are made in the future and derive from profits." For social network sites, user labor is the source of profit, and without users' activities, the financial value of SNSs, including Facebook and Twitter, cannot be substantial. Fuchs (2012c, 638; 2014, 255) especially argues that "on corporate social media, users create content, browse content, establish and maintain relations with others by communication, and update their profiles." Following Smythe (1977) who stated, "all non-sleeping time of most of the population is work time," Fuchs (2012c, 638) argues that all time users spend on platforms, including Facebook, is work time. What Fuchs also emphasizes is that this work time contains time for social relationship management and cultural activities that generate reputation. Borrowing Bourdieu's terms, Fuchs claims that "users employ social media because they strive to a certain degree for achieving social capital (the accumulation of social relations), cultural capital (the accumulation of qualification, education, knowledge) and symbolic capital (the accumulation of reputation)." Although Fuchs's argument raises some controversies, what we need to consider is that the time that users spend on commercial platforms for generating social, cultural, and symbolic capital cannot be separated from the process of user commodification transformed into economic capital.

COMMODIFICATION OF FACEBOOK USERS

As the Internet has been a primary tool as a social networking system in the 21st century, the degree to which users' activities (use value) have been transformed into valuable commodities (exchange value) has also been remarkable in the social media era. As Mosco (2009) articulates, extensive commodification refers to the way in which market forces shape and re-shape life, entering spaces previously untouched, or mildly touched, by capitalist social relations. The process of commodification in Facebook is clear. On the one hand, use-value is determined by a product's ability to meet individual and social needs; on the other hand, exchange-value is determined by what a product can bring to the marketplace. Facebook users do not voluntarily sell data about themselves; however, through searching for their favorite ads and clicking the keyboard, the users have turned themselves into valuable commodities. As Fuchs (2014, 117) aptly argues, "the emergence of 'playbour' implies that surveillance as a coercive means of work control is to a certain degree substituted or complemented by ideological forms of control, in which workers monitor and maximize their own performance or monitor themselves mutually. Surveillance thereby transformed into control of the self. Playbour is an actual control strategy of humans that aims at enhancing productivity and capital accumulation."

When we compare Facebook with other technology-driven corporations, such as Apple, Microsoft, and Google, it is evident that Facebook is one of the most effective in terms of the generation of per capita revenue through the commodification of its users. As Figure 6.4 shows, in 2012 with 4,619 employees Facebook's total annual revenue was recorded at $5.1 billion.

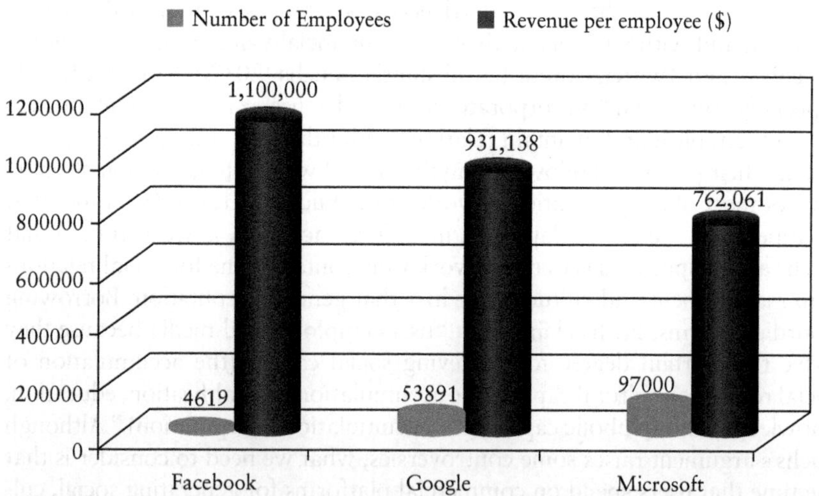

Figure 6.4 Revenue per Employee among New Media Corporations (2012)
Source: Facebook (2012b); Google (2012b); Microsoft (2012).

This means that the revenue per employee was $1.10 million, which was higher than that of Microsoft with 97,000 employees ($762,061) and Google with 53,891 employees ($931,138).

Facebook's relative advantage has not obviously been the number of employees that create value for the company, but the number of its active users who share millions of photos, texts, and videos on a daily basis worldwide. Facebook does not (or hardly ever) pay its users for the production of content. One accumulation strategy is to give users free access to services and platforms, let them produce content, and then to accumulate a large number of producers that are sold as a commodity to third party advertisers (Fuchs, 2010). As Cote and Pybus (2007, 97) argue, the commodified user of Facebook has shifted from Smythe's conception of the audience as discrete, measurable quanta in the chain of production and circulation to a dynamic, productive composition of bodies as aggregate networked information and communication technologies. As Smythe (1977, 7–8) emphasized, people were brought into this commodity relation by working (unconsciously, uncoerced, and unpaid) during supposedly nonwork times to carry out the demands of advertising. As consumers, people enable the transvaluation of their leisure activity into this commodity. To this extent, Smythe proposed that "audience work produces value for the consciousness industry" (Maxwell, 1991, 31).

Of course, with respect to the term labor, it can no longer only be seen as a factor in industrial relations; it must also be understood as a larger category with which to analyze many:

> "The contemporary life compels us as audiences for ever more recombinant forms of entertainment and new programming, to labor on ever-multiplying numbers of texts (as readers and Facebook fans). When such labor is subsequently repurposed by traditional producers of information and entertainment products, the producing/consuming prosumer is born. Additionally, as individuals are subject to precarious, unstable forms of employment that demand they put their personalities, communicative capacities and emotions into their jobs, they are encouraged to see their intimate lives as resources to be exploited for profit and, as a consequence, new forms of labor on the self are brought into being."
>
> (Burston et al., 2010, 215)

More specifically, SNS owners and corporations have rapidly appropriated users as free labor, while providing some productive resources. For Smythe (1977, 3), this joint process embodies a principal contradiction. On the one hand, the information, entertainment and educational materials transmitted to the audience are an inducement (gift, bribe, or free lunch) to recruit potential members of the audience and to maintain their loyal attention. The appropriateness of the analogy to the free lunch in the old-time saloon or cocktail bar is manifest: "the free lunch consists of materials which whet the prospective audience members' appetites and thus (1) attract and keep them attending to the program, newspaper or magazine, and (2) cultivate a mood conducive to favorable reaction to the explicit and implicit advertisers' messages" (Smythe, 1977, 5).

On the other hand, in economic terms, the audience commodity is a non-durable producers' good which is bought and used in the marketing of the advertiser's product. The work which audience members perform for the advertiser to whom they have been sold is to learn to buy particular brands of consumer goods, and to spend their income accordingly. In short, they work to create the demand for advertised goods which is the purpose of the monopoly capitalist advertisers. Whereas doing this, audience members are simultaneously reproducing their own labor power (Smythe, 1977, 6).

What differentiates Facebook users, therefore, SNS users, from television audiences in Smythe's' analysis is that SNSs directly change user values to exchange values for commercial profits. Media corporations make billions of dollars by gathering detailed information about Internet users and by subsequently claiming it as their private property. Participation in cultural activities has been a commoditized activity; however, the current form of appropriation is beyond what the users imagine. As Mejias (2013) argues, participation in digital platforms produces inequality because it is asymmetrical. For instance, while users surrender their privacy for the sake of convenience, platform owners are increasingly opaque about the ways in which they use the information they collect. "The full range of inequalities that participation in digital networks can produce has not been fully indexed, but it includes dynamics such as the transformation of public goods into private goods once they are uploaded to the platform; the way in which small social media projects are acquired by corporations who capitalize on the social labor of the site's existing communities" (Mejias, 2013, 4–5).

The information gathering process is made easier by "the current climate of self-disclosure facilitated by interactive technology, including blogging and social networking that help generate a trove of information for data miners, whether for advertising or policing purposes" (Andrejevic, 2007, 178). Although playfulness and joy are major features for users, use-values ultimately become subordinate to exchange-value. For many corporations, users are the new economy because they do not just buy their goods and services, but they convince their friends to give them a try through their activities. Thus, the commodification of SNS users is produced not only by users themselves but also by corporate strategies as SNSs have vehemently utilized users as commodities to be sold.

CONCLUSION

This chapter has critically analyzed the process of commodification of Facebook users as free labor. It has especially engaged with audience commodity theory to frame an analysis of free labor in an era of social media. Smythe's view that would see "individual audience members as undertaking unpaid work when they watch television programs" might not be appropriate in the social media era (Hesmondhalgh, 2010, 278). However, it is also true that audiences are increasingly required to participate audibly and physically, albeit that their activities require a subtle eye on the part of the observer, and audience commodities are still very useful in understanding new technologies. Smythe's concepts have gained a renewed saliency amidst the emerging practices and celebratory rhetoric of Web 2.0. In the case of audience commodity theory, the work of the audience is materially embedded in, and articulated through, the capitalist application of communication technologies in the 21st century (Comor, 2010).

In fact, this chapter has argued that the terms audience commodities and audience work warrant a new look due to the importance of the changing nature of Web 2.0 participants, unlike audience commodity theory previously emphasizing the role of audiences in mass communication, such as television and newspapers. The novelty of the concept of the audience commodity gives some ideas to see the transformative qualities of the concept of audience towards users in the new economic era (Coté and Pybus, 2007). When we extend the theory to social media, we are able to find that it has provided a solid groundwork for the understanding of the commodification of users.

However, as Bermejo (2009, 149) points out, "it is important to pay attention to the specification of the actual work performed by the audience. Whereas it can be argued that the audience is working to create the demand for advertised goods, the specific work performed by the audience has changed, or at least has become more complex. Clearly, this change is reflected in the different pricing models used currently in online advertising." This means that, as Andrejevic (2004) also argues, watching—that is, being exposed to advertising—cannot be considered as the only work of the online audience that is appropriated by the media; activities such as clicking and typing also should be considered as labor. Unlike TV and radio, social media is able to target specific user groups much more effectively. This is done through powerful computing algorithms that filter user data according to a range of different advertising oriented criteria (Bohm et al, 2012).

In addition, it is critical to understand that the real value produced by Facebook users is economically relevant as long as the credibility of user commodities and associated exploitation have been seriously considered in the market. Facebook users feel joy and create their own cyber culture; however, Facebook is used to refine the process of delivering Internet users to advertisers. The users proactively participate in producing and consuming knowledge and information, and users interact with each other on an open platform through which someone can create and consume content. Therefore, Facebook users can be seen as confirming the pre-eminence of exchange-value in Facebook, as audiences in television have, but as more affective customers (Jin, 2012). Facebook users are free labor, instead of affective labor, because the immaterial production that Hardt and Negri (2008) emphasize is increasingly outside of capital with the partial exception of creative/originating workers with nonemployee legal status, little more than an example of wishful thinking (Camfield, 2007, 129).

Finally, as Facebook evolves in relation to an environment of commodification, it seems likely that Facebook users will continue producing the inescapable inequalities between capital and themselves as free labor primarily because corporations have utilized the users as commodities, which are not-paid workers. The users of interactive media freely agree to turn over control of information about themselves to Facebook:

> "There is no external compulsion to use Facebook—such decisions are generally portrayed as a matter of choice, convenience, and personal pleasure. However, conditions of estrangement may still obtain since the commercial character of online social network sites means that users will still be subject to detailed forms of data-gathering and ongoing controlled experiments in target marketing designed to more effectively influence their behavior without their knowledge."
>
> (Andrejevic, 2011, 96)

Facebook users add and/or create value to what they consume by clicking the keyboard and dragging the mouse with no monetary reward, resulting in an asymmetrical relationship between Facebook and its users.

NOTES

1. Of course, as Eran Fisher (2012) argues with the notion of Dallas Smythe's audience commodity, some researchers attempt to combine these two different perspectives under Marxist theory. In fact, Marxist-inspired research on the new media environment has focused almost exclusively on audience exploitation. Simultaneously, mainstream (liberal) research has tended to reaffirm the common-sense and ideological construction of SNSs as facilitating de-alienation by offering users opportunities for self-expression; authenticity; communication; collaboration with others; and deep engagement with, and control over cultural, social, and economic ventures. As Fisher (2012, 174) points out, "both these trends—seemingly contradictory—are in fact dialectically linked. Exploitation and de-alienation are not simply two contrasting interpretations of SNS; rather, Marxist theory encourages us to accommodate them within a single analytical framework. SNS give audience more opportunities for objectification by allowing self-expression, authenticity, and communication and collaboration with others. As the communication and sociability of users are commodified, so does their labor become a source for exploitation."
2. Google is explicit at how it generates revenue and how advertisers pay the company. Advertisers pay only a few dollars to join the Google AdWords Auction System. They submit text-based advertisements and bid for keywords. Advertisers only pay Google when the link is clicked. Google aims to deliver relevant

advertisements to users and deliver potential consumers to advertisers. Google hires as many people in sales and advertising as in engineering. Google constantly emphasizes that search results are not influenced by the amount of money that advertisers pay, but larger advertisers have a better chance to have their advertisements listed next to the search results because they have the money to bid for more keywords at a higher price (Lee, 2010, 914).

REFERENCES

Andrejevic, M. (2007). *iSpy: Surveillance and Power in the Interactive Era*. Lawrence, KS: University of Press Kansas.

Andrejevic, M. (2011). Social network exploitation. In Z. Papacharissi (ed.), *A Networked Self: Identity, Community, and Culture on Social Network Sites*. pp. 82–101. London: Routledge.

Arvidsson, A. & Colleoni, E. (2012). Value in informational capitalism and on the Internet. *The Information Society* 28: 135–150.

Bermejo, F. (2009). Audience manufacture in historical perspective: From broadcasting to Google. *New Media and Society* 11(1 & 2): 133–154.

Bohm, S., Land, C., & Beverungen, A. (2012). The value of Marx: Free labour, rent and primitive accumulation in Facebook. Working Paper.

Bolin, G. (2010). Symbolic production and value in media industries. *Journal of Cultural Economy* 2(3): 345–361.

Bonsu, S. & Darmody, A. (2008). Co-creating *Second Life:* Market–consumer cooperation in contemporary economy. *Journal of Macromarketing* 28(4): 355–368.

boyd, d. (2011). Social network sites as networked publics: Affordances, dynamics, and implications. In Z. Papacharissi (ed.), *A Networked Self: Identity, Community, and Culture on Social Network Sites*. 39–58. London: Routledge.

Burston, J., Dyer-Witheford N. & Hearn, A. (2010). Digital labour: Workers, authors, citizens. *ephemera: theory & politics in organization* 10(3/4): 214–220.

Camfield, D. (2007). The multitude and the kangaroo: A critique of Hardt and Negri's theory of immaterial labor. *Historical Materialism* 17: 21–52.

Castells, M. (2009). *Communication Power*. London: Oxford University Press.

Cohen, N.S. (2008). The valorization of surveillance: Towards a political economy of Facebook, *Democratic Comunique* 22(1): 5–22.

Comor, E. (2010). Digital prosumption and alienation. *ephemera: theory & politics in organization* 10(3/4): 439–454.

Cote, M. & Pybus, J. (2007). Learning to immaterial labour 2.0: MySpace and social networks. *ephemera: theory & politics in organization* 7(1): 88–106.

Dowling, E. (2007). Producing the dining experience: Measure, subjectivity and the affective worker. *ephemera: theory & politics in organization* 7(1): 117–132.

Dowling, E., Nunes, R. & Trott, B. (2007). Immaterial and affective labour: Explored. *ephemera: theory & politics in organization* 7(1): 1–7.

Edwards, J. (2014). Facebook shares surge on first ever $1 billion mobile ad revenue quarter. http://www.businessinsider.com/facebook-q4-2013-earnings-2014-1#ixzz3ClY3Njdt.

eMarketer (2013a). Facebook U.S. mobile ad revenue soaring. Press release. 3 April.

eMarketer (2013b). Worldwide Facebook revenues by source, 2009–2013. Press release, 29 August.

Facebook (2013a). Facebook reports second quarter 2013 results. Accessed http://investor.fb.com/releasedetail.cfm?ReleaseID=780093.

Facebook (2013b). Facebook's growth in the past year. https://www.facebook.com/photo.php?fbid=10151908376831729&set=a.10151908376636729.1073741825.20531316728&type=1&theater.

Facebook (2013c). Facebook reports fourth quarter and full year 2012 results. Menlo Park, CA: Facebook.

Facebook (2013d). S-1 filing with the U.S. Securities and Exchange Commission: Form S-1 Registration Statement. New York: SEC.

Facebook (2012a). Newsroom. Accessed September 17, 2012. http://newsroom.fb.com/content/default.aspx?NewsAreaId=20.

Facebook (2012b). S-1 filing with the U.S. Securities and Exchange Commission: Form S-1 Registration Statement. New York: SEC.

Fisher, E. (2012). How less alienation creates more exploitation? Audience labour on social network sites. *tripleC: Communication, Capitalism & Critique. Open Access Journal for a Global Sustainable Information Society* 10(2): 171–183.

Fuchs, C. (2010). Labor in informational capitalism and on the Internet. *The Information Society* 26(3): 179–196.

Fuchs, C. (2011). *Foundations of Critical Media and Communication Studies*. London: Routledge.

Fuchs, C. (2012a). Dallas Smythe Today—The audience commodity, the digital abour debate, Marxist political economy and critical theory. Prolegomena to a digital labour theory of value. *tripleC: Communication, Capitalism & Critique. Open Access Journal for a Global Sustainable Information Society* 10(2): 692–742.

Fuchs, C. (2012b). The political economy of privacy on Facebook. *Television and New Media* 13(2): 139–159.

Fuchs, C. (2014). *Social Media: A Critical Introduction*. London: Sage.

Fuchs, C. (2012C). With or without Marx? With or without capitalism? A rejoinder to Adam Arvidsson and Eleanor Colleoni. *tripleC: Communication, Capitalism & Critique. Open Access Journal for a Global Sustainable Information Society* 10(2): 633–645.

Geron, T. (2012). Facebook prices third-largest IPO ever, valued at $104 billion. *Forbes*. 15 May. http://www.forbes.com/sites/tomiogeron/2012/05/17/facebook-prices-ipo-at-38-per-share/.

Google (2008). 2008 annual report of Google. Mountain View, CA: Google Inc.

Gots, J. (2012). Jaron Lanier: Why Facebook isn't free. 18 May. Bid Think. http://bigthink.com/humanizing-technology/jaron-lanier-why-facebook-isnt-free.

Gregg, M. (2009). Learning to (love) labour: Production cultures and the affective turn. *Communication and Critical/Cultural Studies* 6(2): 209–214.

Hardt, M. & Negri, A. (2000). *Empire*. Cambridge, MA: Harvard University Press.

Hardt, M. & Negri, A. (2004). *Multitude: War and Democracy in the Age of Empire*. New York, NY: Penguin.

Hardt, M. & Negri, A. (2009). *Commonwealth*. Cambridge, MA: Harvard University Press.

Hasmondhalgh, D. (2010). User-generated content, free labour and the cultural industries. *ephemera theory & politics in organization* 10(3/4): 267–284.

Jhally, S. (1987). *The Codes of Advertising: Fetishism and the Political Economy of Meaning in the Consumer Society*. New York: St. Martin's.

Jin, D.Y. (2013a). The construction of platform imperialism in the globalization era. *tripleC: Communication, Capitalism & Critique. Open Access Journal for a Global Sustainable Information Society* 11(1): 145–172.

Jin, D.Y. (2014b). Critical analysis of user commodities as free labor in social networking sites: A case study of Cyworld. *Continuum: Journal of Media and Cultural Studies.*

Jin, D.Y. and A. Feenberg (accepted, 2015). Commodity and community in social networking: Marx and the monetization of user-generated content. *The Information Society* 31(1): 52-60.

Lanier, J. (2010). *You Are Not a Gadget*. New York: A.A. Knopf.

Lazzarato, M. (1996). Immaterial labor. In P. Virno and M. Hardt (ed.), *Radical Thought in Italy: A Potential Politics*, 133–147. Minneapolis: University of Minnesota Press.

Lee, M.K. (2011). Google ads and the blindspot debate. *Media, Culture and Society* 33(3): 433–437.

Mansson, D. & Myers, S. (2011). An initial examination of college students' expressions of affection through Facebook. *Southern Communication Journal* 76(2): 155–168.

Manzerolle, V. (2010). Mobilizing the audience commodity: Digital labour in a wireless world. *ephemera: theory & politics in organization* 10(3/4): 455–469.

Maxwell, R. (1991). The image is gold: Value, the audience commodity, and fetishism. *Journal of Film and Video* 43(1–2): 29–45.

McGirt, E. (2007). Facebook's Mark Zuckerberg: Hacker, dropout, CEO. Accessed September 17, 2012. http://www.fastcompany.com/magazine/115/open_features-hacker-dropout-ceo.html.

Meehan, E. (1990). Why we don't count: The commodity audience. Logics of television: Essays in cultural criticism. Patricia Mellencamp (ed.). 117–137. Bloomington: Indiana University Press.

Microsoft (2012). *2012 Annual Report*. Redmond, WA: Microsoft.

Miller, T. (2003) (ed.), *Television: Critical Concepts in Media and Cultural Studies*. London: Routledge.

Milberry, K. & Anderson, S. (2009). Open sourcing our way to an online commons: Contesting corporate impermeability in the new media ecology. *Journal of Communication Inquiry* 33(4): 393–412.

Mosco, V. (2nd ed., 2009). *The Political Economy of Communication*. London: Sage.

Google (2012a). S-1 filing with the U.S. Securities and Exchange Commission: Form S-1 Registration Statement. New York: SEC.

Google (2012b). *Annual Report on Form 10-K*. Mountain View, CA: Google Inc.

Ritzer, G. & Jurgenson, N. (2010). Production, consumption, prosumption: The nature of capitalism in the age of the digital prosumer. *Journal of Consumer Culture* 10(1): 13–36.

Saleem, M. (2010). Visualizing six years of Facebook. Mashable. 2 October. http://mashable.com/2010/02/10/facebook-growth-infographic/.

Satell, G. (2013). How much is Facebook really worth? *Forbes*, 11 February. http://www.forbes.com/sites/gregsatell/2013/02/21/how-much-is-facebook-really-worth/.

Shimpach, S. (2005). Working watching: The creative and cultural labor of the media audience. *Social Semiotics* 15(3): 343–360.

Smythe, D. (1977). Communication: Blindspot of western Marxism. *Canadian Journal of Political and Social Theory* 1(3): 1–27.

Smythe, D. (1981). *Dependency Road*. Norwood, NJ: Ablex.

Smythe, D. (1994).Communications: Blindspot of western Marxism. In D. Smythe and T. Guback (1994, eds.), *Counterclockwise: Perspectives on Communication*, 266–291. Boulder: Westview.

Socialbakers (2013). Facebook statistics by country. http://www.socialbakers.com/facebook-statistics/.

Terranova, T. (2000). Free labor: Producing culture for the digital economy. *Social Text* 18(2): 33–58.

van Dijck, J. (2012). Facebook as a tool for producing sociality and connectivity. *Television and New Media* 13(2): 160–176.

Vincos Blog (2012). World map of social networks. Accessed April 4, 2013. http://www.vincos.it/world-map-of-social-networks/.

7 Challenge to the Global Digital Divide

INTRODUCTION

In the early 2010s, as SNSs, smartphones, and relevant ideologies and cultures have taken primary roles, the global digital divide cannot be the same as that of the 1990s and the early years of the 21st century because of social media's enormous potential, not only for capital accumulation for software developers and owning countries, but also for socio-cultural opportunities. "The virtuous circle of easy access to computers, related skills and social support, entails a vicious circle for those who lack those things: these inequalities are likely to extend into the world of social networking" (Couldry, 2012, 11). As Castells (2001, 3) pointed out, "the digital divide was the concept based on the Internet-based economy and culture," however, the social media era relies on platforms, such as SNSs and smartphones, including operating systems, as well as the Internet. This means that we have to comprehend the global digital divide as the various causes and consequences that our global society witnesses with the growth of smartphones and SNSs.

In particular, nation-wide capital accumulation occurring as a consequence of the use of social media and intellectual property (IP) rights and cultural aspects relevant to the global digital divide should be considered as some of the most significant issues because they are the critical causes and effects of disparities in the social media era, resulting in intensifying inequalities among nations. As van Dijck (2012) points out, the overall importance of the phenomenon is not only for the economy, but also for social inequalities which can be increased due to the digital divide. Unlike previous works that primarily focused on the disparity in economy, we emphasize new perspectives in understanding the global digital divide driven by platform technologies as the disparity between the U.S. and the majority of developing countries.

This chapter attempts to develop new perspectives in the existing body of knowledge on the issue of the global digital divide by discussing its significant pertinence to digital platforms. The goal is not to provide more statistical data on ICT indicators to the dimensions of the divide. Instead, as Tsatsou (2011) clearly points out, the digital divide must be revisited in order to better contextualize it and that less linear explanations of the divide phenomenon should be developed. It thus discusses the theoretical examination of a few significant standards, such as smartphones in conjunction with software (operating systems), big data, intellectual property, and symbolic hegemony as some of the most significant socio-cultural and ICT-related issues in determining the degree of the global digital divide. Hegemony in this context implies domination through ideology or discourse as a symbolic domination, instead of a narrow-minded, political domination, which is one of the major elements in constructing the dominant power of TNCs (Gramsci, 1971; Johnson, 2010). It begins with a discussion of inequalities in people's access to, and use of, two of the most significant platforms, smartphones and Facebook, not only as technologies but also as symbols of the knowledge economy. Based on that, it explores the chief reasons why these new measures as the nature of the problem itself and the manner in which it should be resolved are significant in the current debates on the global digital divide, and what the implications are in our networked society.

FROM INTERNET DIVIDE TO PLATFORM DIVIDE: TRANSITION OF THE GLOBAL DIGITAL DIVIDE

Since the late 1990s, a digital divide has become one of the most discussed agendas, both nationally and globally.[1] Admitting diverse variances and dimensions, the digital divide commonly refers to discrepancies between social groups based on income, race, ethnicity, age, and education in access to, use of, and empowerment by networked computers and the Internet (van Dijck, 2012, 196; 2006). The idea of a digital divide was originally popularized with regard to the disparity in Internet access (Castells, 2001), and addressing the digital divide within a country has been a major agenda for policy makers and researchers (Gunkel, 2003). However, the digital divide is not only within one country, as the global divide has also existed for a long time between developed and developing countries, and the global digital divide deals with divergence of access to Internet between nations (Norris, 2001; International Telecommunication Union, 2005; Vehovar, 2006).

Whereas there are several different ideas, the global divide is commonly concerned with absolute differences between countries' telecommunications infrastructures, information transmission capacity, aggregate number of computers, website hosts, telephone users, and the like (Couldry, 2009, 384). Pippa Norris (2001), for example, defines the global digital divide as a divergence of Internet access between industrialized and developed societies. As the OECD (2001) highlighted, the uneven distribution in opportunities to access and use ICTs exists not only amongst diverse population groups, such as individuals, households, and businesses but also geographical areas.

Globally, the majority of developing countries have limited access to other socio-economic resources and continue to struggle in their efforts to become digital. They have also found difficulties in resolving numerous barriers such as access, skill, and infrastructure, which make the situations of these countries worse (Quan-Hasse, 2013). The global digital divide has been particularly significant because it can further widen the economic gap between developed and developing nations (Marriott, 2006; Deichmann et al., 2006; Ayanso et al., 2010, 304). With the recent growth of digital platforms, including social network sites and smartphones, the global digital divide has been further worrisome for many developing countries. It asks us to critically rethink the global digital divide in order to reflect the milieu surrounding the growth of platform technologies.

More specifically, previously two major problems were identified in the realm of the digital divide: one focused on inequalities in material access to ICTs, and the other focused on inequalities in the skills necessary to use ICT effectively (Selwyn, 2004; Bradbrook and Fisher, 2004). Many policy makers, researchers, and ICT practitioners have paid attention to the subject of unequal access to and use of the Internet due to its tremendous influences on people's socio-economic lives, especially between developed countries and developing countries. It is obvious that the major reason for the concern raised by the digital divide is the value of information. In the networked society, "information is considered as one of the most significant goods, both material and immaterial, that is so essential for the survival and self-respect of individuals that it cannot be exchanged for other goods, such as a basic (survival) level of income, life chances, freedoms and fundamental rights. Information has become a primary good in contemporary society even though the minimum amount that is required appears hard to assess and is likely to differ according to the type of society" (van Dijck, 2006, 231).[2]

As the former secretary-general of the UN states, too many of the world's people remain untouched by the information technology revolution. Kofi Annan (2003) says that "a digital divide threatens to exacerbate already-wide gaps between rich and poor, within and among countries. The stakes are high indeed. Timely access to news and information can promote trade, education, employment, health and wealth. One of the hallmarks of the information society—openness—is a crucial ingredient of democracy and good governance. Information and knowledge are also at the heart of efforts to strengthen tolerance, mutual understanding and respect for diversity." The issue is that the current form of the global digital divide in the platform era has intensified the divide because only a few platform owners and their nations have greatly benefited from their dominant power.

Global Digital Divide

The global digital divide has become nuanced, reflecting different standards for measuring global disparities in tandem with the growth of technologies, including digital platforms. Therefore, those narrowly defined notions implying a bipolar division between the haves and the have-nots, as well as the connected and the disconnected, cannot explain the multiplicity of the recent global dynamics (Mansell, 2002; Warschauer, 2003,

2004; Vehovar, 2006; Ayanso et al., 2010; Epstein et al., 2011). As Epstein et al. (2011, 92) aptly put it, "the digital divide not only covers different kinds of disparities with different sorts of consequence, but it also obscures the variety of ideas about the nature of the problem itself and the manner in which it should be resolved." Taking an example of the Chinese working-class in conjunction with ICTs, Jack Qiu (2009) points out that "the binary model is inadequate to reflect the technosocial dynamics in a rapidly industrializing society." Tsatsou (2011, 323) also correctly argues that "the linear, simplistic and normative character largely overlooks the role of socio-cultural and political capital and the importance of their connections for how people adopt ICTs and for social implications of ICT adoption:"

> "That is to say that research has hardly touched upon the role of ... agencies, such as political agencies, and their interconnections in the distribution of symbolic capital that relates to new technologies and effects on social life. This is because economic and technological factors are given more emphasis to explain digital divides and to justify the role of such divides in people's socio-economic status and positioning."
>
> (Tsatsou, 2011, 323)

With the rapid growth of ICTs in the 21st century, several initiatives attempted to come up with a broad policy framework aimed at closing this global digital divide. Whereas these attempts mainly focused on the ways to reduce inequalities in material access to ICTs and in the skills necessary to use ICT, they also consequently asked to develop a handful of conceptual ideas reflecting the swift change in the information society. Among the most prominent of these initiatives was the World Summit on the Information Society (WSIS) sponsored by the International Telecommunication Union (2005). The WSIS was organized into two phases, hosted in Switzerland in 2003 and in Tunisia in 2005. During the second meeting, the WSIS portrayed a desperate picture:

> "We recognize that access to information and sharing and creation of knowledge contributes significantly to strengthening economic, social and cultural development, thus helping all countries to reach the internationally-agreed development goals and objectives, including the Millennium Development Goals. This process can be enhanced by removing barriers to universal, ubiquitous, equitable and affordable access to information. We underline the importance of removing barriers to bridging the digital divide, particularly those that hinder the full achievement of the economic, social and cultural development of countries and the welfare of their people in developing countries."
>
> (WSIS, 2005)

Similarly, the World Intellectual Property Organization (WIPO, 2007) aimed to create a database to match specific intellectual property–related development needs with available resources, thereby expanding the scope of its technical assistance programs, aimed at bridging the global digital divide. Although WIPO tries to enforce strict IP rules, which eventually benefits Western countries as the developed world serves as host to IP owners while the developing world houses the users (Pang, 2006), this initiative by WIPO at least emphasizes the importance of the transfer and dissemination of technology to the benefit of developing countries and the role of IP rights in the debates of the global digital divide.

As such, the United Nations, WIPO, and World Trade Organization have taken initial steps by adopting policy statements and publicly declaring their commitment. However, these institutions, and hundreds of NGOs, struggle to balance the growing demand for access with inadequate resources and the need to protect intellectual property (Menschel, 2011). The primary challenge in devising such a policy framework is in understanding the distinct and meaningful profiles of different nations and regions so that effective policies could be articulated and implemented (Ayanso et al., 2010). In addition, newly developed conceptual frames are needed to deal with the contemporary digital divide occurring primarily due to discrepancies between nations in the social media era.

From the Internet Divide to the Platform Divide

Given the importance of smartphones and SNSs in the era of platforms, it is essential to compare the penetration rate of these technologies with the Internet to derive the conceptual ground of the new perspective of digital divide. To begin with, the global digital divide, in terms of access to and use of the Internet between developed and developing countries, has continued over the last decade, although it is reduced in several countries. The falling price of laptops, more computers in public schools and libraries, and the newest generation of hand-held devices that connect to the Internet have all contributed to closing the divide (Marriott, 2006).

As Table 7.1 shows, among selected countries, several North American and Western European countries achieve a higher penetration rate than non-Western countries.[3] As of June 2012, developed countries, such as the Netherlands (92.9%), Sweden (92.7%), Australia (88.8%), the U.K., Canada, Germany, France, Japan, and the U.S., comprise the top 10 countries in the realm of Internet penetration rate. Only Korea from the category of developing nations was part of the list. Several developing countries, such as India (11.4%), South Africa (17.4%), Indonesia (22.1%), Thailand, and the Philippines are still far behind. This data proves that with very few exceptions, developing countries in general cannot achieve what Western countries have fulfilled in terms of penetration.

As Benkler (2006) pointed out, perhaps the digital divide in many countries is less stark today than it was in the late 1990s. As ICTs become more central to life, they seem to be reaching higher penetration rates, and growth rates among underrepresented groups are higher than the growth rate among the highly represented groups. The disparity between the haves and the have-nots in terms of technology access, which constitutes the basic digital divide, has been somewhat resolved. As the access gap shrinks in many countries, it becomes less relevant in discussions of social inequalities (Tranter and Willis, 2002, cited in Ji and Skoric, 2013). Strover (2003) also argued that, with the rapid growth of ICTs globally, the digital divide in many countries has been arguably resolved, and it has been on the sidelines in the early 21st century. However, the digital divide with regard to basic access and skills within many economies is still significant. As Couldry (2012, 10–11) clearly points out, "within the apparently infinite expansion of global connectivity, new hidden forms of disconnection are emerging.... Disconnection becomes even more acute when we look outside the West, where the percentage of monthly salary necessary to buy a computer varies widely."

More importantly, the digital divide in the realm of digital platforms between developed and developing countries has just started, which is a new concern in the networked society. A platform is not only about technological disparities but also about cultural and legal inequalities. On the one hand, the disparity of smartphones is conspicuous. As of April 2013, developed countries, such as Sweden (85%), Australia (72%), Japan (62%), the U.K. (56%), and the U.S., are global leaders in penetration rate, as in the case of the Internet. Several developing countries, such as India (3%), Egypt (8%), Indonesia (11%), Mexico (13%), the Philippines, and China record among the lowest in this category (see Table 7.1).

Table 7.1 Global Digital-Social Divide (unit: %)

Country	*Internet*	*Smartphone*	*Facebook*
Netherlands	92.9	54	45.2
Sweden	92.7	85	54.4
Australia	88.8	72	53.1
U.K.	83.6	56	52.3
Canada	83	44	52.7
Germany	83	30	31.2
Korea	82.5	66	20.5
France	79.6	41	39
Japan	79.5	62	13.5
U.S.	78.1	54	52.9
Taiwan	75.4	30	57
Hong Kong	74.5	85	56.4
Spain	67.2	39	37.4
Argentina	66.4	26	45.1
Poland	64.9	23	22.7

(*Continued*)

Country	*Internet*	*Smartphone*	*Facebook*
Malaysia	60.7	41	46.6
Italy	58.4	31	37.9
Saudi Arabia	49	53	22.1
Russia	47.7	13	3.8
Turkey	45.7	17	39.3
Brazil	45.6	27	26.4
China	40.1	18	0.05
Mexico	36.5	13	33.5
Egypt	35.6	8	14.5
Philippines	32.4	16	28.8
Thailand	30	20	26.4
Indonesia	22.1	11	20.6
South Africa	17.4	21	12.8
India	11.4	3	5.2

Source: Internet Penetration June 2012; Smartphone Penetration April 2013; Facebook Penetration December 2012. Internet World Stats 2013; Communities-dominate.blogs.com 2013.

Only a few developing countries, including Hong Kong (85%) and Korea (66%) show higher penetration rates than most Western countries. Whereas the penetration rate of mobile phones is getting higher in many developing countries, smartphones yield a new form of digital divide because people cannot afford them in many developing countries. Whenever new forms of media technologies appear in our society, we cannot avoid the global digital divide, mostly because only a few developed countries create these new technologies, resulting in a higher penetration rate in these countries than developing countries, with a few exceptions.

As Jack Qiu (2009, 56) correctly observes, China has rapidly grown in the wireless sector and many workers use mobile phones to access the Internet. Therefore, including wireless access, the Internet penetration rate in China would be higher than this figure. Likewise, China has substantially developed its mobile communication system and working class members in urban areas that are rapidly switching from feature phones to smartphones, which will change the overall picture in the realm of platforms in the near future. Of course, this does not mean that China will resolve the global digital divide anytime soon because "access to mobile phones, although beyond the traditional boundaries of elite-based landline systems, is still limited to those who can pay," and smartphones are much more expensive than mobile phones for migrant workers.

Meanwhile, the penetration rate of Facebook—which is one of the most significant social media in terms of socio-cultural influences on people's daily activities—shows a very similar trend. Facebook has maintained its rate of growth and generates thousands of new user registrations every day. The number of total users has grown from 585 million in December 2010 to 1.15 billion in June 2013. About 699 million daily active users on average visited Facebook in June 2013. Approximately 80 percent of active users are outside the U.S. and Canada (Facebook, 2013a). Among those countries analyzed, developed countries including Sweden (54.4%), Australia (53.1%), U.S. (52.9%), Canada (52.9%), and U.K., are global leaders. In contrast, China (less than 1%), India (5.2%), South Africa (12.8%), Egypt (14.5%), and Indonesia are lowest in Facebook penetration.[4]

As explained previously, according to the World Map of Social Networks, which shows the most popular SNSs by country and is based on Alexa and Google Trends for website traffic data, Facebook has rapidly expanded its dominance in many countries. In fact, Facebook is the market leader in more than 90 percent of countries. These numbers are significant because they have contributed to the high valuation assigned to Facebook. With a few exceptions in Mixi (Japan), Cyworld (Korea), and QQ (China), as well as VK (Russia), Facebook has managed to overtake local incumbent SNSs in many countries, including Brazil, and has rapidly penetrated the majority of countries in the world.

SNSs have gained tremendous attention as popular online spaces in recent years, but disparities in both access to and use of Facebook and Twitter have expanded. As Colin Sparks (2013, 37–38) observes, "the developments known as Web 2.0 have greatly expanded and supplemented the communication functions that characterized the earlier days of the Internet as a mass phenomenon." However, platforms are mostly about applications, and many users in developing countries just get the basic services of these platforms, compared to those who are rich so that they can buy value-added services, resulting in the expansion of the global digital divide. SNSs also symbolize the new form of capital accumulation for a few developers and countries possessing ownership, unlike previous ICTs.

DISPARITIES IN CAPITAL GAINS BETWEEN DEVELOPED AND DEVELOPING COUNTRIES

In the early 21st century, American-based SNSs have rapidly penetrated the world and enjoyed enormous financial benefits. Facebook is one of the most dynamic in terms of its monetization based on its popular global usage. Facebook is a platform that plays an advanced role in aggregating several services. Facebook has rapidly expanded its dominance in many countries, resulting in another form of disparity, not only because it is a new digital technology but also because it is a commodity that the U.S. company monetizes.

The U.S. is the largest country in terms of the number of Facebook users; however, other countries have swiftly increased their userbases. As of April 2013, Brazil became the second largest country with 70.1 million users, followed by India (62.9 million) and Indonesia. Mexico, Turkey, U.K., France, and Germany were also among the top 10 countries. Facebook will continue to grow in these countries because Brazil (34.8%), India (5.3%), and Indonesia

(20.6%) have huge populations, but their penetration rates will be much lower than that of the U.S. (52.9%). While Facebook has become a dominant power, the concentration of capital into a few U.S.-based SNS start-ups continues. A handful of U.S.-owned platforms, including Twitter, have rapidly expanded their control in the global market, which has caused the asymmetrical gap between a few Western countries and the majority of non-Western countries, in addition to the asymmetrical relation between the corporation and users.

Individually, having a Facebook account means participation and solidarity with virtual friends. In the social media–driven society, social inclusion occurs because of owning the Facebook account (and in general social media). Facebook becomes positioned as a space of self-expression and social participation, if used fairly and creatively. Participating as a virtual community member provides not only affection but also necessary information. Those without access to social media will be isolated in future society (van Dijck, 2012). Murdock and Golding (2004, 246) already argued that "full digital citizenship [as the right of full participation in social life in the digital age] is not simply a matter of guaranteeing basic access, but it requires command over the resources that underwrite people's capacity to use the Net creatively as a space of self-expression and social participation." Unlike the Internet, however, access to Facebook creates a new form of disparity because the increasing rate of penetration guarantees the soaring capital gains for Facebook, Inc.—an American owned company.

More specifically, Facebook (and other social media) has become one of the major social media accentuating inequality between a handful of developed countries and the remaining countries, because of its role as a commodity. Starting in 2005, the value of Facebook as a tool to monetize its resources—mostly Facebook users—has been increasing. Advertisers have focused more on Facebook as an alternative advertising medium in the social media era. In a world where social structure is everything, "connections become the prime economic value" (van Dijck, 2012, 169–170). Facebook consequently garners the profits. Facebook's revenue has been soaring due in large part to its advertising component based on user activities. As discussed in previous chapters, Facebook's (2013b) total revenue during 2012 was $5.08 billion, up from $3.7 billion in 2011. Out of this, advertising revenue during 2012 accounted for $4.27 billion (84%), up from $3.1 billion in 2011. Payments and other fees, including revenue from social games, were $810 million in 2012. Approximately 50.8 percent of Facebook's 2012 revenue came from the U.S. However, it went down to 46 percent, while the rest of the world accounted for 54 percent in 2013. The proportion from the U.S. decreased from 70 percent in 2008 (Facebook, 2013b, 86; Facebook, 2014), meaning that Facebook has rapidly increased its revenues from foreign countries. This change is primarily due to factors including a faster growth rate among international users (see Figure 7.1).

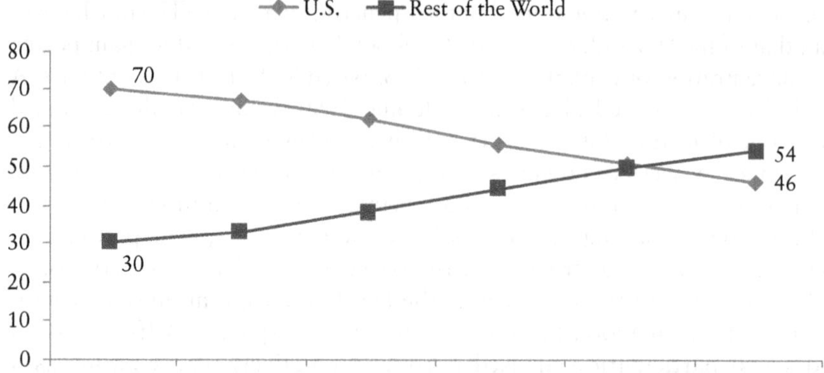

Figure 7.1 Facebook's Global Revenue from 2008 to 2013 (unit: %).
Source: Facebook (2014). Annual Report. Facebook (2013b). S-1 filing with the U.S. Securities and Exchange Commission. New York: SEC; Facebook (2012). S-1 filing with the U.S. Securities and Exchange Commission. New York: SEC.

Facebook has been increasing its advertising revenue while other countries, in particular developing countries, advance their domestic penetration rate. Unlike previous ICTs, such as the Internet, fixed and mobile phones, which have nothing to do with advertising revenues for the developers, Facebook has created a new form of capital gains in the global markets. The disparity of the Facebook haves and the Facebook have-nots creates several significant inequalities, including in economic, political, and cultural activities.

As Ayanso et al. (2010, 304) pointed out, "the digital divide has sparked serious debates along the lines of economic disparity among world nations," and Facebook has intensified inequalities among nations. In the platform era, two different forms of the global digital divide occur. One is the disparity of the penetration rate, as usual, and the other is the disparity in benefiting capital gains in favor of the U.S.-based corporations. The increasing penetration rate in social media is supposed to resolve the digital divide; however, this development has ironically intensified inequalities in capital accumulation through not only advertising but also big data and intellectual property.

THE BIG DATA DIVIDE IN PLATFORMS

Social media corporations are heavily benefiting from big data because they gather all kinds of data that users send. Users just click their mouse and input some information with their fingers. However, due to the increasing number of users, platform corporations have tremendous data as a form of either structured or unstructured information so that they sort out data as commodities. Unstructured data comes from information that is not organized or easily interpreted by traditional databases or data models, and typically, it's text-heavy. Metadata, Twitter tweets, and other social media posts are good examples of unstructured data (Arthur, 2013). The emergence of platforms in the middle of the 2000s created opportunities to utilize social and cultural processes and dynamics in new ways, because for the first time, "we can follow imaginations, options, ideas, and feelings of hundreds of millions of people" (Manovich, 2012, 462).

The key in utilizing big data are the algorithms that social media corporations control. As Gilliespie (2014, 167) points out, "algorithms designed to calculate what is hot or trending or most discussed skim the cream from seemingly boundless chatter that's on offer." Search engines like Google and social network sites, including Facebook, certainly utilize algorithm to benefit from data gathered by users. Algorithms turn meaningless numbers into actionable insights. Facebook and Google extract signals and patterns of data through intelligent algorithms (Lorentz, 2013). As Lev Manovich (2012, 464) points out, "only social media companies have access to really large social data, especially transactional data." For example, Google does not offer any service that would allow a user to analyze patterns directly in all data. Google's Terms of Service, which was modified on April 14, 2014, clearly said:

> "You must follow any policies made available to you within the Services. Don't misuse our Services. For example, don't interfere with our Services or try to access them using a method other than the interface and the instructions that we provide. You may use our Services only as permitted by law, including applicable export and re-export control laws and regulations. We may suspend or stop providing our Services to you if you do not comply with our terms or policies or if we are investigating suspected misconduct."
>
> (Google, 2014b)

In the era of data abundance, the economic control of information relied upon endeavors to reinforce dominant ideologies that accorded with the interests of those who possess power. Likewise, in the big data era, power belongs to platform developers and owners because they control information, in particular, in an economic sense, such as pricing and production. Therefore, those with access to data, expertise, and processing power are positioned to engage in increasingly powerful, sophisticated, and opaque forms of sorting that can be "powerful means of creating and reinforcing long-term [or newly generated] social differences" (Lyon, 2002, 1, cited in Andrejevic, 2014). "People are palpably aware that powerful commercial interests shape the terms of access that extract information from them" (Andrejevic, 2014, 1685).

boyd and Crawford (2011, 13) therefore argue that "the current ecosystem around Big Data creates a new kind of digital divide: the Big Data rich and the Big Data poor." In other words, the platform era opens up a new form of digital divide: that between those with access to the datasets, which are information, and those without, both nationally and globally. Only a few social media corporations, such as Google, Facebook, and Twitter control access to the data gathered: restrict access to their data entirely and sell the privilege of access for a high fee, for instance (boyd and Crawford, 2013).

Of course, as discussed, the digital divide, in this case the big data divide, is not simply between database haves and have-nots; it is also about asymmetric sorting processes and different ways of thinking about how data relate to knowledge and its application (Andrejevic, 2013, 2014). As discussed, only platform corporations such as Google and Facebook have database access they gather through users' activities, and they also control the ability to capture and mine ample amounts of data, which is a new resource for capitalization. While there are many sources that create and gather data, social media is the forerunner because hundreds of thousands of users send their information on a daily basis. Since these platforms first monopolize their access and analysis, they are the big winners, which makes a new form of the digital divide in the era of platforms.

Finally, it is not difficult to predict that the big data divide will intensify the global digital divide between a few Western countries and other countries because "the primary goal of big data is to be predictive. Find patterns deep in the data and expect that, barring significant structural changes, they will tell us what the future will be like. Determining why is less important than predicting what will be," as Vincent Mosco (2014, 181) aptly puts it. We are indeed entering a world of constant data-driven predictions where we may not be able to explain the reasons behind our decisions (Mayer-Schonberger and Cukier, 2013, cited in Mosco, 2014). This implies that only a few platform owners and their governments, including Google, Facebook, and Twitter, are able to correctly predict the future based on datasets they gather and access. Since these platform corporations analyze and forecast future human behavior, they continue to develop new technologies and scientific knowledge more than non-Western countries, and so their economic and ideological hegemony last longer than expected, resulting in the growth of the global digital divide.

DIVIDE IN INTELLECTUAL PROPERTY RIGHTS

Intellectual property has been significant due to its creativity and capital gains. It is not a new realization that a few developed countries have benefited from IP rights. However, the dominant position of a few developed countries, in particular the U.S., in the realm of IP has become larger than during previous decades with the rapid growth of digital platforms. As discussed in Chapter 5, the U.S. has created massive profits from hardware, software, and services, all of which are protected by IP laws, including copyright, patent, and trademark laws. Technological innovation drives industrial growth and helps raise living standards. Therefore, the importance of intellectual property rights in the 21st century cannot be doubted.

As the significance of IP grows for the global knowledge economy, the disparity between developed and developing countries in the realm of IP is widening. According to the U.S. Department of Commerce (2011, 2012, 2013), the total amount of royalties and license fees that the U.S. received from foreign countries in 2012 was $124.1 billion. However, royalties and license fees that the U.S. paid to foreign countries during the same period was $39.8 billion. The net profits in 2012 were recorded as being as much as $84.2 billion. Therefore, the U.S. has certainly benefited from intellectual property rights (see Table 5.2).

As global computer networks and global trade in software products develop, the dramatic changes ushered in by cutting-edge technologies have significantly increased the magnitude and relevance of IP rights. Consequently, there is an increasing tension between developed countries as IP owners and developing countries as IP users, particularly in platforms due to their unique roles not only as computational infrastructure, but also as the software framework that allows software to run on the platforms (Tech Coders, 2012; Gillespie, 2010).

It is crucial to adequately and reasonably transfer and disseminate technology invented in developed countries to the benefit of developing countries; however, this is not simple because of the intensification of global IP rights. Fair intellectual property rules are necessary for the growth of ICTs; however, we cannot deny the increasing disparity occurring due to IP rights. Most technological breakthroughs happen in developed countries because they have know-how and capital. Whereas some developing countries, including Korea, China, and Taiwan, advance their smartphone technologies, they cannot compete with a few developed countries in the field of software, which has been dominated by the U.S. corporations.

In particular, there is no doubt that the disparity of worldwide research and development (R&D) expenditures—as one of the most significant indicators that we can predict for the future of ICTs will be widening between a few developed and the majority of developing countries. Worldwide R&D expenditures totaled an estimated $1,276 billion in 2009, up from $641 billion in 1999. Global R&D performance remains highly concentrated in a few countries. Three countries account for more than half of global R&D. The U.S. is by far the largest R&D performer ($402 billion in 2009), accounting for about 31 percent of the global total, but down from 38 percent in 1999. China became the second largest performer ($154 billion) in 2009, accounting for about 12 percent of the global total. Japan moved down to third at 11 percent ($138 billion) (National Science Foundation, 2012). The European Union performers spend comparatively less: Germany ($83 billion, 6%), France ($48 billion, 4%), and the U.K. ($40 billion, 3%).

The most recent figure available for Korea is for 2008, with $44 billion of R&D—in recent years Korea has typically been among the top seven R&D performing countries, representing 3–4 percent of the global total. Taken together, these top seven countries account for about 71 percent of the global total. Russia, Italy, Canada, India, Brazil, Taiwan, and Spain comprise the next lower rung, with national R&D expenditures ranging from $20 billion to $33 billion. The remainder, approximately 10 percent, reflects the R&D of countries in the regions of Central and South America, Central Asia, Middle East, Australia/Oceania, and Africa (National Science Foundation, 2012). While some developed countries continue to invest money in developing new technologies, including social media, developing countries have no choice but to consume social media created and designed by these developed countries. Although several non-Western countries have advanced their own software and platforms, the lop-sided interaction between Western and non-Western countries remains unchanged and perhaps is even more magnified today than in the past.

It is often argued that the integrated use of ICTs will contribute to wealth creation through increased access to knowledge and information on developmental issues. However, such aspirations usually overlook the barriers to use of and access to knowledge. Intellectual property protection tends to "reinforce rather than resolve some of the more critical impediments to knowledge resources and information" (Ngenda, 2005, 71). The adoption of IP rights as a prerequisite for the transfer of technology provides the setting in which regulation of ICTs is advocated. This fortifies the intersection of IP rights and regulation of information technology, and particularly reinforces the process by which the former makes it conducive to promulgate the latter. As a result, while developments in information technology afford new media the rapid dissemination of information, they also entrench the hegemony of Western legal models (Ngenda, 2005, 71).

The high cost of digital platforms puts certain technologies out of reach for many low income individuals in developed nations and the majority of the population in the developing world. Without affordable access options, "people face a choice between foregoing the technology altogether or accessing the technology, but in violation of IP rights" (Menschel, 2011, 164). "Discourse on transfer of technology is rife with references to the need and desire to 'bridge the knowledge gap' between developed and developing countries for which information and communication technology is seen as the prime panacea" (Ngenda, 2005, 71). Despite numerous efforts to make technologies more affordable for people in many countries, intellectual property in the era of platform sometimes prevents developing countries from enjoying the benefit. The exploitation of digital platforms is increasingly seen as an enabler of socio-economic development.

For instance, under the Draft ICT Policy for Zambia, it is envisioned that the integrated use of information and communication technologies will contribute to wealth creation through increased access to knowledge and information on health and developmental issues. Such aspirations usually overlook the barriers to use of and access to knowledge. Foreign direct investment and transfer of technology is often contingent upon adoption of intellectual property rights (Wolfard, 1990, cited in Ngenda, 2005). Intellectual property protection tends to reinforce rather than resolve some of the more critical impediments to knowledge resources and information (Ngenda, 2005). With strict IP rules, people in developing countries cannot enjoy the benefits of digital/social technologies, which is a serious problem in the global digital divide debates.

DISPARITIES IN SYMBOLIC HEGEMONY

In the platform era, one of the most significant disparities comes from an intangible idea known as symbolic hegemony. Hegemony refers to a process of moral and intellectual leadership, and hegemony implies domination through ideology or discourse as symbolic domination or as power largely operating semiotically (Johnson, 2007). As Epstein et al. (2011) claim, again, the digital divide not only covers different kinds of disparities with different kinds of consequences, it also obscures the variety of ideas about the nature of the problem itself and the manner in which it should be resolved. This says that, although we cannot identify all ideologies in the realm of digital divide, symbolic hegemony in conjunction with innovation plays a key role because it is one of the most significant ideas in understanding innovative technologies and now digital platforms. Which countries are more innovative than others, and therefore, which countries are influencing other countries with their ideas are crucial factors in the platform era because the fast mover armed with innovation dominates the global market, not only with its own technologies but also its own ideas, as in the cases of Apple's iPhones and Mark Zuckerberg's Facebook.

Indeed, the notion of entrepreneurship has been rooted in economics and business management, and "entrepreneurship represents a dynamic process of change brought by the implementation of new ideas and creative solutions, based on the vision to recognize opportunities, take calculated risks, and build a solid business plan" (Otmazgin, 2011, 261). Since SNSs and smartphones deal with youth culture and digital economy, the work of entrepreneurs has wider social and cultural implications for consumers. Unlike their counterparts in other fields, in SNS and smartphone entrepreneurs not only generate value in the economic sense,[5] but also value in terms of feelings, identifications, and perceptions. They are likely to express new aspirations and provide the context for people to fulfill a wide range of social and personal attributes and purposes. SNSs and smartphones promote messages and narratives, which have a wider potential to shape people's thoughts, identities, and even views of space.

Entrepreneurs dealing in SNSs and smartphones, thus, not only construct mechanisms for commodifying and marketing popular culture, but unintentionally disseminate ideas, emotions, and sensibilities together with the commodities (Gramsci, 1971; Otmazgin, 2011). Unlike political and/or military imperialism, platform imperialism has especially become significant because of the entrepreneurship of inventors and corporations that develop social networks and smartphones due to the significance of their spirits that influence corporate culture, consumers, and information technology developers around the world. Since the 19th century, hegemony commonly has been used to indicate political predominance, usually of one state over another (Williams, 1985). However, instead of following a rigid Marxist base–superstructure dichotomy, emphasizing the major role of the base (economy), for Gramsci, hegemony was a form of control excised primarily through a society's superstructure, as opposed to its base or social relations of production of a predominately economic character (Postcolonial Studies @ Emory, 2013). Gramsci's notion of hegemony clearly applies to the transfer of ideological entrepreneurship.

Whereas many CEOs in the platform sector are role models for many college students and start-ups, Mark Zuckerberg and Steve Jobs are much stronger than others due to their distinctive innovative entrepreneurship. As entrepreneurship emphasizes innovation such as new products, production methods, and forms of organization, some Western entrepreneurs certainly accomplished all of them. This spirit has influenced hundreds of thousands of followers globally. For example, in 2011 Jobs greatly influenced many people through his unique philosophy on the interplay between technology and humanities. When he introduced iPhone 4 in February 2011, he pointed out the importance of the convergence of these two presumably separated areas:

> "It's in Apple's DNA that technology alone is not enough—it's technology married with liberal arts, married with the humanities, that yields us the result that makes our heart sing, and nowhere is that more true than in these post-PC devices."
>
> (Wadhwa, 2011)

What Jobs implied is that good engineering is important, but what matters the most is good design, because we can teach artists how to use software and graphics tools, but it's much harder to turn engineers into artists. Therefore, our society needs liberal arts majors as much as it does engineers and scientists (Wadhwa, 2011).

Steve Jobs' idea has been exclaimed by many followers around the world. Previously, many people chanted what Bill Gates posited. Gates argued that "we need to spend our limited education budget on disciplines that produce the most jobs." He implied that "we should reduce our investment in the liberal arts because liberal arts degrees don't correlate well with job creation" (Wadhwa, 2011). However, with the stunning growth of Apple with iPhones, Jobs' position has been considered the most innovative and one that corporations and entrepreneurs must adapt. For instance, Hwang Chang Gu, a CEO in Samsung Electronics, proclaimed the importance of the interaction of technologies and humanities in his key note speech at MIT Start-up Workshop held in Seoul, Korea in March 2011. Nam-pyo Seo, President of Korea Advanced Institute of Science and Technology (KAIST), also emphasized the importance of the hybridization of technologies and culture in his address at KAIST in March 2011. Since they had previously primarily emphasized the technology sector, these changes are considered to be reflecting Jobs' spiritual idea.

Likewise, Robin Li, Baidu's CEO, also expresses his respect of Gates as his model. During his interview with Bloomberg West's Emily Chang on November 23, 2013, which I saw during my conference in Salzburg in Austria, Li said that, unlike the early 21st century when Steve Jobs and Mark Zuckerberg became role models in the information technology field in the 1990s, when he created the Chinese search engine Baidu with Eric Xu, the "Bill Gates is the only role model" mantra influenced his work greatly[6] (*Bloomberg*, 2013).

Meanwhile, it is significant to acknowledge that the era of post-Fordism can be seen to have been encouraged partly by consumer demand for more varied and individualized products. Therefore, those who are in the realm of consumption are major features in modern society. In this regard, it is interesting to review what Leo Lowenthal (1961) stated with his analysis of biographies. Lowenthal analyzed the biographies printed in American popular magazines in 1941 and found that between 1901 and 1941 a considerable decrease of people from the serious and important professions were featured compared with a corresponding increase of entertainers (1961, 111–112). He defined serious and important professions as those that are connected with production and politics: engineers, industrialists, politicians, and classical artists. By 1941, the American public was being presented, in place of substantive biographical information, with a diet of celebrity tittle tattle, involving professional models, horse race gamblers, the inventors of gadgets [who would later be social network sites developers], and restaurant chain owners. Lowenthal (1961, 115) stated "we called the heroes of the past idols of production: we feel entitled to call the present day magazine heroes idols of consumption."

Jobs and Zuckerberg are indeed the inventors of gadgets and platforms. We could say that these inventors are the heroes of consumption in our digital economy and culture. However, this thesis also can be criticized on the basis that whether the consumer of today is offered anything more than pseudo individualized products is highly questionable and that the move to consumer differentiation was engineered by the producers themselves (Granter, 2009, 163). This means that Jobs and Zuckerberg are also the heroes of production, and their global influence is not debatable because they are both heroes of production and heroes of consumption. Where we live in the era of post-Fordism, platforms have opened a new chapter because we are witnessing new global figures representing both production and consumption.

Overall, entrepreneurships and ideas are significant in establishing empires because they are eventually turned into commodities and become parts of capitals. Several media and telecommunications firms increasingly rely on innovation to remain competitive, as many new technologies quickly turn into commodities. The clearest evidence that corporate media are redirecting their strategies toward the Internet is via their investments. Hegemony is also the name given to the momentum of the objective relationships of forces that exist between different collective social agents (for example, classes, groups, regions, and nations) situated in a determined social space which we observe from a symbolic point of view—that is, where the creation and recreation of meanings take form in the enactment of all social relations (González, 2001). González (2001) believes that we can create a dialogical understanding of our common symbolic existence if we ask questions about how, from where, and between whom specific relations of symbolic authority have been structured, deconstructed, and re-created across a specific history. As Lash (2007, 55) aptly puts it, therefore, "hegemony means domination through consent as much as coercion. It has meant domination through ideology or discourse. It has meant symbolic power."

By attracting millions of people to YouTube, Google amasses a huge potential advertising market (Castells, 2007). Platforms afford an opportunity to communicate and interact for the user, but they also provide an opportunity to sell ads for corporations. Unlike ICTs, although users do not pay for access to Facebook and Twitter, they provide their time and energy for corporations that turn them into commodities they can sell to advertisers.

In technologically mediated space, a power distribution and hegemonic negotiation is always at play. Such assertion of dominance in the new public space of communication occurs through acts ranging from legislation labeling some Internet users as pirates to disseminating symbolic ideas and philosophies to tame non-Western societies as well as their own communities (Castells, 2007). As Gitlin (1980, 11) pointed out, "in corporate capitalist society, the schools and the mass media specialize in formulating and conveying national ideology. At the same time, indirectly, the media—at least in liberal capitalist society—take account of certain popular currents and pressures, symbolically incorporating them, repackaging and distributing them throughout the society.... The media [including social media] create and relay images of order." Scholars, such as Block (2013, 263) and Couldry (2012) have granted the media the potential to generate various sorts of power, primarily symbolic, and with the capacity to impact the ways people construct their reality.

Consequently, innovation and ideas are vital elements in establishing inequalities in economy and culture because they are eventually turned into commodities and become parts of capitals. As van Dijck (2005, 22–23) clearly pointed out, "the digital divide primarily is a social problem, not a technical one. This does not mean that the properties of the technology concerned are irrelevant. Some of these properties support access and others reduce it." However, the digital divide needs to be understood beyond the technical issues because without solving the disparity in these socio-cultural issues, we never overcome the global digital divide. Many firms increasingly rely on innovation to remain competitive, as many new technologies quickly turn into commodities. Web 2.0 technologies have allowed capital itself to be commodified so that a few Western countries, transnational corporations, and more powerful investors can now sell packets of platforms to non-Western countries.

The contemporary world is being deeply damaged by the intensification of the dominance by platforms as several Western-based technologies, such as SNSs and smartphones, as well as software, have taken over the global order. On the one hand, "by the global spread of capitalist relations and commodities, they drive to make the world one big market" (Johnson, 2007, 106). On the other hand, by the intensification of the dominance by platforms, several Western-based technologies have taken over the global order. This platform imperialism has been fuelled not only by technologies, but also spiritual hegemony and legal domination.

Although hierarchies are shifting, they are also maintained in ways that work for the select few who have access and control over ownership and the cultural capital that shapes constructs of identity and ignorance as well as definitions of skilled and unskilled workforces (Gajjala and Birzescu, 2011, 97). This is how platform imperialism plays out through the weaving of the online and offline. We therefore need to give sufficient weight to the dimension of a new form of digital divide, including IP rights and symbolic hegemony as primary spiritual symbols in the social media era in tandem with platforms, such as Facebook and smartphones. Although the old form of digital divide may be partially gone, Western influences have not been obliterated by globalization. Instead, the platform as a new global order has rapidly replaced the digital divide based on the Internet, because platforms in conjunction with IP and symbolic hegemony have unilaterally influenced the current form of digital divide. The global digital divide will be locked in instead of resolved because it is not only about individual and household issues but also national issues. Since developing countries, other than a handful of exceptions such as China and Korea, cannot secure capital and innovative entrepreneurship in the field of social media, they are consequently influenced by a few developed countries, both materially and psychologically, resulting in the continuing global digital divide between developed and developing countries.

CONCLUSION

This chapter has sought to provide new perspectives on the global digital divide debates in the social media era. The task was to espouse global digital divide discourse in understanding the complexity and nuances of several variances that have been newly identified. Since the inception of the discussion of the digital divide, the global digital divide has been primarily associated with the disparities in economic growth among nations, although there are several significant areas, such as political and cultural realms. Thus, many developing countries have been enthusiastic in embracing ICTs, and the digital divide and its inequalities were seemingly resolved with the rapid growth of ICTs. Many countries have built the necessary infrastructure for the growth of the Internet. The Internet has done much to level the playing field for people looking to launch businesses and even more so those looking to grow them (*Huffpost,* 2013). However, whether the digital divide is further marginalizing already oppressed and disenfranchised individuals and nations is still an ongoing question. The inequalities remain unresolved and some even suggest that the gap is widening. This should not be surprising since, "if economic and social inequalities are among the key determinants of the digital divide in all of its manifestations, internationally these have certainly not been significantly reduced, and in some important cases have increased, as the Internet and social media are undergoing development and diffusion" (Sparks, 2013, 39).

In particular, the greatest benefit that access to several ICTs provides is opportunity, Access to ICTs in developing nations fosters economic opportunities for all (White et al., 2011). However, the opportunity is shrinking in many countries. In the 21st century, digital platforms have been abuzz, and in all likelihood the digital divide will continue as it has. As Warschauer (2004, 7) already pointed out, "the notion of a digital divide implies a chain of causality: that lack of access (however defined) to computers and the Internet harms life chances. Whereas this point is undoubtedly true, the reverse is equally true: those who are already marginalized will have fewer opportunities to access and use computers and the Internet. In fact, technology and society are intertwined and co-constitutive, and this complex interrelationship makes any assumption of causality problematic."

In the platform era, this is clearly the case. Those countries that are already marginalized when it comes to software will have fewer opportunities in developing software, particularly operating systems and SNSs. Measured in terms of access, it is likely that we will again see the fast diffusion of smartphones and SNSs around most of the globe in the coming years, as we witnessed in the case of the Internet (Castells, 2001, 262). However, as long as we are concerned about software and symbols, the existing gap can be widening instead of shrinking because developing countries cannot develop these areas although they rapidly use these technologies and content. As Quan-Hasse (2013, 135) also identifies, the more salient barriers that exist at both the micro and macro levels are not only a lack of infrastructure, economic barriers, illiteracy, poor computing skills, and lack of supports, but also cultural barriers.

The global digital divide cannot be resolved anytime soon because the majority of developing countries have no available resources, especially when compared to a few Western countries. The majority of developing countries have no opportunity to create, design, and produce their own software and symbols, which perpetuates the discrepancies between developed and developing countries. Only a few developing countries, such as Korea and Taiwan, are partially competing with Western forces, but other countries have no skills and capital. SNSs and smartphones in conjunction with software could leave many developing countries far behind because they are about IP rights and symbolic hegemony as well. This is the overlooked side of the systematic chain of causality described above: that lack of skills and capital to produce platforms harms life chances for the majority of developing countries and their citizens. In other words, this is not an issue of access to, and use of, several ICTs.

In particular, the convergence of big data and ideological dominance has become significant in intensifying the global digital divide. In an era of relative data scarcity, the control of information relied upon attempts to define and reinforce dominant narratives that accorded with the interests of those in power (Andrejevic, 2014). Karl Marx and Friedrich Engels' famous formulation captured this version of ideological control: the ideas of the ruling class are in every epoch the ruling ideas.... The class which has the means of material production at its disposal, has control at the same time over the means of mental production.... Therefore, as they rule as a class and determine the extent and compass of an epoch, it is self-evident that they do this in its whole range, hence among other things rule also as thinkers, as producers of ideas (Marx and Engels, 1970, cited in Andrejevic, 2014). This understanding of the economic control of information meant securing the most accurate and up-to-date information about prices and the variables likely to affect them. "In the era of big data, new strategies of control emerge alongside these: in the financial realm, data collection leads to large-scale strategies of correlation, prediction, and pre-emption that would have been impossible in the pre-digital era, and only a few platform corporations are able to actualize this large-scale strategy" (Andrejevic, 2014, 5).

In sum, the digital divide between developed and developing countries in the era of platform will continue to rise, resulting in the intensification of platform imperialism. Therefore, while how to resolve these fundamental issues is significant, it is also vital to explore the multifaceted approaches, including the need for a more rich, considerate, and systematic assessment of the ways in which socio-economic factors, cultural perceptions, and regulation are interrelated.

NOTES

1. As the Internet became commonplace in the 1990s, officials in the Clinton administration wondered if there should be concern about equity of access to computers and the Information Superhighway. As a result, based on the analysis of Census data about computer/modem ownership and usage collected in 1994, the newly created National Telecommunications and Information Administration (NTIA) prepared and released in 1995 the landmark report entitled

"Falling Through the Net: A Survey of the Have Nots in Rural and Urban America." From there, the discussion of the inequalities of online access as a new aspect of the larger issues of wealth and poverty began and the "Digital Divide" became a major focus in countries around the world (International Communication Association, 2014).

2. As Joo Young Jung (2008, 323) aptly puts it, regardless of the recent scholarly opinion that the digital divide exists beyond access to Internet technology, very few studies have developed a systematic empirical tool to measure such post-access disparities.
3. In this chapter, I selected about 30 countries representing both developed and developing countries, and I identified the penetration rate of three major indicators: the Internet, Facebook, and smartphones.
4. In the case of China, Facebook is not available for political reasons, which explains the low penetration, but there are massively-subscribed-to Chinese alternatives, including QQ and Weibo, which allegedly provide better functionality. China's ruling Communist Party aggressively censors the Internet, routinely deleting online postings and blocking access to websites it deems inappropriate or politically sensitive. Facebook and Twitter were blocked by Beijing in mid-2009 following deadly riots in the western province of Xinjiang that authorities say were abetted by the social networking sites. Regardless of a report saying that Facebook, Twitter, and other websites deemed sensitive and blocked by the Chinese government would be accessible in a planned free-trade zone (FTZ) in Shanghai, since September 2013, The *People's Daily*, the official mouthpiece of China's ruling Communist Party, denied the report by the *South China Morning Post* (Coonan, 2013). Therefore, we need to be very careful to analyze the digital divide only based on the simple penetration with no specificities.
5. Of course, the hardware itself is usually manufactured elsewhere, and Apple is not exceptional because Foxconn, a Taiwanese company in China, produces iPhones. Apple as the U.S.-based transnational corporation has exploited cheap labor in China, which is a typical form of value exchange that brings a lot of profits to the U.S.
6. Robin Li also admitted the significant role of the government in the growth of Baidu. Google came to China in 2006 because the government previously blocked its launch due to the censorship issue. However, Google was too late because Baidu started its business in China in 2000 and had already become a strong market leader in the Chinese search engine market that Google could not break.

REFERENCES

Annan, K. (2003). Secretary-general's message to the net world order: Bridging the global digital divide conference. Delivered by Amir Dossal, Executive Director, UN Fund for International Partnerships. New York, 18 June.

Ayanso, A., Cho, D.I., & Lertwachara, K. (2010). The digital divide: Global and regional ICT leaders and followers. *Information Technology for Development* 16(4): 304–319.

Benkler, Y. (2006). *The Wealth of Networks: How Social Production Transforms Markets and Freedom*. New Haven, CT: Yale University Press.

Block, E. (2013). Culturalist approach to the concept of the mediatization of politics: The age of media hegemony. *Communication Theory* 27(3): 259–278.

Bloomberg (2013). Baidu CEO Robin Li talks with Bloomberg's Emily Chang about social media and Google in China. He speaks with Emily Chang on Bloomberg Television's "Bloomberg West." http://www.businessweek.com/videos/2013-10-29/chinas-third-richest-man-bill-gates-is-my-model.

Bradbrook, G. & Fisher, J. (2004). *Digital Equality: Reviewing Digital Inclusion Activity and Mapping the Way Forwards*. London: Citizens Online.

Castells, M. (2001). *The Internet Galaxy: Reflections on the Internet, Business, and Society*. New York: Oxford University Press.

Coonan, C. (2003). China won't allow Twitter, Facebook access in Shanghai Free Trade Zone after all. *The Hollywood Reporter*, 26 September. http://www.hollywoodreporter.com/news/china-wont-allow-twitter-facebook-636927.

Couldry, N. (2009). Communicative entitlements and democracy: The future of the digital divide debate. In R. Mansell, C. Avgerou, D. Quah, and R. Silverstone (eds.), *The Oxford Handbook of Information and Communication Technologies*, 383–403. New York: Oxford University Press.

Couldry, N. (2012). *Media, Society, World: Social Theory and Digital Media Practice*. Cambridge: Polity.

Deichmann, J.I., Eshghi, A., Haughton, D., Masnghetti, M., Sayek, S., & Topi, H. (2006). Exploring breakpoints and interaction effects among predictors of the international digital divide. *Journal of Global Information Technology Management* 9(4): 47–71.

The Economist (2005). A survey of patent and technology: A market for ideas. October 20.

Epstein, D., Nisbet, E. & Gillespie, T. (2011). Who's responsible for the digital divide? Public perceptions and policy implications. *The Information Society: An International Journal* 27(2): 92–104.

Facebook (2013a). Newsroom: Key facts. Accessed August 30, 2013. http://newsroom.fb.com/Key-Facts.

Facebook (2013b). S-1 filing with the U.S. Securities and Exchange Commission: Form S-1 Registration Statement. New York: SEC.

Facebook (2012). S-1 filing with the U.S. Securities and Exchange Commission: Form S-1 Registration Statement. New York: SEC.

Facebook (2014). Annual report 2013. Menlo Park, CA: Facebook.

Gitlin, T. (1980). *The Whole World Is Watching: Mass Media in the Making and Unmaking of the New Left*. Berkeley: University of California Press.

Gillespie, T. (2010). The politics of platforms. *New Media and Society* 12(3): 347–364.

González, J. (2001). Cultural fronts: Towards a dialogical understanding of contemporary cultures. In J. Lull (ed.), *Culture in the Communication Age*, 106–131. New York: Routledge.

Gramsci, A. (1971). *Selections from The Prison Notebooks*, Quintin Hoare and Geoffrey Nowell-Smith (eds. and trans.). New York: International Publishers.

Granter, E. (2009). *Rethinking Classical Sociology: Critical Social Theory and the End of Work*. Surrey, UK: Ashgate Publishing Group.

Gunkel, D. (2003). Second thoughts: Toward a critique of the digital divide. *New Media and Society* 5(4): 499–522.

Halliday, J. (2011). Samsung and Microsoft settle Android licensing dispute. *The Guardian*. 28 September.

Huffpost (2013). Coming to terms with a global digital divide. 21 May.

IDC (2013). Apple cedes market share in smartphone operating system market as Android surges and Windows phone gains. 7 August. http://www.idc.com/getdoc.jsp?containerId=prUS24257413.

International Telecommunication Union (2005). *Building Digital Bridges*. Geneva: ITU.

Ji, P. & Skoric, M. (2013). Gender and social resources: Digital divides of social network sites and mobile phone use in Singapore. *Chinese Journal of Communication* 6(2): 221–239.

Johnson, R. (2007). Post-hegemony? I don't think so. *Theory, Culture & Society* 24(3): 95–110.

Lash, S. (2007). Power after hegemony: Cultural studies in mutation? *Theory, Culture & Society* 24(3): 55–78.

Levine, D. (2011). Apple sues Samsung over Galaxy products. *Reuters*. 18 April.

Lowenthal, L. (1961). *Literature, Popular Culture, and Society*. Palo Alto, CA: Pacific Books.

Mansell, R. (2002). From digital divides to digital entitlements in knowledge societies. *Current Sociology* 50(3): 407–426.

Marriott, M. (2006). Digital divide closing as Blacks turn to Internet. *New York Times*. 31 March.

Menschel, B. (2011). One web to unite us all: Bridging the digital divide. *Cardozo Arts & Entertainment Law Journal* 29(91): 143–177.

Murdock, G. & Golding, P. (2004). Dismantling the digital divide: Rethinking the dynamics of participation and exclusion. In A. Calabrese and C. Sparks (edd.), *Toward a Political Economy of Culture: Capitalism and Communication in the Twenty-First Century*, 244–260. Lanham: Rowman & Littlefield.

National Science Foundation (2012). *Science and Engineering Indicators 2012*. Arlington: NSF.

Ngenda, A. (2005). The nature of the international intellectual property system: Universal norms and values or western chauvinism? *Information & Communications Technology Law* 14(1): 59–79.

Norris, P. (2001). *Digital Divide: Civic Engagement, Information Poverty, and the Internet Worldwide*. New York: Cambridge University Press.

Organization for Economic Cooperation and Development (2001). *Understanding the Digital Divide*. Paris: OECD.

Otmazgin, N. (2011). Commodifying Asian-ness: Entrepreneurship and the making of East Asian popular culture. *Media, Culture and Society* 33(2): 250–274.

Pang, L. (2006). *Cultural Control and Globalization in Asia: Copyright, Piracy, and Cinema*. London: Routledge.

Postcolonial Studies@Emory (2013). Hegemony in Gramsci. http://postcolonialstudies.emory.edu/hegemony-in-gramsci/#ixzz2k5pQDU8d.

Quan-Hasse, A. (2013). *Technology and Society: Social Networks, Power, and Inequality*. Ontario: Oxford University Press.

Qui, J. (2009). *Working-Class Network Society: Communication Technology and the Information Have-less in Urban China*. Cambridge, MA: The MIT Press.

Selwyn, N. (2004). Reconsidering political and popular understandings of the digital divide. *New Media and Society* 6(4): 341–364.

Sparks, C. (2013). What is the digital divide and why is it important. *Javnost-the Public* 20(2): 27–46.

Strover, S. (2003). Remapping the digital divide. *The Information Society* 19(4): 275–277.

Tsatsou, P., Pruulmann-Vengerfeldt, P. & Murru, M. (2009). Digital divides and children in Europe. In S. Livingstone and L. Haddon (eds.), *Kids Online: Opportunities and Risks for Children.* 107–119. Bristol: Policy Press.

Tsatsou, P. (2011). Digital divides revisited: What is new about divides and their research? *Media, Culture and Society* 33(2): 317–331.

U.S. Department of Commerce (2011). *Survey of Current Business.* Washington DC: Department of Commerce.

U.S. Department of Commerce (2012). *Survey of Current Business.* Washington DC: Department of Commerce.

U.S. Department of Commerce (2013). *Survey of Current Business.* Washington DC: Department of Commerce.

van Dijck, J. (2012.). *The Network Society.* London: Sage.

van Dijck, J. (2006). Digital divide research, achievements and shortcomings. *Poetics* 34: 221–235.

van Dijck, J. (2005). *The Deepening Digital Divide: Inequality in the Information Society.* London: Sage.

van Dijck, J. (2012). Facebook as a tool for producing sociality and connectivity. *Television and New Media* 13(2): 160–176.

Vehovar, V., Sicherl, P., Hsing, T., & Dolnicar, V. (2006). Methodological challenges of digital divide measurements. *The Information Society* 22(5): 279–290.

Vincos Blog (2012). World map of social networks. http://www.vincos.it/world-map-of-social-networks/.

Wadhwa, V. (2011). Engineering vs. liberal arts: Who's right—Bill or Steve? http://techcrunch.com/2011/03/21/engineering-vs-liberal-arts-who's-right—bill-or-steve/.

Warschauer, M. (2004). *Technology and Social Inclusion: Rethinking the Digital Divide.* Boston, MA: MIT Press.

Warschauer, M. (2003). Dissecting the digital divide: A case study in Egypt. *The Information Society* 19(4): 297–304.

White, S., Gunasekartan, A., Shea, T., & Argiuzo, G. (2011). Mapping the global digital divide. *International Journal of Business information Systems* 7: 207–219.

Williams, R. (1985). *Keywords: A Vocabulary of Culture and Society.* New York: Oxford University Press.

World Intellectual Property Organization (2007). *The 45 Adopted Recommendations under the WIPO Development Agenda.* Geneva: WIPO.

World Summit on the Information Society (2005). *Document WSIS-II/PC-3/DT/12(Rev.4)-E.* Tunis: WSIS.

Yang, J. (2011). Samsung counter sues Apple as patent dispute deepens. *Bloomberg.* 22 April. http://www.bloomberg.com/news/2011-04-22/samsung-sues-apple-on-patent-infringement-claims-as-legal-dispute-deepens.html.

8 The Future of Digital Platforms

The rapid growth of digital platforms and political cultures in the early 21st century has significantly changed our society. Platforms are known as digital intermediaries, and they have influenced people's daily activities. In the era of globalization, platforms have especially gained significance for capital accumulation, which turns platforms into some of the most important technologies in the digital economy and digital culture. By developing a critical interrogation of the global hegemony of digital platforms, this book has analyzed whether the dominant position of the U.S. has intensified an increasingly unequal relationship between a few Western countries, of course, driven by the U.S. and the remaining non-Western countries. With the analysis of three major domains in digital platforms, including computational, cultural values embedded in designs, and communication and commercial domains, it has attempted to verify whether the world has become further divided into a handful of Western states, in particular the U.S., which have developed platforms, and a vast majority of non-Western states, which do not have advanced platforms in the early 21st century.

Several countries, both developed and developing, have created their own platforms such as SNSs and smartphones, and they have competed with each other in the global markets. We cannot deny it. "The massive switch to the digital economy has indeed provided a surplus for several emerging powers, including China, India, and Korea with which to challenge the longer-term U.S. dominance" (Boyd-Barrett, 2006, 24). These countries have presumably competed with Western countries, and they are supposed to build a new global order with their advanced digital technologies. However, there are serious doubts as to whether non-Western platforms have reorganized the global flow and constructed a balance between the West and the East. Even if several non-Western countries, including Korea and China, invent some platforms, the use of these platforms is limited within their nation or diaspora instead of penetrating Western countries.

Unlike previous ICTs that some countries eventually advanced through their technologies, as in the cases of Walkman in Japan, semi-conductor in Taiwan, and television monitors in Korea, these countries have not become major players in the era of platform with a very few exceptions. Non-Western countries have not, and likely cannot, construct a balanced global order because Google (including its Android operating system), Facebook, Twitter, Apple's iPhones (and iOS), and YouTube are indices of the dominance of the U.S. in the digital economy. These platforms have penetrated the global market and expanded their global dominance. The growth of platform technologies and big data continues a process of building a global informational capitalism by concentrating production and distribution, as well as gathering and accessing databases in a handful of transnational corporations who are closely working with governments. These TNCs benefit from global consumption as the users of these platforms soar globally. Since only one country—the U.S.—controls the absolute majority of the global market—as Facebook accounting for about 95 percent and two American-based operating systems accounting for more than 85 percent of the global markets exemplify—it is safe to say that American dominance has been continued and intensified with platforms. Some believed that the panacea of technology might reduce imperialism and domination to vestiges of the past. However, technology has always been the reality of human hierarchy and domination (Maurais, 2003; Demont-Heinrich, 2008). Digital platforms have furthermore bolstered U.S. hegemony.

When scholars in media studies and sociology analyzed previous forms of dominance with capital, culture, and news, they could not say only one country, of course the U.S., controlled the entire world. Although the U.S. accounted for the majority of dominance of several fields, such as military and popular culture, it was not the true meaning of majority. Instead it meant only 50 percent, and sometimes even less than a half. However, as in the case of platforms such as operating systems in smartphones, search engines, and social network sites, the U.S. alone accounts for more than 80–90 percent of the global market. Our history has never seen this kind of absolute dominance. As such, platforms have functioned as a new form of distributor and producer that the U.S. dominates. Therefore, we are still living in the imperialist era. The U.S., which had previously controlled non-Western countries with its military power, capital, and later cultural products, now seems to dominate the world with platforms, benefiting from these platforms in terms of both capital accumulation and spreading symbolic ideologies and cultures.

In the 21st century, Lenin's analysis continues to explain what is happening in the world. The new concept of imperialism functions through digital technologies, first information and then platform technologies in the 21st century, which were not seen in Lenin's imperialism. The platform imperialism is much different from previous forms of imperialism, even information imperialism. Unlike the notion of information imperialism, in which hardware played a primary role in the formation of the asymmetrical relationship between a few Western and many non-Western countries, platform imperialism primarily is about software known as applications. In addition, the hegemonic power of American-based platforms is significant because only one country—the U.S.—has substantially increased its dominant role in the realm of platforms. Unlike the hardware era, software needs several supports from the government, including intellectual property and research and development (R&D), and the U.S. has positioned itself as the fast mover. In addition, platforms are not only gathering information from users but also commercializing user information as commodity, resulting in massive capital accumulation for the owners of these platforms and their countries. This implies that users are critical assets for digital platforms, and their activities are commodified by platform owners who are based in a handful of Western countries, although user activities are mainly voluntary in platforms. Although we cannot deny the fact that platforms, including social network sites, provide the space in which people can communicate and express themselves, platforms also work as a vital element in the circuit of capital accumulation, both nationally and globally.

Consequently, a critical investigation of the global hegemony of platforms proves that the dominant position of the U.S. has intensified an increasingly unequal relationship between the West and the East. In the 21st century, the world has become further divided into a handful of Western states, in particular the U.S., which have developed platforms and a vast majority of non-Western states which do not have advanced platforms. Therefore, it is certain that American imperialism has been renewed with platforms, like the old form of American imperialism supported by politics, economy, and military, as well as culture.

At the time of Lenin, "there was certainly a connection between communication—cable and telegraph systems—globalization and capitalist imperialism" (Winseck and Pike, 2007, 1). In the 21st century, again, there is a distinct connection between platforms, globalization, and capitalist imperialism. Platforms can be situated within more general capitalist processes that follow familiar patterns of asymmetrical power relations between the West and the East, as well as between workers and owners, commodification, and the harnessing of user power. However, platform imperialism needs to be understood within a multiplicity of relations.

Most of all, the nation-state has continued to be a significant player in the growth of platform technologies. The pressures of economic, cultural, and political globalization ushered in by the rapid growth of ICTs, in this case platform technologies, in conjunction with neoliberalism have challenged the sovereignty of nation-states by weakening their ability to control major national affairs and to protect their citizens. Far from the nation disappearing with globalized commerce, again, "hyper-nationalism and a semi-secret state presence are integral to many countries and even to the U.S. cultural industries and crucial to its empire" (Miller, 2010, 143).

As discussed in Chapter 5 in the case of Google affairs between the U.S. and China, although it is seemingly a private sphere, two powerful governments must be in the front line in order to guarantee their national benefits. The U.S. government—the strongest supporter of neoliberal globalization, emphasizing a small government regime—did not hesitate to take a primary role representing the private sector, as it did many times previously in the name of democracy and humanitarianism, and also capitalism. In addition, the Chinese government also jumped into the tug-of-war, as expected, in the name of nationalism. This implies that whether democratic or socialistic, the role of government remains key in the era of neoliberal globalization in tandem with platforms.

Over the past five centuries, technological change has progressively reduced the barriers to international integration. Transatlantic communication, for example, has evolved from sail power to steam, to the telegraph, the telephone, commercial aircraft, and to the Internet. Yet states have become neither weaker nor less important during this odyssey. On the contrary, in the countries with the most advanced and internationally integrated economies, governments' ability to tax and redistribute incomes, regulate the economy, and monitor the activity of their citizens has increased beyond all recognition. This has been especially true over the past century (Wolf, 2001).

Secondly, the recent growth of an intellectual property (IP) regime based on new platforms shows an asymmetrical relationship of interdependence between the West, primarily the U.S., and many developing countries. In the early 21st century, it is not unusual to witness the U.S. expanding its dominance in the global markets, not only with cultural products but also with intellectual properties based on its advanced technologies. The dramatic changes ushered in by cutting-edge digital/social technologies have significantly increased the magnitude and relevance of the phenomenon of the diffusion of IP rights infringement. Therefore, as global computer networks and global trade in software products and cultural genres develop, there is an increasing tension between developed countries as IP owners and developing countries as IP users. This is due to the unique roles of platforms, not only as computational infrastructure but also as software framework that allows software to run (Jin, 2013).

The smartphone patent wars underscore the difficulty we face in enacting fundamental discussion of mobile media platforms (Goggin, 2012). We could see patents as a relatively inefficient way to demonstrate the interdependent, collaborative nature of technology innovation—underscoring how adaptation happens, with PDAs blurring into early smartphones, begetting iPhones which are close relatives of Androids, and so on. Of course, manufacturers and media companies alike veer between rivalrous self-assertion of the unique inventive genius of one firm, on the one hand, and the smiling partnerships and alliances (Symbian, Open Handset Alliance) on the other hand. "Yet the slew of [law]suits over smartphone patents would be farcical if they did not so palpably enact the desire of some of the most wealthy companies in the world to seize control of the future of mobile media—with nary a nod to the claims of the three billion citizens globally who use today's technology, and who surely care about the affordance and prospects for what follows" (Goggin, 2012, 749).

Intellectual property rights have played a key role in accumulating capital in the hands of a few Western-based platform developers and owners. While a few non-Western countries are developing their own platform technologies and expanding their market share in the global markets, IP rights are some of the most difficult hurdles that they have to surmount. As Western countries, in particular the U.S., have influenced several global agencies in order to make very strict IP norms that are favoring these countries, non-Western countries are experiencing two fundamental challenges: the development of their own platform technologies comparable to Western-based ones and the utilization IP laws which have resulted in capital accumulation for a few Western corporations. In the field of platform technologies, as Facebook, Twitter, Google, and smartphones (in the case of operating systems) prove, American dominance has been expanding on a large scale, which has been intensifying asymmetrical power relations between Western and non-Western countries.

Thirdly, this book critically analyzed the process of commodification of Facebook users as free labor. It especially engaged with audience commodity theory to frame an analysis of free labor in an era of social media. Smythe's view that would see "individual audience members as undertaking unpaid work when they watch television programs" might not be appropriate in the social media era (Hesmondhalgh, 2010, 278). However, it is also true that audiences are increasingly required to participate audibly and physically, albeit that their activities require a subtle eye on the part of the observer, and audience commodities are still very useful in understanding new technologies. Smythe's concepts have arguably gained a renewed saliency amidst the emerging practices and celebratory rhetoric of Web 2.0. In the case of audience commodity theory, the work of the audience is materially embedded in, and articulated through, the capitalist application of communication technologies in the 21st century (Comor, 2010).

In fact, this book argued that the terms audience commodities and audience work need to gain a new look due to the importance of the changing nature of Web 2.0 participants, unlike audience commodity theory previously emphasizing the role of audiences in mass communication, such as television and newspapers. The novelty of the concept of the audience commodity gives some ideas to the transformative qualities of the concept of audience towards users in the new economic era (Coté and Pybus, 2007). SNS users are counted, packaged, and sold to advertisers and industrial capitalists, while engaging in various forms of producing through posting their pictures and texts in the case of Facebook.

However, as Bermejo (2009, 149) points out, it is important to pay attention to "the specification of the actual work performed by the audience." Whereas it can be argued that the audience is working to create the demand for advertised goods, the specific work performed by the audience has changed, or at least has become more complex. Clearly, this change is reflected in the different pricing models used currently in online advertising.

This means that, as Andrejevic (2004) also argues, watching—that is, being exposed to advertising—cannot be considered as the only work of the online audience that is appropriated by the media. Activities such as clicking and typing also should be considered as labor. When Smythe located the audience within the media production process, the work of the audience came after content was produced by producers (Cohen, 2008); therefore, the concept of audience commodity could not explain the interactive nature of consumption and production in SNSs. In other words, while TV and radio mass broadcasting platforms are only able to produce very broad audience commodities whose profiles and characteristics can then be sold to advertisers, social network sites, such as Facebook, Twitter, and Google, are easily able to target specific user groups much more effectively. This is done through powerful computing algorithms that filter user data according to a range of different advertising-oriented criteria (Bohm et al., 2012).

In addition, it is crucial to understand that the real value produced by Facebook users is economically relevant as long as the credibility of user commodities and associated exploitation have been seriously considered in the market. Facebook users feel joy and create their own cyber culture; however, Facebook is used to refine the process of delivering Internet users to advertisers. The users proactively participate in producing and consuming knowledge and information, and users interact with each other on an open platform through which someone can create and consume content. Therefore, Facebook users can be seen as confirming the pre-eminence of exchange-value in Facebook, as audiences in television have, but as more affective customers (Jin, 2013). Social network sites users are free labor, instead of affective labor, because the immaterial production that Hart and Negri (2008) emphasize is "increasingly outside of capital with the partial exception of creative/originating workers with non-employee legal status, little more than an example of wishful thinking" (Camfield, 2007, 129). Platforms also utilize other business models; therefore, it is also imperative to understand platforms from diverse perspectives.

As Facebook evolves in relation to an environment of commodification, it seems likely that Facebook users will continue producing the inescapable inequalities between capital and themselves as free labor primarily because corporations have utilized the users as commodities, which are not-paid workers. Facebook users add and/or create value to what they consume by clicking the keyboard and dragging the mouse with no monetary reward, resulting in an asymmetrical relationship between Facebook and its users. This implies that digital platforms, again both social network sites and search engines, prove their original cultural values as commercial entities. In other words, both the commercialization of these platforms and the commodification of users prove that the platform's values are embedded in design. Technologies are not value neutral but reflect the cultural bias, values, and communicative preferences of their designers, as several scholars indicate (Feenberg, 1991; Ess, 2009). Platforms often "reinforce the values and preferences of designers," either explicitly or implicitly, while sometimes "clashing with the values and preferences" of their intended uses (Ess, 2009, 116).

Finally, we need to seek new perspectives on the global digital divide debates in the social media era. The task was to espouse global digital divide discourse in understanding the complexity and nuances of several variances that have been newly identified. Since the inception of the discussion of the digital divide, the global digital divide has been primarily associated with the disparities in economic growth among nations, although there are several significant areas, such as political and cultural realms. Thus, many developing countries have been enthusiastic in embracing ICTs, and the digital divide seemed to partially resolve these inequalities with the rapid growth of ICTs. Many countries have built the necessary infrastructure for the growth of the Internet; therefore, the Internet has done much to level the playing field for people looking to launch businesses and even more so those looking to grow them (*Huffpost*, 2013).

However, whether the digital divide is further marginalizing already oppressed and disenfranchised individuals and nations is still an ongoing question. Inequalities remain unresolved and even suggest that the gap is widening. This perhaps should not be surprising since, "if economic and social inequalities are among the key determinants of the digital divide in all of its manifestations, internationally these have certainly not been significantly reduced, and in some important cases have increased, as the Internet and social media are undergoing development and diffusion" (Sparks, 2013, 39). In particular, the greatest benefit that access to several ICTs provides is opportunity, because access to ICTs in developing nations fosters economic opportunities for all (White et al., 2011). However, the opportunity is shrinking in many countries. In the 21st century, social media has been abuzz, and in all likelihood, the digital divide will continue as it has.

In the platform era, this is clearly the case. Those countries that are already marginalized when it comes to software will have fewer opportunities in developing software, particularly operating systems and SNSs. "Measured in terms of access, it is likely that we will again see fast diffusion of smartphones and SNSs around most of the globe in the coming years, as we witnessed in the case of the Internet" (Castells, 2001, 262). However, as long as we are concerned about software and symbols, the existing gap can be widening instead of shrinking because developing countries cannot develop these areas although they rapidly use these technologies and content. As Quan-Hasse (2013, 135) also identifies, the more salient barriers that exist at both the micro and macro levels are not only a lack of infrastructure, economic barriers, illiteracy, poor computing skills, and lack of supports, but also cultural barriers.

The global digital divide cannot be resolved anytime soon, because the majority of developing countries have no available resources, especially when compared to a few Western countries. Only a few developing countries, such as Korea and Taiwan, are partially competing with Western forces, but other countries have no skills and capital. SNSs and smartphones in conjunction with software could leave many developing countries far behind, because SNSs and smartphones are about IP rights and symbolic hegemony as well. This is the overlooked side of the systematic chain of causality described above: that lack of skills and capital to produce platforms harms life chances for the majority of developing countries and their citizens. In other words, this is not an issue of access to, and use of, several ICTs.

The more serious problem is that the majority of developing countries have no opportunity to create, design, and produce their own software and symbols, which perpetuates the discrepancies between developed and developing countries. The digital divide between developed and developing countries in the era of platform will continue to rise. Therefore, while how to resolve these fundamental issues is significant, it is also vital to explore the multifaceted approaches, including the need for a more rich, considerate, and systematic assessment of the ways in which socio-economic factors, cultural perceptions, and regulation are interrelated.

All these factors explain how the profitability of platforms is centered on establishing proprietary systems for which they control access and the terms of relationship, not the idea of platforms being as open as possible (McChesney, 2013). Whereas platforms are part of digital revolution, these new technologies have rapidly replaced old technologies, such as television, the Internet, and mobile telephones. Technical standards and values embedded in platforms will continue to grow, and their influences in our global society will similarly be growing. Instead of developing a public sphere, these platforms are enhancing the corporate sphere, which needs to be checked. As new technologies are invented, the global hegemony of the U.S. has been intensifying and platform owners in the U.S. have dominated the global network society.

Platform imperialism is real and will remain as one of the most significant frameworks in explaining our society, no longer driven by only the Internet through the Web, but also driven by platforms through applications. Platform imperialism will intensify the asymmetrical power relationships between countries possessing platforms and countries using platforms invented in the U.S. The major reason is not only because platforms themselves are technological breakthroughs but because of their commercial and ideological values embedded in platforms. As platforms are primarily considered as some of the most significant tools to accumulate capitals, platform owners and host countries intensify their dominance through intellectual property rights and state power. Platform owners especially appropriate hundreds of thousands of users in order to make financial profits. Once they learn of the importance of platforms as capitalist tools, they don't look back while developing new methods to utilize platform users as free labor.

With or without any intention to be imperialistic, platforms enjoy the sweet price of success, which must be checked. Unlike other ICT sector manufacturers, such as television set and semi-conductor companies, platform companies do not produce many products because platforms work as digital intermediaries. Users are actually producing content. As some argue that the Internet constitutes a new form of public sphere, several works emphasize the significance of platforms. However, as Ulises Mejias (2013) clearly points out, the Internet has become almost completely subordinated to the forces of the market instead of sustaining its major role as a public sphere.

Likewise, the growth of platforms is supposed to provide a new opportunity for people to enjoy their platforms to "discuss and debate politics as equals free of both government scrutiny or interference and the dominant corporate economic institutions" (McChesney, 2013, 66). In fact, in the early stages of social media platforms, the question arose whether this new kind of mediated sociality presented a new type of public sphere. Terms such as democracy, collectivity, and participation implicitly borrowed Habermas' model of political communication to argue the value of these platforms as new carriers of the public sphere (van Dijck, 2012). Barlow (2007) also points out that social networks sites, being freed of institutional confines, provided semi-public ways to enact relationships and express opinions. What is commonly argued is that "social media platforms are untainted by state forces at the level of political communication and untouched by market forces at the level of political economy, something that has prevailed for quite some time, despite ardent criticism" (van Dijck, 2012, 163).

However, platforms have become a new tool for the corporate sphere instead of the public sphere. The global usage of platforms gives us an impression of the overall wealth and innovative capacities of contemporary society; however, due to the imperialization by a few Western countries, in particular the U.S., new achievements remain limited to certain classes and don't benefit all (Fuchs, 2008). With continuous commercialization attempts by platform owners, users' participations do not function as part of public discussions leading towards the discussions of public affairs. Even if so, users' participation as prosumers has been monetized. In particular, a few U.S.-based platforms actualize the same commodification process of participation in other countries, resulting in the accumulation of capital in the hands of these U.S.-based platform corporations. The future of platforms primarily relies on global users. As platforms as intermediaries aggregate the sum of the activities of the users (Zittrain, 2008), it is crucial for platforms to reward users by providing the role of public sphere. If it is not avoidable to see the intensification of platform imperialism, we must protect users from platform owners who are utilizing them as proprietary rights.

In conclusion, the rapid integration of platforms in the digital economy spawns new disparities between countries. As Armand Mattelart (2000, 98) argued, "although the north/south dividing line no longer suffices to make sense of the world, the structural inequalities criticized in earlier decades have not disappeared" in the network society. More significantly, the concentration of capital accumulation in the era of platforms shows that a few U.S.-based transnational corporations and start-ups have tremendously dominated the remaining countries, which cannot be seen in other areas. The current form of platform politics is not only about the massive penetration of platforms in terms of their computational functions, but also about critical junctures with several relevant issues in cultural and commercial values, such as intellectual property, symbolic hegemony, and platform users as free labor. The great powers, encompassing both the nation-state and transnational corporations, have played pivotal roles in the construction of platform imperialism, which has resulted in the expansion of the global platform divide.

REFERENCES

Barlow, A. (2007). *The Rise of the Blogosphere*. New York: Praeger.

Bermejo, F. (2009). Audience manufacture in historical perspective: from broadcasting to Google. *New Media and Society* 11(1&2): 133–154.

Fuchs, C. (2008). *Internet and Society: Social Theory in the Information Age*. London: Routledge.

Mattelart, A. (2000). *Networking the World, 1794–2000*. In Liz Carey-Libbrecht and James A. Cohen (eds.), Minneapolis, MN: University of Minnesota Press.

Mejias, U. (2013). *Off the Network: Display the Digital World*. Minnesota, MN: University of Minnesota Press.

Zittrain, J. (2008). *The Future of the Internet and How to Stop It*. New Haven, CT: Yale University Press.

Index

For Product Safety Concerns and Information please contact our EU representative GPSR@taylorandfrancis.com Taylor & Francis Verlag GmbH, Kaufingerstraße 24, 80331 München, Germany